DISCOVER WESTERN EUROPE

Reader's Digest

PUBLISHED BY THE READER'S DIGEST ASSOCIATION LIMITED

LONDON   NEW YORK   MONTREAL   SYDNEY

DISCOVER WESTERN EUROPE

Translated and edited by Toucan Books Limited, London
for Reader's Digest, London

Translated and adapted from the French
by Antony Mason

For Reader's Digest
Series Editor: Christine Noble
Editorial Assistant: Caroline Boucher

Reader's Digest General Books
Editorial Director: Cortina Butler
Art Director: Nick Clark

ISBN 0 276 42443 3

Discover the World: WESTERN EUROPE
was created and produced by M L Editions, Paris, for
Selection Reader's Digest S.A., Paris, and first published
in 1998 as *Regards sur le Monde: L'EUROPE DE L'OUEST*

©1998 Selection Reader's Digest, S.A.
212 boulevard Saint-Germain, 75007, Paris

CONTENTS

IRELAND

UNITED
KINGDOM

THE
NETHERLANDS

GERMANY

BELGIUM

LUXEMBOURG

AUSTRIA

FRANCE

LIECHTENSTEIN

SWITZERLAND

MONACO

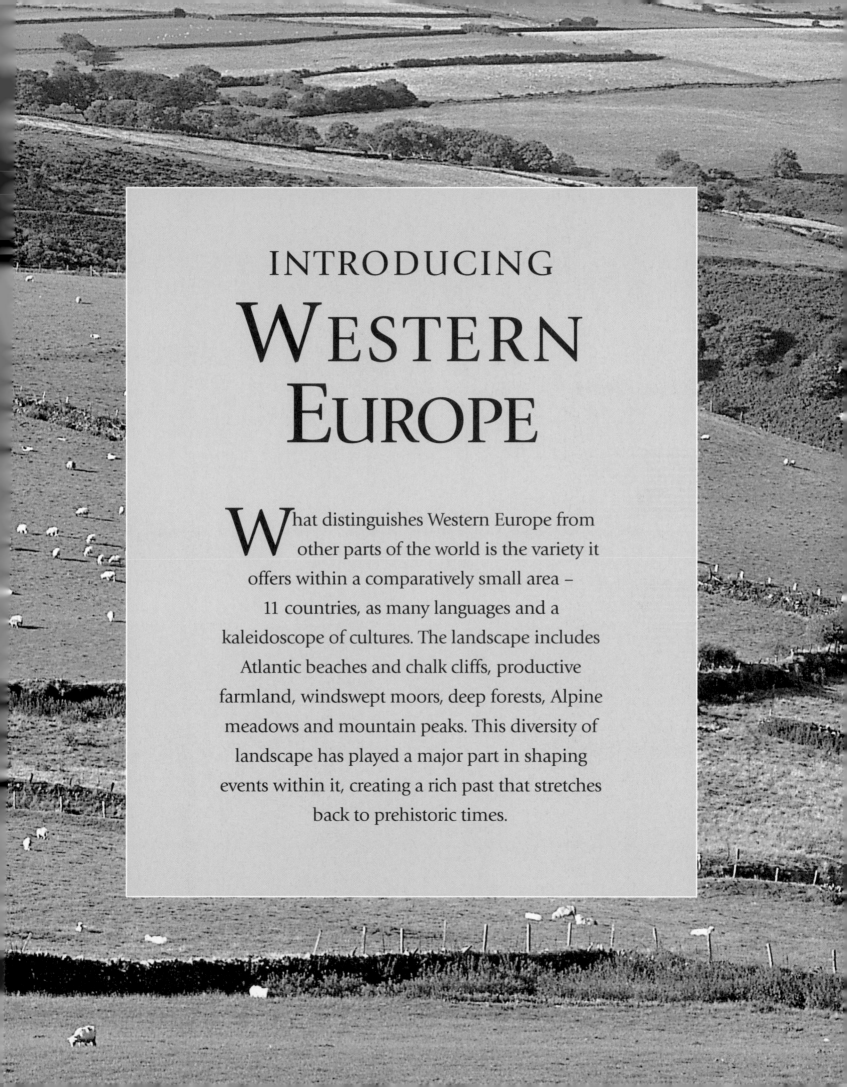

INTRODUCING
WESTERN EUROPE

What distinguishes Western Europe from other parts of the world is the variety it offers within a comparatively small area – 11 countries, as many languages and a kaleidoscope of cultures. The landscape includes Atlantic beaches and chalk cliffs, productive farmland, windswept moors, deep forests, Alpine meadows and mountain peaks. This diversity of landscape has played a major part in shaping events within it, creating a rich past that stretches back to prehistoric times.

Images of a continent

If the map of the world were redrawn today, Europe would probably not be called a continent at all as it is really little more than an appendage tacked onto the landmass of Asia. But when the continents were defined, Europe was seen as a self-contained unit, characterised not just by its geography but also by its unique culture and industry – qualities that made Western Europe the power-house of the world for many centuries.

The landscape played a major role in this. Western Europe is surrounded by sea, which has always provided the means to trade and to conquer. It also has an equable climate, fertile lands, and is rich in natural resources such as timber and minerals. Much of the landscape consists of plains and rolling hills, covered with pasture and arable farmland. The North European Plain, rarely rising above 330 ft (100 m), stretches virtually uninterrupted from Flanders to the Urals deep within Russia, which mark the dividing line between Europe and Asia. The highest mountains of the region are thrust to the rim, in the Alps and the Pyrenees.

Civilisation may have been forged in the warmer climes of Mesopotamia and Egypt, but the Europeans adopted their technologies of iron-working and farm-ing to goad their own lands into high levels of productivity. The success of the European agricultural economy gave rise to towns and cities, a key feature of the European identity. Some have histories dating back over 2000 years: Marseilles, in southern France, for example, has been a trading port since 600 BC.

Western Europe was the birthplace of the Industrial Revolution, and when this began to unfurl in the 18th century, the trend towards urbanisation accelerated. Over time, Western Europe has become not only one of the richest but also one of the most densely populated regions of the world. The Netherlands, for exam-ple, has 940 inhabitants per sq mile (362 per km²), compared to the USA's 75 per sq mile (29 per km²).

Growing populations, technical skill, curiosity and greed combined to induce the people of Western Europe to expand outwards. This was initially motivated by trade. In the late 15th century, the desire to find the sources of valuable luxury goods from the East led to the discovery of the New World, as well as sea routes to India and South-east Asia. As fast as maps were drawn for North America, southern and eastern Asia, Africa, Australia and the South Pacific, they were filled in with the colours of Britain, France and the Netherlands, and later Germany and Belgium. Confident of the superiority of their civilisations, their technology and their religion, Christianity, the countries of Western Europe ruled vast tracts of the world and brought to these – for better or for worse – their own forms of administra-tion, systems of justice, industry and export-oriented economies.

Yet for all their claims of civilisation, the expansion of the European nations also rested on a willingness to use brute force. This savagery came home to roost when they turned their guns on each other in the two world wars of the 20th century. Since then, the Europeans have retreated from their colonies, and instead have turned their energies towards co-operation within the European Union.

But the distinctive qualities of each nation survive, woven into the texture of their historic towns and monuments, their languages, foods, festivals and tra-ditions. Differences persist and are care-fully protected, sometimes to the point of conflict, as between the loyalist and nationalist communities in Northern Ireland, or between the Flemish and the Walloons in Belgium. But one of the defining elements of the continent of Europe has always been its diversity.

Space-age view *A satellite photo shows the degree to which Western Europe has been shaped by the sea, an element that has influenced the region's history and culture.*

The great divide   The Atlantic Ocean has battered a path through the chalk landscape on either side of the English Channel. The cliffs of the Caux region of eastern Normandy (above) are mirrored by the White Cliffs of Dover on the English side. Between them lies one of the world's busiest shipping lanes. The Channel represents a vital maritime link – serving Rotterdam, Antwerp and London – as well as a historic cultural divide.

Once a lake   Until 10 000 years ago the Baltic Sea (right) was a freshwater lake draining glacier-fed rivers. Now it is linked to the Atlantic by the straits that separate Denmark from the Scandinavian peninsula. But the sea retains the legacy of its past in its small tides and comparatively low salt content.

Transcontinental artery *The Rhine is not just the longest river in the region, but also a bustling waterway that has played a key role in Germany's economic history. Medieval castles stand guard on hilltops along the central stretch of the river, amid vineyards where some of Germany's finest wine is produced. Since the Rhine-Main-Danube canal was completed in 1992, barges have been able to travel from the North Sea to the Black Sea, a distance of 2175 miles (3500 km).*

The rooftop of Europe *Western Europe reaches its highest point in the Alps at Mont Blanc (top), whose summit stands at 15 770 ft (4807 m). Lying on the border between France and Italy, this massive mountain is surrounded by more delicate peaks called aiguilles (needles). Mont Blanc was first conquered by climbers in 1786, and is still held in special regard as the birthplace of mountaineering. Although the region is visited by thousands of climbers, it is as perilous as ever, and a dozen or more people die every year, usually victims of the fickle weather and merciless crevasses. The lower slopes are more forgiving, famed for the mountain walks that link the valley floors to upland pastures where alpine flowers such as edelweiss and gentian grow. In winter, these same pastures are transformed into well-equipped ski-slopes serving resorts such as Chamonix on the French side, and Courmayeur on the Italian side. Since 1962, the two towns have been linked by the Mont Blanc road tunnel. Although just 12 miles (20 km) apart, the two towns retain their distinctly French and Italian characters, illustrating the role that the Alps have played as both a geographical and cultural barrier.*

The imprint of humanity
The landscape of Western Europe has been shaped by human activity since prehistoric times. Even the unspoilt stretches of coast in Cornwall (right), in south-west England, bear the marks of centuries of sheep-grazing, and before that the forest clearance of the iron-working Celts. Only remote islands and the most uneconomic expanses of bog and mountain have been left untouched.

Nature by decree   The Forest of Compiègne (left) in north-eastern France was a royal hunting forest, fastidiously protected in its natural state for the king's pleasure – a privilege that was passed down through generations before the woods were handed to the public at large. Remnants of ancient woodlands such as these give a clue to the central role that forests have played in European myth. While representing precious and vital sources of fuel, timber and game, they were also imbued with mystical powers, the otherworldly domain of fairies, elves, spirits and witches.

A brief history

From Homo erectus to Neanderthal Man

The climate was bitter in Europe when *Homo erectus*, an ancestor of modern humans, ventured into Eurasia from Africa about 1.5 million years ago, in a period of fluctuating cycles of cold known as the Ice Age. The first European hunters left their mark with roughly hewn flint hand axes, fashioned 700 000 years ago. Neanderthals, who appeared about 100 000 years ago, produced more sophisticated flint tools, sheltered in caves, used fires and buried their dead.

Cro-Magnon cave-dwellers

The ancestor of modern Europeans was a form of *Homo sapiens sapiens* known as Cro-Magnon Man. These people (named after a cave in the Dordogne where their remains were first identified) may have lived alongside the Neanderthals for a while, and either crossbred with them or pushed them to extinction. They made tools out of flint, bone and antler, and used their catches of deer and bison for food and to make clothing and covers for huts built of branches or bones. These people also produced cave paintings, and sculptures made of wood, stone, clay, bone and ivory.

End of the Ice Age

As the population grew, family groupings formed communities several hundred strong. They lived a semi-nomadic life, erecting tent-like structures at summer and winter bases, and following the herds of bison, horses, reindeer and mammoths as they migrated each season. The changing seasons also provided edible shoots, roots, fruits, nuts and berries, while fish and shellfish could be netted or collected. Around 10 000 years ago the Ice Age glaciers began to retreat, and as the tundra evolved into forests, the wild boar, deer, wildfowl and other game that adopted this habitat lured humans farther north.

Farming villages

The scene was set for the Neolithic revolution, the New Stone Age, which again originated in the Middle East. By the 5th millennium BC, wheat and barley were being grown in Europe for bread, and flax was cultivated to make linen cloth. Also cattle, sheep and pigs were domesticated. Farming demanded that people settle in one place, and more permanent houses were built. Pottery appeared, and there is evidence of trade, in flint for example, over wide distances, while the massive earth and stone monuments suggest the presence of large, well-organised communities.

Female spirit   The Willendorf Venus, from Austria, was sculpted from limestone some 25 000 years ago.

The coming of metal

During the 2nd millennium BC, new possibilities were opened up by the spread of copper and gold, then bronze (an alloy of copper with a little tin).

Face of the past   This bronze mask and pair of hands, found in Austria, are thought to be Celtic.

These could be made into improved tools and weapons, but they were also used to create jewellery, ornaments, figurines and other vessels that displayed status; for alongside the practical developments came a more hierarchical structure of society. The chiefs were now

Nature study   The paintings at Lascaux, France, are more than 13 000 years old.

Cave art

Some of the earliest known artistic expressions of humankind in Europe are found in the dark recesses of caves, notably in France and Spain, where some paintings may be over 20 000 years old. The fact that most are images of large animals suggests a quasi-religious bond between a hunting culture and the animal world. The cave artists used pigments such as red and yellow ochre and charcoal, and worked by the light of tallow lamps. Their talent for representation reveals acute powers of observation, and well-practised skills in interpreting this in lively and expressive paintings or drawings.

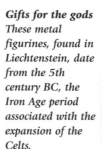

Gifts for the gods These metal figurines, found in Liechtenstein, date from the 5th century BC, the Iron Age period associated with the expansion of the Celts.

Hallstatt and La Tène

In 1824 an ancient burial site was discovered at Hallstatt, a settlement in Austria. Since then over 2000 princely tombs have been excavated, yielding the remains of a rich Celtic culture dating from 800 to 500 BC. Its iron-working skills and geometric design have given rise to the term Hallstatt Style, which coincides with the first phase of the European Iron Age. A more sophisticated use of iron evolved in around 500 BC at La Tène, near Lake Neuchâtel in Switzerland, where Celts had contacts with the Greeks and Etruscans of central Italy. The La Tène culture lasted until the 1st century BC, and followed the expansion of the Celts across most of northern Europe during the Late Iron Age. The curvaceous decorative forms of its metalwork and the use of animal imagery became the hallmarks of Celtic design that spread as far as Ireland and Spain.

Horse culture
This enamel-encrusted harness decoration reflects the central role of the horse in Celtic culture.

Chariot of the gods *Celtic gods ride with a chariot-borne challice, found in Austria. It dates from the 7th century BC.*

buried in elaborate tombs, often with the trappings of their rank such as goblets, shields and armour. Valuable commodities such as copper and salt were mined on an industrial scale and traded, extending contacts over a wide area, at least as far as the Mediterranean.

The Celts

In the middle of the 7th century BC bronze began to be replaced by a new, harder metal from the Middle East: iron. The masters of the European iron trade were the Celts, a broad group of peoples speaking a number of different languages. They learnt their iron-working skills through trading contacts with Mediterranean peoples, and over the next seven centuries their iron-working culture spread across northern Europe.

The Celts sacked Rome in 390 BC; thereafter the Romans seldom had a good word to say about them, describing how they went naked into battle to

Standing stones

Even by Celtic times the vast standing stones that dot the landscape of Western Europe were ancient monuments of immense age, dating back as far as 6000 BC. The product of Neolithic enterprise, some were clearly burial sites, such as the dolmens of Brittany, where underground burial chambers were crowned by immense stone tables. The standing stones or menhirs found in Brittany and the British Isles pose more of a mystery. Some stones stand alone as isolated landmarks; others form circles and alignments that appear to correlate with astronomical observations, suggesting a religious significance perhaps connected to the farming year. Whatever their purpose, the work involved in erecting them represents both a prodigious feat of engineering and a remarkable degree of social cohesion and communal organisation.

Stones of silence *Work on Stonehenge in Wiltshire, in southern England, is thought to have begun in about 3100 BC, and the monument developed in three phases over the next 1500 years.*

The Roman Empire

Map legend:
- at the death of Augustus
- at its height
- fortified borders

Map labels: Antonine Wall, Hadrian's Wall, North Sea, BRITAIN, Rhine, Germania, Agri Decumates, Belgica, Danube, Atlantic Ocean, Lugdunensis, Rhaetia, Noricum, GAUL, Aquitania, Narbonensis, ITALY, SPAIN, Mediterranean Sea, Rome

Engineering an empire
This funerary sculpture (left) of a 2nd-century general in charge of troops in Germania illustrates the Romans' military prowess. Success on the battlefield was supported by outstanding feats of military engineering, such as Hadrian's Wall (above), their northernmost lasting defence. The Pont du Gard aqueduct (right) in southern Gaul, completed in the 1st century AD, is a masterpiece of civil engineering.

the sound of screaming women. In reality they were farming folk. The distinctive designs of Celtic metalwork point to an elaborate and sophisticated society.

Enter the Romans

Rome added Western Europe to its empire comparatively late. It dominated the Mediterranean by 130 BC, but it took its greatest leader Julius Caesar (100-44 BC) to conquer the Celtic peoples, or Gauls, to the north of the Alps. The Alpine Roman provinces of Rhaetia and Noricum (approximately modern Switzerland and half of Austria) were created under Augustus (63 BC-AD 14), while the conquest of Britain began

under Claudius in AD 43. The German tribes were brought to heel by AD 83.

By the second century, Western Europe was part of an empire containing some 50 million people in 44 provinces, and stretching from the Atlantic Ocean to the Euphrates river – an area covered today by some 25 countries. Free men enjoyed the perks of a well-ordered administration, and a disciplined military ensured peace for another 200 years.

The empire in crisis

Even so, there were signs of degeneration even in the early years of the 3rd century AD, when the empire was racked by disputes over who should

rule, and was crippled by social and economic problems. The Germanic tribes (labelled Barbarians in imitation of the unintelligible way they talked) pressed in on the frontiers along the Rhine and Danube. Emperors Diocletian (reigned AD 284-305) and Constantine (AD 306-337) appeared to stop the rot, but this was illusory. In around AD 395, the Roman Empire split in two, the West based in Rome, the East now centring on Byzantium (later called Constantinople, then Istanbul). By this time, many Romans had adopted Christianity.

The collapse of the Western Empire followed as the Germanic Barbarian tribes, such as the Alans, Vandals and

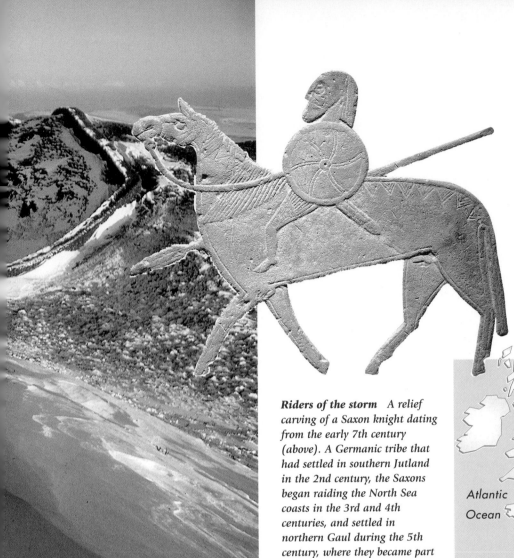

pushed the Celts into Wales and the western fringes. Despite appearances, for most people these changes were not abrupt: local cultures had been allowed to flourish under the Romans, and now they mingled with the new waves of conquerors and settlers. Clovis adopted Christianity in AD 496, thereby conforming to the majority religion of Gaul.

The Frankish empire (the origin of France) was ruled until AD 751 by the Merovingian dynasty, named after an earlier Frankish tribal chief, then by the

Riders of the storm A relief carving of a Saxon knight dating from the early 7th century (above). A Germanic tribe that had settled in southern Jutland in the 2nd century, the Saxons began raiding the North Sea coasts in the 3rd and 4th centuries, and settled in northern Gaul during the 5th century, where they became part of the empire of the Franks. They also settled in southern Britain, along with the Angles, founding the distinctive Anglo-Saxon culture.

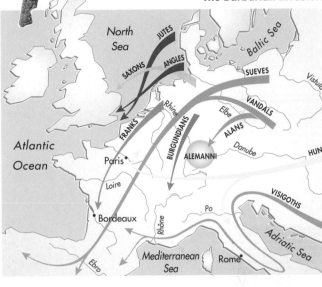

The Barbarian invasions

The rise of the monasteries

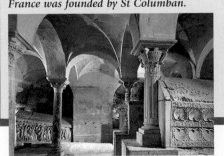

The Italian monk St Benedict is credited with founding the Western tradition of monasticism, at Monte Cassino in about AD 529. The Benedictine Order expanded northwards across Europe. Meanwhile, Celtic Christianity spread out from Ireland. In the later 6th century, a number of Irish monks – such as St Columban, St Gall and St Columba – founded monasteries and abbeys across Frankish Europe, the British Isles and northern Italy. Sustained by legacies and tithes, the monasteries were the main guardians of culture and learning until the Renaissance.

Irish influence The abbey of Jouarre in France was founded by St Columban.

Sueves, moved west, harassed by the Huns pushing in from Central Asia. In AD 406 the Rhine frontier gave way. In the face of chaos, the Romans withdrew from their extended empire; the last Roman soldiers left Britain in AD 407. Three years later the Visigoths, led by Alaric, sacked Rome. They then became Roman allies and helped to repulse the Huns under Attila when he invaded Gaul in AD 451. In AD 476 Odoacer, king of the Ostrogoths, deposed the last emperor of the West. The Roman Empire now survived only in the East.

Barbarian rule

At the start of the 6th century the new force in the region were the Franks, a Germanic tribe that occupied northern Gaul. Their king, Clovis, extended his domain to the Pyrenees, relegating the Celts to Brittany. In the British Isles, the Roman culture evaporated as Angles and Saxons moved in from Jutland, and

Frankish finery The large brooch or fibula, used to secure folds in clothing, offered the jeweller an opportunity to show flair. This 7th-century gold fibula has been lavishly overlaid with garnets and glass cloisonné.

Carolingian dynasty, founded by Charles Martel. The greatest of the Carolingian kings was Charlemagne (reigned AD 768-814), undisputed ruler of a vast empire. But the treasures of the empire's monasteries and the riches of its trading ports attracted a new scourge: the Vikings.

Feudal society

Vikings, or Norsemen, began raiding the coasts of the Frankish and Anglo-Saxon kingdoms in about AD 790. They came mainly from Denmark, while Norwegian

Vikings tended to raid the coasts of Scotland and Ireland. To counter this threat, power was divided up among local strongmen who could provide protection. The result was feudalism, a hierarchy of reciprocal duties in which military services were exchanged for the promise of mutual protection. This was

Charlemagne

On Christmas Day in the year 800, in St Peter's Basilica in Rome, Charlemagne (Charles the Great), king of the Franks and the Lombards, was crowned Emperor of the West by Pope Leo III. This acknowledged that he was the most powerful leader in Europe. From his headquarters in Aachen (in French Aix-la-Chapelle), Charlemagne ruled over much of what is now France, Germany, Belgium, the Netherlands, Switzerland, Austria and northern Italy. But he was also driven by another vision: he saw himself as the heir to the old Roman Empire, as well as the champion of Christianity over the pagans in Europe and the Muslims in Spain. Thus he ruled over what was later referred to as the Holy Roman Empire. Charlemagne died in AD 814. When his empire was divided up by his three grandsons in the Treaty of Verdun in AD 843, the mosaic of modern Europe began to emerge.

Imperial stature A 9th-century bronze of Charlemagne.

War games An 11th-century manuscript conveys the mighty force of arms that could be packed on board a Viking warship. This 12th-century chess piece (left) was carved in the form of a mounted Norse warrior.

the foundation of early medieval society, usually centring on castles owned by one of the nobles, such as a count or duke, supported by his loyal knights. At the tip of the pyramid was the king, whose position depended on the loyalties of the nobility. For the serf at the bottom, life was little different from slavery.

The solace of the Church

One constant feature of the era was the Church, which offered the certainty of faith and the promise of paradise in the next life. Like feudal society, the Church had a pyramidal structure, with the Pope in Rome at its head, and through its wealth, lands and political influence it had a powerful grip on the mindset of

the medieval world. It also had a virtual monopoly on education, attracting many of the greatest minds of the era, and was the principal patron of the arts.

The Church commanded intense devotion. Hundreds of thousands joined the eight Crusades launched between 1095 and 1291 against the infidel, after the shrines of the Holy Land had fallen into Muslim hands.

Medieval prosperity

By the 11th century, the Vikings had settled in Britain, Ireland and northern France, and political stability was returning. Agricultural production

Trade in the 12th and 13th centuries

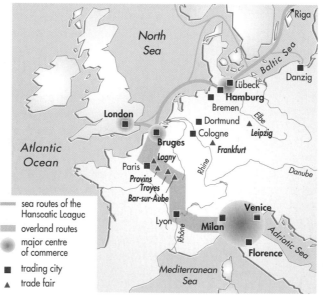

sea routes of the Hanseatic League
overland routes
● major centre of commerce
■ trading city
▲ trade fair

increased, aided by advances such as the wheeled plough and the water mill. Food surpluses led to a revival of the towns, which often developed around markets. Towns became busy centres of craft manufacture, where artisans organised themselves into trade guilds to defend their interests. As the towns took an increasing hold on the economy, they were able to persuade sovereigns to grant them charters that guaranteed their liberties and privileges such as land rights, freedom from taxes and the power to dispense justice. In 1215 a group of barons forced England's King John to sign the Magna Carta, which set limits on the king's powers.

Medieval crisis

'Lord, deliver us from the plague, famine and war' was a familiar prayer of the 14th century. The countryside was already under stress from increasing populations when poor harvests in 1317-19 caused famine for the first time in three centuries. The populace became vulnerable to epidemics, and above all to the bubonic plague which ravaged Europe in 1347-51.

The sudden loss of about a third of the population of Europe contributed to a religious and social crisis. The

Beating death *A procession of flagellants in Tournai (now in Belgium) in the 14th century. The religious practice of self-mortification reached its peak during the Black Death.*

Once more unto the breach *Henry V of England decisively defeated the French at Agincourt, in northern France, in 1415. Despite vastly superior numbers, the French were routed by the English army's deadly and powerful longbows.*

The emergence of Switzerland

The Romans conquered the land they called Helvetia in 58 BC. Later it was taken over by the Alemanni, Burgundians and Franks before being subsumed into the Holy Roman Empire in 1033. The cantons had a large degree of autonomy, and resented the imposition of authority, particularly from the Austrian Habsburg dynasty after 1273. On August 1, 1291, a pact of mutual assistance was signed by three cantons, Schwytz, Unterwald and Uri, to oppose Austrian interference. This is the origin of the Swiss Confederation, which grew as other cantons joined. A long struggle for liberation lay ahead, reflected in the legends of William Tell, whose tale of revolt against the Austrians is set in the 14th century. By the end of the 15th century, the Swiss Confederation had won effective independence within the Holy Roman Empire.

Church's authority had been undermined by internal feuds and corruption, which had persuaded the French-born Pope Clement V (1305-14) to shift the papacy headquarters from Rome to Avignon. The decision to return to Rome in 1378 resulted in the period known as the Great Schism, with rival popes in Avignon and Rome until 1417.

The Hundred Years' War (1337-1453), in which the English kings tried to win control of France, brought sieges and pillage to France, and higher taxes in both countries. The combination of plague, war and social turmoil resulted in the first popular revolts, such as the Jacquerie peasants' rising in central France in 1358, and the Peasants' Revolt in south-eastern England in 1381.

Humanism and the Renaissance

With the gradual easing of the power and authority of the Church, scholars and artists began to ask new questions about the world around them, and to

The Norman Conquest

In AD 911 Charles III of France ceded the lands of the lower Seine to a band of Viking or Norse settlers – the Normans – thus creating the Duchy of Normandy. In 1066, when Edward the Confessor, King of England, died without an heir, his cousin Duke William of Normandy claimed the English throne. The English earl Harold Godwinson assumed the crown, and William launched an invasion of England. Harold was defeated by William at the Battle of Hastings on October 14, 1066. When William the Conqueror was crowned king of England at Westminster on Christmas Day, the Anglo-Saxon period of English history came to a close.

Stitches in time *The Bayeux tapestry tells the story of the Norman invasion of England.*

reassess the work of the classical world. It was clear that the Greeks and Romans had made extraordinary advances in science, architecture, art and philosophy, but the medieval mind had to come to terms with the fact that this had happened within a non-Christian framework. Nonetheless, by the mid-15th century, scholars and artists – first in Italy, and then in northern Europe – had begun to delve into the classical

The Virgin Queen *Elizabeth I of England (reigned 1558-1603), daughter of Henry VIII and Anne Boleyn, ruled over a period of prosperity and confidence, providing the foundations for Britain's later growth as an imperial power.*

The genius of printing

In 1455 the first edition of a printed Bible emerged from the workshop of Johann Gutenberg in Mainz, Germany. Not only was this a vast and elaborate work, the product of 15 years of secret labour, it was also the first book to be printed in Europe. Gutenberg developed a system whereby letters were individually cast in metal, so could be made up into words or blocks of type, then broken up and the letters re-used. Previously, all books had to be copied by hand, one by one, but now they could be manufactured in their hundreds on printing presses. This in turn allowed learning to shift from the Church to the new universities.

heritage. Scientists began to take a new look at astronomy and the human body. Artists began painting portraits and scenes from everyday life or history, and architects adopted the styles of Greek and Roman architecture.

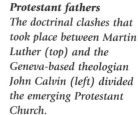

The result was a new era of intellectual and artistic endeavour that came to be called the Renaissance, or Rebirth.

The Reformation

By the early 16th century, the failings of the Church were becoming increasingly transparent. One flagrant abuse was the sale of indulgences, a practice by which forgiveness of sins was promised in return for payment. In Germany, the theologian Martin Luther (1483-1546) returned to the New Testament scriptures to formulate his own doctrine. Luther's campaign

Protestant fathers
The doctrinal clashes that took place between Martin Luther (top) and the Geneva-based theologian John Calvin (left) divided the emerging Protestant Church.

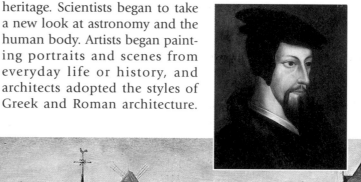

The St Bartholomew's Day Massacre

In France the Huguenots, much influenced by the teachings of John Calvin, found support among the ruling classes, but their intrigues at court created enemies and led to a massacre at Wassy near Paris in 1562, when supporters of the Catholic Guise family slaughtered 60 Huguenots, thereby triggering 35 years of civil war known as the Wars of Religion. One of the most infamous incidents of the war occurred in 1572. Catherine de Medici, mother of the French king Charles IX, agreed to a plot to assassinate the influential Huguenot Admiral Gaspard de Coligny, but the assassination attempt failed. Fearing that her role would be revealed, Catherine persuaded Charles to order the death of all the Huguenot leaders, who were assembled in Paris to celebrate the marriage of Marguerite de Valois, her daughter, to the Protestant Henry of Navarre. The murder of the leaders on August 24, St Bartholomew's Day, turned into a massacre of Huguenots in which thousands were slaughtered.

Death at dawn *On the signal of a church bell, French Huguenots were put to the sword.*

The sport of kings *Every aspect of Louis XIV's life was designed to reinforce his divine right to rule. This painting shows him hunting with his Spanish wife, Marie-Thérèse.*

The legacy of Charles V

When Charles V became Holy Roman Emperor in 1520, he was ruler of Spain, Austria, Germany, Burgundy and the Low Countries, Naples and Sicily. Spain conquered Mexico and Peru, bringing home ships laden with silver and gold, and Charles defeated the French and the Turks. His reign coincided with a period of high Renaissance art, architecture and learning in northern Europe. It was this legacy that his son Philip II of Spain took over in 1555. A fanatical Catholic, Philip sent the Inquisition into the Low Countries to eradicate the Protestants, who rallied to William of Orange. After 50 years of religious strife, the Protestants formed the United Provinces (the Netherlands) while the Catholics stayed in the Spanish Netherlands (Belgium).

Tireless warrior
Charles V at the Battle of Mühlberg, painted by Titian.

for Church reform, listed in his 95 theses in 1517, won support in Germany. Luther's excommunication by the Pope in 1521 polarised the emerging divisions in the Church. In 1536, the French theologian John Calvin (1509-64) began to spread his own version of Protestantism. Like Luther, he rejected the authority of the Pope. He also advocated the doctrine of predestination – the theory that the salvation of individuals has already been determined by God. Calvin's teachings soon became popular in France and the Low Countries.

The Reformation in England was linked to Henry VIII's conflict with papal authority. His first wife Catherine of Aragon bore six children, but only one (the future Mary I) survived. Henry was desperate for a son and sued for divorce, which the Pope refused to grant. Henry broke with Rome in 1533 and made himself head of the Church in England.

Sun symbol
A decoration at Versailles.

The consequences of religious discord in England were comparatively light compared to those in France, which suffered 35 years of upheaval in the Wars of Religion (1562-98). Germany was ravaged by the Thirty Years' War (1618-48), a conflict between the Protestant princes, backed by Sweden, and the Holy Roman Empire.

Courtly extravagance

Over all the hardships and daily grind in the late 17th century shone the splendour of the court of Louis XIV, the Sun King. Louis XIV believed himself to have been appointed by God, and hence had the gift of Divine Right: his every move was divinely sanctioned, his power was absolute, and his very being sacred. He centralised the administration of France and encouraged industry.

The Enlightenment

During the 17th century, scientists and philosophers began using scientific analysis and rational thought to reassess their subjects. The new era later

Habeas corpus

In 1679, the English parliament passed the Habeas Corpus Act, which guaranteed the individual against unlawful imprisonment. The Latin phrase, which means 'you shall have the body', was inherited from the Magna Carta signed by King John in 1215, which had stated that no freeman could be imprisoned except by the lawful judgment of his peers. Introduced after the turbulent times of the English Civil War and the Restoration, the Act limited the power of the king and marked an important victory in the people's fight for dignity.

Food for thought   The French philosophers of the Enlightenment, such as Voltaire (with raised hand), were socially much in demand.

became known as the Enlightenment. The English philosopher Thomas Hobbes (1588-1679) argued that people give up their freedom in exchange for the protection of a sovereign. In other words, the power of the king is derived from the people, and is upheld by a social contract. This challenged the concept of the divine right of kings to rule. Such arguments had a direct bearing on politics in England. King Charles I, a believer in the divine right of kings, tried to assert his will over Parliament, leading to the Civil War of 1642-6. The Parliamentarians under Oliver Cromwell

defeated the Royalists and Charles was executed in 1649, but the monarchy was restored in 1660.

The French philosophers of the Enlightenment, such as Voltaire (1694-1778), Montesquieu (1689-1755) and Jean-Jacques Rousseau (1712-78), advocated reforms to eradicate inequalities and injustices, and to ensure a fair social contract between citizens and their rulers. The Enlightenment had become a revolutionary tinderbox.

The French Revolution

The French Revolution erupted in 1789 and swept the *ancien régime* of Louis XVI from power. Histories of the Revolution tend to highlight the pitiless slaughter of the nobility at the guillotine, the repression of the Terror (1793-5), and the

Encyclopaedic knowledge

The spirit of enquiry of the Renaissance led to the belief that all things might one day be known, and various scholars put their minds to creating compendiums of knowledge known as encyclopaedias. The father of modern encyclopaedias is said to be Ephraim Chambers, whose *Cyclopaedia* was first published in England in 1728; but the most influential was the French *Encyclopédie*. Published between 1751 and 1772, it was the work of the mathematician Jean d'Alembert and the philosopher Denis Diderot, and presented history, art, philosophy and science for a broad readership. The *Encyclopaedia Britannica* was first published in 1771.

Illustrated knowledge   A plan of a wine press from the Encyclopédie.

Enlightened despots

Joseph II, Austrian Holy Roman Emperor from 1765 to 1790, considered himself to be the very model of a modern ruler. 'Since gaining the throne', he declared, 'I have made philosophy my empire's legislator.' He centralised his administration, abolished serfdom, developed an embryonic public health service and granted greater freedom to the press. He also permitted freedom of worship and freed education from the Church. However, these reforms were achieved through the edicts of an authoritarian regime. Joseph was, like Frederick II the Great of Prussia (reigned 1740-86), an enlightened despot. Although admired by liberals, he alienated the Church and conservative Catholics as well as more radical reformers.

Starting gun   The storming of the Bastille prison, in Paris, on July 14, 1789, marked the start of the French Revolution.

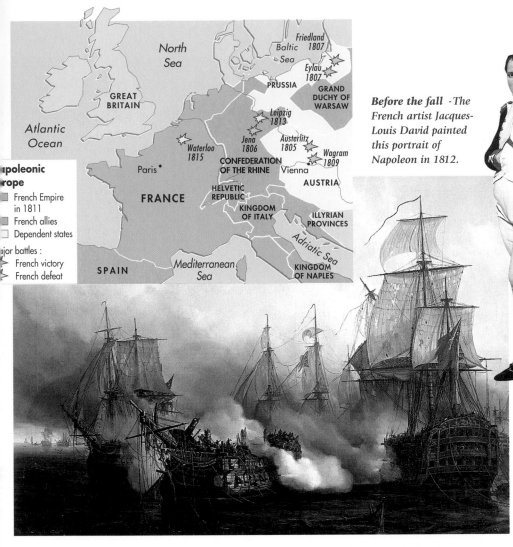

Before the fall - *The French artist Jacques-Louis David painted this portrait of Napoleon in 1812.*

reorganise the legal system along egalitarian principles, brought together in the 2251 articles of his Napoleonic Code, which are still the basis of French law.

The Revolutionary Wars (1792-1802) had netted the Austrian Netherlands (Belgium), Switzerland, the United Provinces and much of Italy. War broke out again in 1803, and Britain formed a coalition with Austria, Russia, Sweden and Prussia. By 1811, the French Empire covered half the continent of Europe. The tide turned against France with British victories in the Peninsular War in Spain and Portugal (1808-14), and the disastrous retreat from Moscow in 1812. Napoleon was defeated by a coalition at Leipzig in 1813. Then, after his comeback from Elba, he was defeated for a final time at Waterloo in 1815.

At the Congress of Vienna of 1814-15, the French Empire was redistributed among European monarchs, with the idea of re-creating the pre-Revolutionary world. But in just 25 years, Europe had undergone a radical transition from which it would never look back.

Nelson's triumph Admiral Horatio Nelson became a revered British hero when he lost his life leading the British fleet to victory over the French and Spanish at Trafalgar, off south-western Spain, in 1805. He was shot by a sharp-shooter on La Redoutable (centre).

Manufacturing boom

Europe was undergoing a social and economic transformation. The Industrial Revolution had begun in England in the mid 18th century, and spread across

anarchy of the Directoire (1795-9). But the Revolution brought in significant innovations. Key ideas, embodied in the Declaration of the Rights of Man of 1789, included equality before the law, in taxation, in military service, and inalienable rights of the individual to liberty, property and security. Power was transferred from the king to the nation, represented by those elected by the people to run it.

However, before Europe could draw breath, a new figure emerged from the Revolution and set about projecting his own grand vision across a vast new empire: Napoleon Bonaparte.

Napoleon

Artillery captain in 1793, commander and victor in the Italian campaign of 1796-7, First Consul after the coup in 1799, First Consul for Life in 1802, and Emperor of the French in 1804, Napoleon Bonaparte epitomised the

meteoric rise to power. He adapted the tenets of the Revolution to centralise the government, reform the tax system and

Carving up the Continent After Napoleon's defeat at Leipzig in 1813, European monarchs met at the Congress of Vienna to redistribute his empire. The congress was still sitting when Napoleon escaped from exile on Elba and made another bid for empire, only to be defeated at Waterloo.

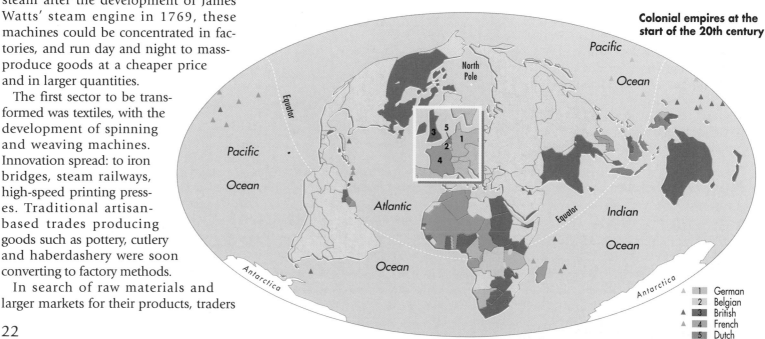

Industrial Revolution *The rapid progress in technology promised an exciting and dynamic world of achievement, captured in William Turner's innovative* Rain, Steam and Speed – the Great Western Railway *(above), painted in 1844. But it also entailed a grim world of gruelling factory labour (left), which drew workers out of the countryside and into overcrowded and insanitary cities. Resentment boiled up in frequent riots, rebellions and strikes, often savagely repressed. In the late 19th century, the workers' struggle for better conditions was increasingly channelled into the trade union movement.*

Europe, to Belgium after 1810, France after 1830, and Germany after 1850. The key to the revolution was machinery capable of manufacturing goods at a far more rapid pace than the individual artisan. Powered first by water, then by steam after the development of James Watts' steam engine in 1769, these machines could be concentrated in factories, and run day and night to mass-produce goods at a cheaper price and in larger quantities.

The first sector to be transformed was textiles, with the development of spinning and weaving machines. Innovation spread: to iron bridges, steam railways, high-speed printing presses. Traditional artisan-based trades producing goods such as pottery, cutlery and haberdashery were soon converting to factory methods.

In search of raw materials and larger markets for their products, traders took their goods abroad, tapping into and enlarging the European colonial possessions that formed ever greater empires for Britain, France and the Netherlands, and later Germany and Belgium. But back at home a large working class was often labouring long hours in dreadful conditions for wages that kept them barely off the bread line.

In the late 1840s a combination of poor harvests, social inequality, dissatisfaction with the conservative regimes of

Colonial empires at the start of the 20th century

▲	1	German
	2	Belgian
▲	3	British
▲	4	French
	5	Dutch

the new monarchies, and the newly forged socialist ideas, created an inflammable atmosphere across Europe. An uprising in Paris in February 1848 was the catalyst for a string of revolts in Berlin, Vienna, Prague and Budapest. However, after some concessions, many of these uprisings heralded a period of dictatorial rule, as in France under Louis Napoleon, and Austria under Emperor Franz Josef.

Nonetheless, the revolts widened the debate about political representation, and set an agenda for reformers. The coming decades saw a gradual movement towards democracy, greater access to education and a steady liberalisation of the Press.

one problem threatened the status quo: the breakup of the Ottoman Empire of Turkey, across the strategically vital eastern Mediterranean. The vacuum led to serious clashes, such as the Crimean War (1854-6) in which Britain, France and Turkey took on the Russians.

Another source of concern was Germany. Kaiser Wilhelm II (reigned 1888-1918) was ambitious to make Germany a powerful imperial nation, and set about constructing a navy to rival that of Britain, the acknowledged ruler of the waves. The result was an

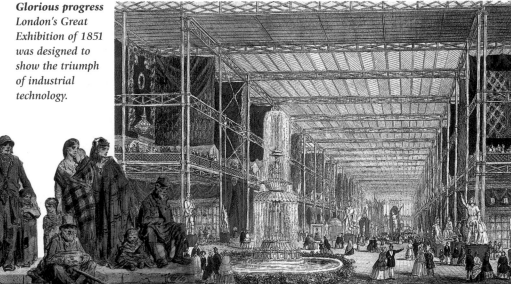

Glorious progress London's Great Exhibition of 1851 was designed to show the triumph of industrial technology.

During this era the modern political parties began to take shape, such as the Conservatives in Britain, and the Social Democratic Party in Germany. By the 1890s Britain, France, Germany, Switzerland and Belgium all had electoral systems based on extensive adult male suffrage; Austrian men had to wait until 1907.

Imperial rivalry

The colonial ambitions of the Western European nations led to confrontations, but by and large they stayed within their agreed spheres of influence. However,

Streets of London The distress and hardship at the heart of the British Empire was captured by the French artist Gustave Doré in around 1870. A survey in the 1880s-90s found that nearly a third of Londoners were living in dire poverty.

arms race that gathered pace after 1900. Meanwhile, France and Germany remained at loggerheads over Alsace-Lorraine, ceded to Germany in 1871. Peace was maintained only through the big-power alliances between Germany,

Paris in flames The mood of revolution in Europe in 1848 erupted in riots in Paris, forcing the abdication of King Louis-Philippe.

A united Germany, in France

On January 18, 1871, a new country appeared on the map of Europe: on that day, bolstered by his rapid victory in the Franco-Prussian War, the Prussian chancellor (prime minister) Otto von Bismarck announced the creation of the German Empire. Since his appointment as chancellor in 1862, Bismarck had campaigned for a united Germany, bringing together over 30 states. First he had shaken off the grip of Austria, which was defeated at Sadowa (Königgrätz) in 1866; this allowed Bismarck to forge the North-German Confederation of states. Then, in 1870, he exploited French obstinacy over succession to the Spanish throne to goad France into war. This persuaded the southern German states of Bavaria, Württemberg and Baden to join the confederation. However, the new empire did not encompass all German-speaking people: it omitted the Germans of Austria and included large minorities of Poles, Danes and the people of Alsace-Lorraine.

This failure to encompass all German-speaking people under one nation had serious consequences when the Pan-German movement was translated into an aggressive form of nationalism during the 20th century.

Victory salute Wilhelm I was proclaimed German emperor in Versailles, following his victory in the Franco-Prussian War.

Austria-Hungary and Italy on the one hand, and Russia and France on the other. Britain remained aloof.

This was the setting for the belle époque, the Edwardian era of the early years of the 20th century – an Indian summer for the European colonial powers, before catastrophe struck.

The First World War

It was in the Balkans, the volatile borderlands of the old Ottoman Empire, where the first shot was fired. The assassination at Sarajevo of the heir to the Habsburg throne called in the complex structure of international alliances, and pushed almost all of Europe and their overseas colonies into war. On August 3, 1914,

War on an industrial scale

The First World War was unlike any previous war. Locked in a stalemate, the world's most powerful industrial nations hurled at each other all the industrial might they could muster. Guns could now fire shells of huge explosive power at an enemy beyond the range of vision; machine guns, armoured tanks and bombardments from aircraft heightened the impersonalised destructive power of the contending nations. Hundreds of thousands of soldiers were pressed into the quagmire of the trenches before being dispatched in wave after wave of doomed assaults on the enemy. The casualties on both sides mounted relentlessly: 1.2 million at the Somme in 1916; 890 000 at Verdun in 1916; 500 000 at Passchendaele in 1917. Some 8 million died altogether.

The pity of war Otto Dix's experiences in the German army during the First World War coloured his painting thereafter. His anti-military sentiments caused his work to be banned by the Nazis.

Sarajevo, 1914 The assassination of Archduke Franz Ferdinand by a Serb nationalist sparked off the war.

German forces breached Belgian neutrality to invade France. Their advance was halted by French and British forces; each side dug in and faced one another in lines of trenches. Germany and Austria-Hungary (the Central Powers) launched an attack to the east against Poland, Russia and Romania. As the conflict escalated, 32 countries were dragged into what became known as the Great War.

Goaded by German U-boat activity against ships trading with Britain,

the US entered the war on the Allied side in April 1917. The Russian Revolution reduced pressure on the eastern front and allowed Germany to concentrate on the west. A German push in March 1918 met with some success, but an Allied counter-offensive in August, assisted by US divisions, knocked the Germans back. The Central Powers now began to crumble across the whole theatre of war, from Europe to the Middle East. On November 11, 1918, the

Germans surrendered, and an armistice was signed. Over 8 million servicemen had died.

An uneasy peace

The peace conditions imposed by the victors in the Treaty of Versailles of 1919 were uncompromising. Germany had to admit responsibility for the war. France, which had lost 1.4 million men in the conflict, was determined to ensure that Germany would never threaten its security again: it won the return of Alsace-Lorraine and insisted on occupied and demilitarised buffer zones in the

Rhineland. The German armed forces were restricted to 100 000 men, and deprived of any significant armaments. Prussian Poland and much of West Prussia was awarded to Poland. Germany also had to give up its colonies. It was a humiliation for Germany, added to which the demands

New dimension *The potential of flight for reconnaissance and bombardment was discovered during the First World War.*

The Great War: the Western Front

The Allied Powers
Germany

Fronts :
— end of 1914
--- July 1918
--- September 1918
—— November 1918
☆ Battle

North Sea
Passchendaele 1917
Ypres 1914 1915
NETHERLANDS
Brussels
Neuve-Chapelle 1915
Meuse
GERMANY
BELGIUM
Somme
Somme 1916
LUXEMBOURG
Chemin des Dames 1917
Rethondes
FRANCE
Verdun 1916
Saar
Oise
Reims
Metz
Seine
Marne 1914 1918
Strasbourg
Paris
Toul

Women's work *Women took on a broad range of wartime responsibilities.*

for heavy reparations drained the means to reconstruct its economy.

The whole of Europe was slow to recover. There was a slump in the early 1920s caused by over-production, which led to massive unemployment, lockouts and labour unrest. Britain was paralysed by a brief General Strike in 1926, evidence of the growing power of the trade unions. Meanwhile, the well-to-do and Bright Young Things were dowsing memories of the Great War in a high-spending tearaway whirl of cocktail parties, American jazz and the Charleston. But the Roaring Twenties came to an abrupt close in the slump that followed the Wall Street Crash of 1929.

For Germany the Crash created yet greater economic difficulties. The communists advocated a restructuring of society along the lines of the revolutionary Soviet Union. By contrast, the National Socialists (Nazis), led by Adolf

Historical reflections *The Treaty of Versailles, signed in June 1919, imposed heavy reparations on the defeated Germany.*

Hitler, appealed to German nationalism. Identifying the Germans as an Aryan master race, they advocated restoration of national pride through militaristic discipline and persecution of the Jews, who were charged with profiting from Germany's economic plight and supporting communism. Hitler achieved power in 1933, pushing aside the faltering Weimar Republic to declare the Third Reich (empire). He immediately turned Germany into a totalitarian state and adopted the title Führer (leader). He stripped the Jews of their rights in 1935,

Votes for women

The drive for equality in law, marriage rights, taxation and work was the focus of women's movements in many countries in the late 19th century. The British suffragettes, led by Mrs Emmeline Pankhurst, opted to focus on women's right to vote. They campaigned from 1903 onwards, but in 1914 they still had not achieved the vote. Their willingness to abandon the campaign and throw their energies into the war effort persuaded the government to relent in 1918. Women won the vote in Germany in 1918, and in the Netherlands in 1920, but French women had to wait until 1945.

British suffragettes.

the central planks of the Nazi agenda was to annihilate the Jews throughout Germany and all occupied territory. Hitler's initial intention was to work the Jews to death in concentration camps, but many thousands were simply shot. These methods were soon considered inefficient, so in January 1942 the Nazi leadership devised the so-called Final

The road to freedom *The towns of Normandy were devastated after the Allied landings of 1944. By the end of the war a year later, much of Europe lay in ruins.*

and began re-arming. In 1936 Hitler remilitarised the Rhineland, then in March 1938 he annexed Austria, claiming common Germanic bonds.

The Second World War

On September 1, 1939, Germany launched a *Blitzkrieg* ('lightning war') on Poland. Britain and France, which had guaranteed Polish sovereignty, were obliged to declare war on Germany. On May 10, 1940, the Germans invaded neutral Luxembourg, Belgium and the Netherlands, outflanking the Maginot Line built by France to protect its border with Germany. The British evacuated 338 000 troops from Dunkirk at the end of the month. France capitulated on June 22, and negotiated a settlement by which the northern half of France would be under German occupation, and the rest ruled by a pro-German French government under Marshal Pétain from Vichy in central France.

From August to November 1940, Britain came under repeated attack from the air in preparation for a German invasion, but its Royal Air Force, bolstered by pilots from Canada, New Zealand, Australia, South Africa, the USA, Poland, Czechoslovakia, Belgium, Holland and France, inflicted heavy losses on the Germans and won the Battle of Britain. London was now the headquarters of the resistance to Hitler, sheltering Queen Wilhelmina of the Netherlands and General de Gaulle, leader of the Free French, and numerous other refugees.

Occupied Europe

The Germans conducted an occupation policy of ruthless exploitation, commandeering labour, and executing hostages in reprisals for resistance activity. One of

---

Resistance

In occupied countries ordinary people faced a dilemma. Would the Germans stay for ever? Was it wiser to cooperate and play the long game? Was resistance worth the horrific reprisals it could provoke? Despite the dangers, many people joined the resistance, inspired by national pride and by the injustices of Nazi rule. Escape networks spirited downed Allied airmen to safety, ordinary people became obstructive. Bands of men and women led guerrilla campaigns of sabotage and beamed intelligence reports to the Allies. There was also resistance in Germany. In July 1944, a group of officers tried and failed to kill Hitler. They suffered the same kind of fate of any opponent of the Nazi regime: they were hanged with piano wire.

Faces of war *Revellers in Piccadilly Circus, London, celebrate VE Day. The inhumanity of the Nazi regime had been exposed by the liberation of the concentration camps, such as Auschwitz in Poland (above).*

The will to unite *The Treaty of Rome, signed on March 25, 1957, established the European Economic Community and laid the foundations for the European Union.*

Solution: the gas chambers of the extermination camps. This genocidal policy, later called the Holocaust, took the lives of over 6 million Jews.

D-Day

The fortunes of the European war shifted when the USA joined forces with the Allies after Pearl Harbor had been attacked by the Japanese in December 1941. In the autumn of 1942, British troops under General Montgomery began a successful counter-offensive in North Africa, and in the following winter the Soviet Union devastated the German Sixth Army at Stalingrad and began their push west. On June 6, 1944, the Allies launched the D-Day landings on the beaches of Normandy, securing a foothold on Europe. They had to fight all the way to Berlin before Hitler committed suicide and Germany surrendered on May 8, 1945.

Europe divided and united

Among the victors there was relief and jubilation at the end of a war that had cost somewhere between 50 and 60 million lives. But the Soviet Union took the opportunity to impose communist puppet governments in the countries of Eastern Europe under its control, including the eastern half of Germany. Western Europe and the Soviet bloc now stood on two sides of a divide that Winston Churchill, in 1946, dubbed the Iron Curtain.

Europe to the West of the Iron Curtain now set about reconstruction, greatly aided by funds supplied by the USA under the Marshall Plan. To encourage

The end of empire

The prestige of the European colonial powers was damaged by the war, particularly by the Japanese conquest of the Far East. After the war, the British, Dutch and French tried to reclaim their Far Eastern colonies, but were resisted by nationalist movements. The Dutch left most of Indonesia in 1949; the French lost Indochina and were defeated in Vietnam in 1954; the British granted independence to India and Pakistan in 1947, Burma in 1948 and Malaya in 1957. Independence for the African colonies followed.

cooperation and reconciliation, six countries – France, Germany, Belgium, Luxembourg, Italy and the Netherlands – formed the European Steel and Coal Community in 1952. In 1957 they signed the Treaty of Rome to form the European Economic Community (EEC). In 1973 Denmark, the United Kingdom and Ireland joined. By the end of the 1990s the European Community had become a European Union of 15 nations.

When the communist regimes of Eastern Europe and the Soviet Union

Joined in remembrance *François Mitterrand of France and Helmut Kohl of Germany remember their countries' war dead.*

The Wall comes down *Reviled as a symbol of communist tyranny, the Berlin Wall was breached on November 9, 1989.*

collapsed in 1989-90, West Germany reunited with East Germany. At the turn of the new millennium, Western Europe is continuing on a path of integration, yet the history of each nation ensures that the national identities forged over centuries will never be expunged.

The Normandy landing beaches: June 6, 1944

English Channel

AMERICAN SECTOR | BRITISH/CANADIAN SECTOR

Cherbourg

Ste-Mère-Église

UTAH OMAHA GOLD JUNO SWORD

Carentan Isigny Port-en-Bessin Arromanches

St-Lô Caen

Coutances Orne

Front line by June 12

Front line by July 25

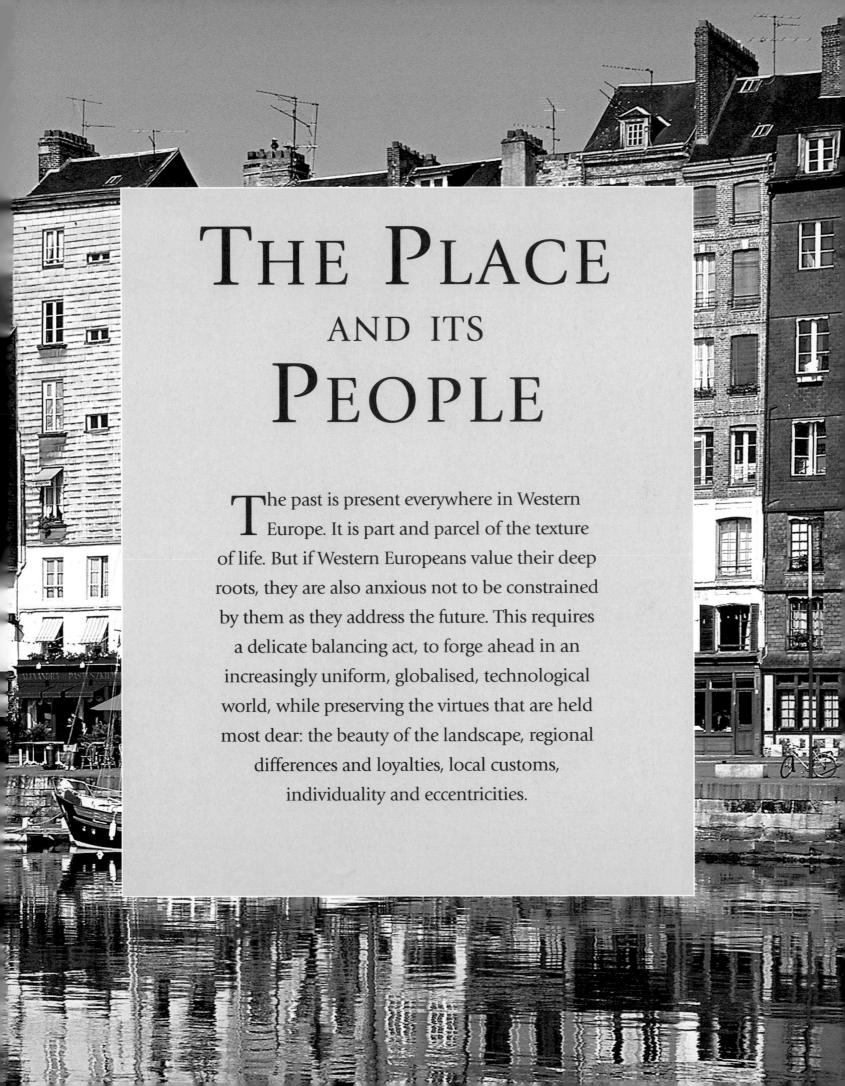

THE PLACE
AND ITS
PEOPLE

The past is present everywhere in Western Europe. It is part and parcel of the texture of life. But if Western Europeans value their deep roots, they are also anxious not to be constrained by them as they address the future. This requires a delicate balancing act, to forge ahead in an increasingly uniform, globalised, technological world, while preserving the virtues that are held most dear: the beauty of the landscape, regional differences and loyalties, local customs, individuality and eccentricities.

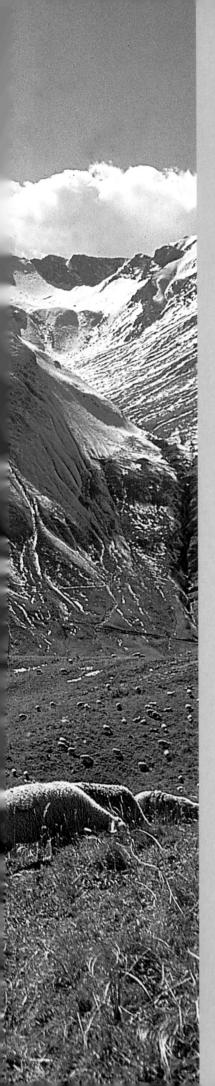

CHAPTER 1

EUROPE'S NATURAL BEAUTY

Journeying through the diverse landscapes of Western Europe, the observer becomes aware of their variety – dense German conifer forests; soft green Norman pastures; long white Belgian beaches; the jagged, rock-flanked inlets of the Mediterranean with limpid pools of ultramarine and turquoise; broom-covered moors of the Celtic lands; and lush alpine meadows. The nuances of change are usually gradual, but now and then they provide a shock, such as the chaos of granite on the Brittany coast, or the wild rock-strewn beauty of Connemara, or the sun-crisped ravines of Corsica.

The people of Western Europe have an ambiguous attitude towards nature. They claim to love the wild, yet they cannot stop themselves from trying to tame it. But while the imprint of human activity spreads relentlessly and becomes increasingly threatening, so the respect for nature deepens, and sharpens the desire to preserve what is left.

Col d'Allos, in the Alpes-de-Haute-Provence, France.

The Celtic fringe: hard lands, soft weather

The remote outer fringes of Western Europe once provided refuge for the Celts from land-hungry Romans and Anglo-Saxons. Today this very remoteness, and the untamed ruggedness of the landscape, are essential elements of their charm.

Wild West *Ireland's rocky Dingle Peninsula is one of the most westerly points of Europe.*

The west coast of Ireland can be bathed in a gentle misty drizzle, reducing visibility to a few feet, for days on end. It is weather that the Irish beguilingly call 'soft', a term which chimes with the climate generally. Warmed by the Gulf Stream, which funnels across the Atlantic from the Caribbean, the temperature rarely drops below 5°C (40°F), and winters are never severe. Because there is so little frost, country lanes are lined with fuchsia hedges, and woodlands are awash with rhododendrons.

Geometric rocks *The Giant's Causeway in Northern Ireland was formed when lava entered the sea, cooled and split into 40 000 hexagonal pillars.*

All this rain provides the inland pastures with a carpet of rich green grass, the ultimate source of Ireland's famous butter and other dairy products, as well as the sobriquet 'the Emerald Isle'. In less well-drained areas, millennia of damp vegetal debris have created vast expanses of peat bog, with a wild beauty all of its own. But nothing quite prepares the visitor for the contrast between these inland landscapes and the ferocious surging and churning of the ocean along the coast, where the Atlantic collides with breathtaking ramparts of sheer cliffs and tumbled rocks. On the coast of County Clare, the spectacular Cliffs of Moher present a curtain of rock 650 ft (200 m) high, running in serried pleats for a full 6 miles (10 km).

A family of landscapes

All the old Celtic lands on the extremities of Western Europe share a broadly similar blend of rugged coastline and a well-watered inland mosaic of marsh, heath, pasture and woodland. The differences are primarily in height: Scotland and Wales have mountains – rising to 4406 ft (1343 m) in the case of Ben Nevis, Britain's highest peak, and 3560 ft (1085 m) for Snowdon. By contrast Cornwall's highest point is the granite moorland of Bodmin, which reaches 1377 ft (419 m) at Brown Willy. Cornwall is said to have two landscapes. The north coast is rugged, and lined with cliffs and rocky inlets. The south is altogether softer, where meadows and oak woods drop down to tidal estuaries, gathering the warmth of the sun with their south-facing aspect.

Brittany is also divided into two: the deeply chiselled coastline facing the Atlantic is known as Armor (Breton for 'Land of the Sea'), while the inland area around the regional capital Rennes is called Argoat ('Land of the Woods'). Once a mighty mountain, known as the Massif Amoricain, dominated the region, but over 300 million years this has been whittled down from an estimated 13 000 ft (4000 m) to a landscape of undulating hills rising to no more than 1132 ft (345 m) at the Monts d'Arrée in the north-west.

The sea is a defining element of Brittany, with its numerous picturesque fishing ports and countless islands, including several larger ones, such as Ouessant and Belle-Île, famed for their windswept beauty. As elsewhere in these Celtic lands, Bretons are fiercely proud of their separate identity, expressed in their language (closely related to Cornish), and their customs, such as the women's lace headdresses, seen on special occasions like pilgrimage processions and festivals.

The legend of King Arthur

The English imagine King Arthur, Queen Guinevere, Sir Lancelot and Merlin in the misty landscapes of ancient Britain. But the Welsh also have their versions of the Arthurian legend, and so do the French. Both Tintagel in Cornwall and Cadbury Castle in Somerset are claimed to be the site of Camelot. In Brittany, the Forest of Brocéliande is famed as the place where Merlin lived and died, and where Arthur received Excalibur from the fairy Vivian, the Lady of the Lake. Whatever the version, these myths reflect the mystical quality of the Celtic landscape, redolent of ancient times.

Wizardry *These rocks in Brittany are said to mark Merlin's tomb.*

Connemara's wild beauty

Connemara: the name alone sings of the poetic beauty of this corner of Galway in western Ireland. Bereft of economic resources, for centuries its poverty was the cause of painful migration and yearning. Today it has found new riches in its natural beauty, for this wild paradise has become a celebrated tourist destination.

The landscape of Connemara is dominated by a low crown of mountains visible for miles around, and constantly changing with the play of mist and the shadows of fleeting clouds. These are the Twelve Bens, or Pins, girdled by a crescent of lakes and by large expanses of peat bog, where pools of water reflect the sky like a million glinting mirrors. Clifden, a pretty little market town, is the largest settlement of the region and self-styled capital of Connemara. Fishing villages lie scattered along the ragged coastline, once the haunt of a famous pirate queen of Elizabethan times, Grace O'Malley. In many villages the main language is still Irish, a Gaelic tongue.

The view from on high

To the north of Clifden lies the Connemara National Park, with miles of steep trails leading up through pastures, where Connemara ponies roam, to the heights of four of the Twelve Bens, and vast panoramic views. To the south, and under the protection of the National Park, lies the Roundstone Bog, home to countless marshland flowers and otters.

The Aran beetle *Fishermen carry their tar-coated currachs to safety beyond the reach of the tide.*

The Aran Islands

To the south of Connemara, in the mouth of Galway Bay, lie three islands celebrated for their rugged and remote beauty: Inishmore (the large island), Inishmaan and Inishsheer – the Aran Islands. Traditional life was hard, for it depended on the treacherous sea and on coaxing crops out of the barren limestone land made fertile with seaweed. Today the Aran Islands live mainly by tourism, but they still retain the charm of their whitewashed thatched cottages and miles of dry-stone walls, absorbing the warmth of the mild climate in the lee of the Atlantic winds.

The gift for horses

Devotees come from all over the world to buy Connemara ponies – a breed famous for its gentle temperament and hardy constitution. The Irish have a famous affinity for horses, witnessed at the great thoroughbred races at The Curragh, Leopardstown, Galway, or on the beach at Laytown. Today all kinds of horses are brought to Ballinasloe in County Galway for the October horsefair, where theatrical bouts of bargaining are refereed by a 'tangler', then sealed with 'luck money' given to the buyer. However, even this event pales when compared to the horsefairs of the 18th century, when most European nations sent agents to Ballinasloe to buy thousands of horses for their cavalries.

Splendid isolation *Lough Inagh is one of a chain of lakes lying below the Twelve Bens.*

Protecting nature

The national parks and nature reserves of Western Europe are museums of the natural world. From Ireland to Austria, millions of square miles of spectacular landscapes have been cordoned off and placed under government protection. But a dilemma remains over quite how much of this heritage should be accessible to the public.

Blunt needle *The flat-topped Mont Aiguille (Mount Needle) dominates the eastern flank of the Parc Régional du Vercors near Grenoble, south-eastern France.*

Waste paper and other residues disfigure natural beauty. Take them with you! reads a stern notice in five languages in the Parc Naziunal Svizzer (Swiss National Park). Don't pick a single flower! Leave your dog at home! There are many other prohibitions in this high and spectacular region of the Alps in south-eastern Switzerland: no fishing, hunting, skiing, camping, berry-picking – or even loud noises. The plants and animals – the alpine flowers, marmots, ibex, chamois, red deer and roe deer – are to be left entirely to their own devices, and have to do their best to ignore the thousands of hikers who crowd the signposted trails during the summer months.

National parks and nature reserves have to strike a delicate balance. On the one hand, they are there to protect landscapes of outstanding natural beauty from damage by human activity, especially industrial exploitation, mining, logging – and also tourism. On the other hand, they are public property, and receive at least some of their funds from entrance permits and other contributions by users. The parks need the public, but must also protect themselves from being over-used.

Pristine setting *Hohe Tauern, in the eastern Alps, is Austria's largest national park. It was founded in 1971.*

New phenomenon

Europe's national parks vary enormously in size. The Parc Naziunal Svizzer, for example, covers only 65 sq miles (169 km²), while the English Lake District extends for 880 sq miles (2280 km²). Yet all are dwarfed by the great parks of the USA, where the national park movement was founded with Yellowstone (3468 sq miles/8982 km²) in 1872. The concept took a while to catch on in Europe. In fact the Parc Naziunal Svizzer, established in 1914, was one of Europe's trailblazers. The British national parks came into existence only in 1949: ten areas were set aside in the wake of this during the 1950s, including the Lake District, Snowdonia, Exmoor, Dartmoor, the North Yorkshire Moors and the Yorkshire Dales. (Scottish equivalents are called National Scenic Areas.)

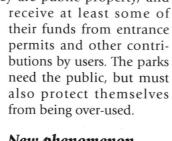

The trust of the nation

The protection of nature depends heavily on private initiative: commercial ventures rarely share the same concerns. One of the most important bodies protecting the natural and historic heritage of England, Wales and Northern Ireland is the National Trust. (Scotland has its own organisation.) Founded as a private venture in 1895, the Trust is wholly funded by entrance fees, legacies, and the subscriptions of its 2 million members.

reserves often have their own rules, depending on local conditions.

Each park and reserve has its own unique, highly localised ecosystem; taken together Europe's parks and reserves represent a priceless compendium of the region's wildlife. They play an important role in research, for only in such relatively undisturbed environments can the natural patterns of flora and fauna be closely observed. Their international significance is symbolised by the use of the parks by migrating birds, which do not respect national borders. For example, the nature reserve and bird sanctuary of Het Zwin on the Belgian coast, near Knokke-Heist, may cover only 370 acres (150 ha), but it provides refuge for storks, greylag geese, oyster catchers, avocets and golden orioles. There is now widespread agreement that parks and reserves have a vital role in Europe's agenda. They have become an essential part of the very definition of modern European civilisation.

The six French national parks were instituted in the 1960s and 1970s; the Germans and Austrians followed suit by announcing a series of parks in the 1980s. But the chronology is misleading: not all national parks have the same regime of protection, and much depends on the history, geography and ecology of each site. Some European national parks owe their origin less to the American model than to ancient hunting forests, which were jealously protected for the use of monarchs and the nobility from medieval times onwards. This is the case of the New Forest, in southern England, which became a national park in 1992.

By contrast, De Hoge Veluwe National Park near Arnhem in the Netherlands – home to wild boar, red deer and mouflons (wild sheep) – was created by private benefactors who bought the 13 000 acres (5500 ha) of land in 1909-14; it became a national park in 1935. The Alpine splendour of the Berchtesgaden region of Bavaria has been protected since 1911, but became a national park in 1978. In this case, so legend has it, the magnificent scenery of lakes and mountains was created by angels sent to distribute the world's beauty. They were so startled by a sudden divine command that they dropped their entire cargo here.

Commanding heights The 11th century Prunn Castle rises from an escarpment overlooking the Altmühl Valley, a region of Bavaria famed for its outstanding beauty, and now one of Germany's largest nature parks.

European heritage

Each nation has its own grading system for parks and reserves. France's six primary national parks are all uninhabited areas, while those in Britain include houses, farms, and even whole villages – as well as protected wilderness areas. Smaller

The Parc National des Pyrénées

To the south of Lourdes and lying along some 60 miles (100 km) of the Spanish border, the Parc National des Pyrénées contains some of the most dramatic landscapes in France. Beneath the soaring heights – which include the Sommet du Vignemale, at 10 820 ft (3298 m) the highest peak in the French Pyrenees – there are a series of spectacular cirques (semicircular basins), which drop down to dozens of high-altitude lakes and forested valleys. Created in 1967, the park now has over 200 miles (320 km) of marked trails of varying difficulty for walkers. The park has a wide range of wildlife, including brown bears, marmots, lynxes, chamois (known here as izards), golden eagles and griffon vultures (left).

Colour field *The flat, sandy earth north of Leiden has proved ideal for commercial tulip growing.*

The Netherlands: adapting nature

Each year, between March and May, the bulb-growing region of the Netherlands erupts into a mosaic of vivid colour as the commercially grown flowers come into bloom. Centuries-old expertise has made the Netherlands the world's leading exporter of cut flowers and flower bulbs.

A strip of old dunes, drained lakes and marshland lines the west coast of the Netherlands, sheltering Amsterdam and other cities of the Randstad, the country's principal commercial region. This is one of the most heavily populated areas of Europe, with a landscape moulded, shaped and worked by human ingenuity. Ranks of greenhouses produce lettuces, tomatoes and cucumbers for the vegetable markets of Europe. But what this region is famous for, above all, is flowers – and especially tulips. For 30 miles (50 km) between Leiden and Alkmaar, across a landscape of immaculate flatness, there are countless bulbfields, manicured into neat ranks that blossom suddenly in the spring.

The crocuses open the season in March, followed by the daffodils and narcissi; then come the hyacinths and early tulips, with late tulips flowering through May. Many of the blooms are cut and sold at market, but most are churned up by machines – the industry

By the truck-load Specially designed flower transporters ply the routes to and from the market at Aalsmeer.

Dutch auction   The flower auction rooms at Aalsmeer are highly automated and computerised. As successive lots of flowers are presented on trolleys, prices are shown on large display dials. The buyers can signal what they are prepared to pay by operating electronic buttons on their desks.

is primarily geared to bulb production, and strong healthy bulbs are produced by cutting the natural cycle in its prime.

To market

Bulbs are just one aspect of the region's flower production. The growing year continues with freesias, sweet peas, carnations, roses, chrysanthemums, dahlias, orchids, and potted plants such as cyclamen and begonias. Almost all of this production is sold at the vast Bloemenveiling (flower auction) at Aalsmeer, a town surrounded by acre upon acre of greenhouses just 8 miles (13 km) south-west of Amsterdam. Aalsmeer's auction halls – measuring 7.6 million sq ft (710 000 m^2) – are in the record books as the world's largest commercial building under one roof. Astronomical numbers of flowers pass through this market – 20 million every weekday – many destined for export.

The polders

God made Heaven and Earth, the old saying goes, but the Dutch made Holland. The people of the Low Countries have been reclaiming land from the sea since the 11th century. Their method was straightforward: first they built a surrounding dyke, together with canals and sluice gates; then they pumped the water out of the enclosed area into the canals, leaving behind fertile drained land, known as polders, which served as pasture or arable land. With the advancing technology of the 20th century, ever more ambitious projects were undertaken. Now almost one-fifth of the total land area of the Netherlands is below sea level – including much of its most heavily populated regions. The polders around Aalsmeer, for instance, are 9-15 ft (3-5 m) below sea level.

Polders created :
- before the 20th century
- in the 20th century
- dike

NETHERLANDS

IJsselmeer
Alkmaar
Haarlem • ■ Amsterdam
Leiden • • Aalsmeer
North Sea
■ The Hague
■ Rotterdam
GERMANY
Meuse
Rhine
BELGIUM

Dutch windmills

Windmills are as much a part of the Dutch landscape as tulips, and for good reason. The use of windmills in the 17th and 18th centuries revolutionised the construction and maintenance of the nation's polders. Previously, drained land had been kept free of water by bucket elevators powered by animals, but pumps operated by windmills – driven by the breezes blowing across the flat landscape – worked far more efficiently. Some windmills in the Netherlands were used for grinding grain, or even sawing wood, but most of the 10 000 that once crowded the landscape were built as water pumps.

Wind power   There are still about 300 working windmills in the Netherlands.

Dealing with the forces of destruction

Western Europe has a temperate climate, and seldom features in accounts of the world's greatest natural disasters. Nonetheless, it has its share of destructive weather. An equally troubling threat, however, comes from the damage caused by human activity and negligence.

Every little helps *Sorting domestic waste makes recycling more efficient and effective.*

In Western Europe the destructive forces of nature usually manifest themselves in bouts of intemperate weather. On October 16, 1987, a hurricane-force wind swept across southern Britain, flattening thousands of trees, cutting power lines, killing 17 people and causing £300 million worth of damage. In late January 1995 the great rivers of northern Europe – the Rhine, Main, Moselle and Meuse – swelled and burst their banks, causing widespread flooding and 30 deaths, and forcing some 250 000 people in the Netherlands to evacuate their homes. Similar devastation occurred in Germany in July 1997 after record-breaking rainfall caused the River Oder to flood. In places the river spread to 330 yd (300 m) wide and became 20 ft (7 m) deep, inundating towns and villages, as well as the city of Frankfurt an der Oder. In February 1999 record snow

Black tides

There can hardly be a more vivid illustration of the dangers of pollution than the sight and stench of beaches sticky with a blanket of crude oil, and oil-smothered seabirds gasping to draw breath. The coasts of Western Europe have been hit by a series of catastrophic oil spills. In 1978 the *Amoco Cadiz* ran aground off the coast of Brittany. As the ship split in two, it released

The price of petrol *Birds are the sad victims of oil spills.*

230 000 tons of oil onto 70 miles (110 km) of the coastline, including some of France's most beloved beaches. The wreck of the *Braer* off the Shetland Islands in 1993 poured oil into one of Britain's richest areas for wildlife, the habitat of seals, otters and numerous birds.

Overflowing waters *In the floods of 1997, the bridges are all that show the usual path of Germany's River Oder.*

falls in the Alps provoked a series of avalanches, including one near the French town of Chamonix that buried a group of chalets and claimed 12 lives.

In many cases of freak weather there is a suspicion that human activity is somehow to blame. Has pollution – global warming even – affected weather patterns? Has too much building altered the natural drainage of the soil and rivers? The Mer de Glace (the second largest glacier in the Alps) has retreated measurably over recent decades, coinciding with expansion of the nearby town of Chamonix. No one yet knows why the glacier is shrinking, but it could be because of human impact on the environment, either locally or globally.

Pollution

There are many signs elsewhere of the damaging effects of human activity. Every household in Europe annually generates a ton of rubbish, which has to be disposed of somewhere in the environment. Meanwhile factories, power stations and motor vehicles pour sulphur dioxide and nitrogen oxide into the air, where it combines with water vapour to form acid rain. Some 50 per cent of forests in Germany and Switzerland have been damaged by acid rain, which also has the effect of slowly

Jostling for space *Industry and beach huts compete for a share of the shore at IJmuiden in the Netherlands.*

killing fish in rivers and lakes. Another source of damaging pollution for Europe's rivers is the run-off from farmers' fields that have been treated with chemical fertilisers, herbicides and pesticides. These pollutants kill insect larvae, plants and algae, wiping out the bottom rungs of the food chain on which all river life depends.

Fire *A forest burns in France.*

Accidents and simple acts of negligence also play their role. Each year over 5000 fires destroy some 111 000 acres (45 000 ha) of sun-dried scrub and forest in the garrigues or maquis of southern France. The coastlines of Western Europe have been regularly hit by devastating oil spills. The urgency of the need to address environmental pollution has placed the issue at the centre of the European Union's agenda, with particular attention on improving air quality, and the quality of bathing and drinking water.

The principle behind EU legislation is that the polluter pays, conferring responsibility on industry, local authorities and governments. Since the 1970s individuals also have become increasingly aware of the part they can play in helping to diminish environmental damage, from the use of unleaded petrol to the recycling of domestic waste. Schemes vary from country to country; in the Netherlands, for example, the authorities save organic waste and turn it into compost for gardeners.

The wolf returns

Ecosystems throughout Europe have been depleted by the loss or extinction of both plants and animals. In recent years efforts have been made to reintroduce certain species, such as beavers in Switzerland, and otters in parts of the UK. Large predators are more controversial. For 50 years France had no wolves. But in 1992 a breeding pair was reintroduced from Italy in the Parc National du Mercantour, in the southern Alps. They settled in well, and six years later there were some 20 wolves in the park.

The Belgian tundra

Walkers are warned not to lose their way in the Hautes Fagnes, a mysterious landscape of peat bogs, moors and heaths in south-east Belgium. The soggy microclimate ensures that this remains a strangely deserted world.

Hautes Fagnes – or Hohe Venn as they call it in this German-speaking corner of Belgium – means 'high fen'. It is a vast expanse of marshland, lying at an average height of 1300 ft (400 m) above sea level, and rising to the Signal de Botrange, at 2277 ft (694 m) the highest point in Belgium. A granite substratum prevents the high rainfall from running away, and over millennia has created a peat bog of accumulated sphagnum moss, where trees have difficulty taking root.

Michel Schmitz's inn

Desolate it may be, but this area has been crossed by trade routes since at least the 7th century, as old pillars and milestones testify. The damp atmosphere means that thick mists are a frequent hazard – a danger recognised by one Michel Schmitz, who in the early 19th century built a modest inn in the middle of the moor to lodge anyone caught out by bad weather or nightfall. When the weather closed in, a bell was rung to guide travellers towards the light. L'Auberge de la Baraque-Michel (Michael's hut) is still one of the few man-made landmarks on the plateau of the northern Hautes Fagnes, and today it serves as an information centre for walkers.

In winter the Hautes Fagnes is popular with skiers; the area has an unusual climate, with temperatures that are regularly lower than those of surrounding areas. Since 1971 it has been part of the Deutsch-Belgischer Naturpark, shared between Belgium and Germany, and covering 925 sq miles (2400 km^2).

Water world *Fishermen explore the canals of La Brière by boat.*

La Brière

Once upon a time, so the legend goes, a castle – or some say a hidden treasure – lay surrounded by a vast forest. To get his hands on it, a greedy magician flooded the entire area, and the result was La Brière, a huge area of marshland in western France, between the estuaries of the rivers Vilaine and Loire. A less fanciful theory explains that the landscape was created by the sediment of the two rivers, and the gradual retreat of the sea. Today the area is protected as the Parc Régional de Brière, the heart of which is accessible only by boat.

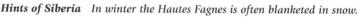

Hints of Siberia *In winter the Hautes Fagnes is often blanketed in snow.*

Corsica: forest and maquis

An island basking in the Mediterranean, Corsica is heady with the perfumes of its eucalyptus trees, citrus groves, herb-scented maquis scrubland, mountain pines and chestnut forests. No other Mediterranean island has such a variety of landscapes, from beaches to mountain peaks capped with snow in midsummer.

Corsica is walking country. A spectacular trail called Fra li Monte ('between the mountains'), or more prosaically GR20, snakes 110 miles (180 km) along the spine of the island – a two-week trek which, because of its height, is open only from June to October. There is uninhabited desert on the north-west coast, the Désert des Agriates, but then just to its south is the island's most fertile zone, the hilly Balagne region, slotted between the coast and Corsica's highest peak, Monte Cinto (8890 ft; 2710 m). Producing olives, oranges and lemons, prickly pear fruits, cheese and wine, La Balagne has been nicknamed the Garden of Corsica.

Much of the island consists of maquis, a dense scrubland of woody shrubs, holm oaks and cork oaks, aromatic with the volatile oils of mint, laurel, myrtle and thyme released by the summer sun. For centuries bandits would retreat into the maquis to evade capture and regroup, a practice taken up by French Resistance fighters during the Second World War.

A vast park

A fifth of the total surface area of Corsica is covered by forest, and over a third is taken up by the Parc Naturel Régional de Corse. Extraordinarily diverse, the park mirrors the full range of Corsican landscape. Most of it occupies the mountainous central region, with deep forest, rolling hills, gushing torrents and soaring peaks. But a western spur reaches down to the coast and includes the maritime nature reserve on the Scandola peninsula. Just to the south, overlooking the Golfe de Porto, rise the spectacular granite rock formations of Les Calanche, with spires of rock soaring to 1000 ft (300 m) above the sea.

Land of chestnuts

During the 16th century, the Genoese rulers of Corsica commandeered the island's grain crop for use back home, forcing the Corsicans to rely on chestnuts for food. So vital did chestnut flour become that the tree was dubbed *larbre pain* ('bread tree'). A key centre of production became known as La Castagniccia (Latin: *castanea*, 'chestnut'). This became one of the island's most prosperous regions, with huge groves of chestnut trees – some 65 ft (20 m) tall – producing thousands of tons of chestnuts every year. Today the chestnuts are used as pig fodder to produce a celebrated kind of pork, but chestnut flour is also still used for pastries.

Free range *Black pigs roam free in the huge forests of Corsica.*

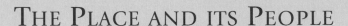

CHAPTER 2

PEOPLE AND RESOURCES

Western Europe was the birthplace of modern industry. The Industrial Revolution spread out from the Midlands of Britain to Belgium, then to France, Germany and beyond. But as technology advanced, and competition shifted first to the USA and then to newly industrialised countries, the old heavy industries of Europe withered. Since the Second World War, the economic structures of Western Europe have had to adapt or die. But the same ingenuity that created the Industrial Revolution helped to reposition the European economy. Emphasis switched to light engineering, financial services and the service industries, and improved agriculture. Manufacturers invited foreign investment; traders went out to reconquer the markets. They reinforced their traditional areas of expertise, such as food and wine, upgraded the infrastructure, renovated, innovated – determined not to be beaten at their own game.

Fishing fleet, Peterhead, Scotland.

Epicentre of wine

Western Europe – and France in particular – is acknowledged as the home of the finest wine traditions of the world. An industry valued in billions, it has fought to modernise and expand without compromising the quality of its greatest labels.

Noble order *The Chevaliers du Tastevin is an elite organisation of the world's foremost wine-tasters.*

The Romans brought vines to Western Europe, establishing vineyards in Burgundy, the Bordeaux region, and on the banks of the rivers Loire and Rhine. After the collapse of the Roman Empire, it fell to the monasteries to maintain the traditions, an association that is still acknowledged on many a wine label today. The complex art of wine-making – choosing and cultivating the vine stocks, harvesting, fermenting, blending, cellaring – evolved over generations, a resource of knowledge still preserved on many family-run estates.

During the 19th century these skills were taken far and wide, to Australia, California, South Africa, Argentina and Chile. At the same time, European wine-makers were plunged into crisis. A root-eating louse called the vine phylloxera, accidentally imported from the USA in 1863, devastated the vineyards of France and Germany. The remedy came in the end from the source of the problem: phylloxera-resistant vines were imported from the USA as rootstock, onto which the old vines could be grafted.

The aristocrats

France now produces around a billion bottles of wine a year. A small portion of this ranks among the finest wine in the world. The elite wines come in particular from the Bordeaux region around the Gironde (the estuary of the Dordogne and Garonne rivers) on the Atlantic coast – and notably the Médoc, a region to the south of the Gironde. This is home to the famous chateau-based estates, such as Chateau Margaux and Chateau Lafite-Rothschild, the real aristocrats of the wine world. The Burgundy region in the centre of France, lining the River Saône, also has its stable of prized estates from regions such as Chablis and Côte d'Or.

Vive la différence!

With a shorter growing season, Germany specialises in white wines from grapes such as Riesling, Müller-Thurgau and Gewürztraminer. The high sugar content imbues a rich and silky fruitiness to the wine. Natural sugars and wine quality depend on the ripeness and the warmth of each season, and this is reflected in specific German rankings such as *spätlese* ('late harvest').

A head for heights *The Valais region, the sunniest in Switzerland, has the highest vineyards in Europe.*

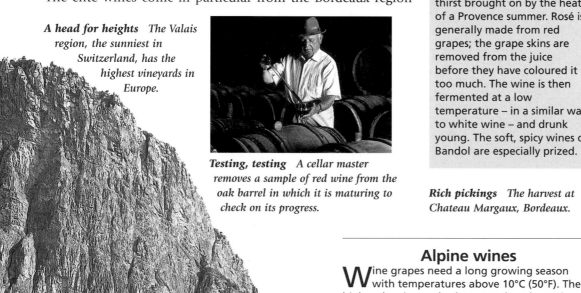

Testing, testing *A cellar master removes a sample of red wine from the oak barrel in which it is maturing to check on its progress.*

In the pink in Provence

The sun-drenched hillsides of southern France are famous for their delicious pink rosé wines – perfect for slaking a thirst brought on by the heat of a Provence summer. Rosé is generally made from red grapes; the grape skins are removed from the juice before they have coloured it too much. The wine is then fermented at a low temperature – in a similar way to white wine – and drunk young. The soft, spicy wines of Bandol are especially prized.

Rich pickings *The harvest at Chateau Margaux, Bordeaux.*

Alpine wines

Wine grapes need a long growing season with temperatures above 10°C (50°F). The higher the vineyards, the more they depend on microclimates and suntraps. Both Austria and Switzerland produce fine wines, mainly Germanic in style. The highest vines are often planted on steep south-facing terraces and surrounded by protective stone walls. Such vineyards are labour-intensive, so their wines tend to be expensive.

Autumn gold   Some grapes are harvested late in the year to produce a rich, sweet wine called 'spätlese'.

Champagne, king of wines

The court of Louis XIV took great pleasure in a white wine from the Champagne region which fizzed in its barrels during the late spring. By summer, however, this second fermentation had run its course and the wine was flat. A monk called Dom Pierre Pérignon devised a method of prolonging the court's pleasure, by trapping the fizz in bottles. Experimenting with tough glass bottles from England and corks from Spain, he induced a second fermentation in the bottle by adding yeast and syrup. There are many imitators around the world using this *méthode champenoise*, but what keeps real champagne ahead of all these is the chalky soil and cool climate of the region around Reims and Épernay.

Cold storage   A champagne cellar at Reims.

The taste of wine depends on countless factors, starting with climate and soil, and the grape varieties that these will sustain. Wine is grown throughout Western Europe, wherever conditions are favourable – in the heights of Switzerland, in the river valleys of Luxembourg, on the south-facing slopes of southern England. Ultimately, wines may be appreciated for very personal reasons, but price is a key factor in this highly competitive industry. Wine-makers have to manage their resources carefully to adopt the techniques that will achieve the right price for their particular market. Despite the romance of its long traditions, its great names, the excitement generated by each new harvest, wine-making is an industry like any other.

The English and claret

English kings ruled the French region of Aquitaine for 300 years following the marriage of Henry II to Eleanor of Aquitaine in 1152. Aquitaine included Bordeaux and some of France's finest wine-growing districts. The English imported wine by the shipload and developed a taste for the light, clear wine they called claret (French: *vin claret*). The French later abandoned the term; the English stuck to it, but by the 20th century it had come to refer to the red wines of Bordeaux generally. The British are still passionate about Bordeaux wines, and rank among their leading buyers.

45

Cereal success *The Beauce plain (top), near Chartres, is not only the premier grain-producing region of France, but of the European Union. Here, as in the Vexin region of Normandy farther north (above), production is highly mechanised.*

The northern plain: breadbasket of Europe

A green-and-yellow agricultural chequerboard spreads from Brittany to the Urals in Russia. Scraped flat by glaciers that began to recede 18 000 years ago, the North European Plain has been a key component in European civilisation.

Paris, the Randstad, the Ruhrgebiet . . . the North European Plain has not only become the region with the highest concentration of population and industrial activity, it is also the granary of Western Europe. Vast acreages produce large yields of wheat, corn (maize), barley, oats, beet and oil-seed rape. The soil of this flat land, however, is not always easy to work. It was shaped by Ice Age glaciers, which in Germany and the Netherlands left pebble-strewn moraines that evolved into marshes and peat bogs, saturated with water. It has taken centuries of hard work to drain and improve these areas.

Dutch agriculture is among the most intensive in the world, producing cattle, pigs and poultry. Holstein-Friesian cows, first bred in the Netherlands and northern Germany, are capable of producing some 1760 gallons (8000 litres) of milk per year each. In the German state of Schleswig-Holstein, the pastures won from the old marshlands are home to some of the most

The shape of the countryside

The rural landscape carries the imprint of history. Once Western Europe was covered in forest, with small clearings for agriculture. Now the reverse is more often the case. This is the result of the evolution of agriculture. With improved crop strains, higher yields and increasingly powerful ploughs, fields have become larger, often consuming the hedgerows and stone walls that once demarcated smaller holdings.

productive dairy farms in the world, renowned for the high quality of their produce.

Natural conditions are more favourable in France. Over half of the land in France is under arable cultivation, with wheat and corn the main crops. This section of the North European Plain has rich alluvial deposits, as seen for example in the Parisian Basin. The leading agricultural nation of Europe, France produces surpluses that make it the world's second largest exporter of agricultural products after the USA.

Organic food: the dietary revolution

The organic food movement offers an alternative approach to food. Spurning the use of chemical fertilisers and pesticides, it is the antithesis of the high-yield agribusiness.

Certified organic.

The debate about intensive farming methods is not new; people have been arguing about the benefits and drawbacks of intensive agriculture since the early years of the 20th century. In the 1920s, the Austrian philosopher Rudolf Steiner began preaching the benefits of traditional agriculture, without artificial fertilisers and pesticides. This led to biodynamic farming, the oldest non-chemical agricultural movement. It promoted a respect for, and protection of, natural ecosystems, the suppression of factory farming, as well as research into crop rotation and the effect of the lunar cycle on yields.

During the late 1960s and early 1970s, the popular revolt against the consumer society brought with it a call for a return to country traditions and self-sufficiency. Rejecting the use of synthetic pesticides and chemical fertilisers, advocates of organic or biological farming argued that their methods were better for the environment, and produced healthier, better tasting foods. These principles were applied not just to vegetables, but also to meat, with emphasis on animal welfare. A number of organisations were set up to promote and monitor organic agriculture, among them the Soil Association in Britain and the Association Française d'Agriculture Biologique in France.

There are now some 40 000 certified organic producers in the European Union. But the spread of the organic movement is uneven. The Belgians are still reluctant: organic agriculture represents only 1 per cent of the food products consumed, with just 41 331 acres (16 727 ha) devoted to it. The French, with 174 500 acres (70 620 ha), have rather more; the Germans have 692 000 acres (280 000 ha). In Britain, 678 340 acres (274 700 ha) are either organic already or undergoing conversion. The champions of all categories are the Austrians: with their 20 000 organic farms, they account for half of the European organic producers.

To a degree, organic farming is a luxury: the volume of cheap food available to all Western Europeans is a product of intensive farming techniques. The public, however, appears increasingly won over to organic products, even though they are generally more expensive.

Hand-picked *Harvesting an organic crop in the UK.*

Organic labelling

The labelling of organic produce has been regulated by the European Union since 1991, at least for vegetables. National organic farming organisations award certificates to farmers that meet their – and the EU's – criteria. To get approval, farmers must let their land rest under grass and clover for three years. Provided they continue to stick to the rules, they have the right to use the organisation's label on their produce – a privilege that is jealously guarded. In the case of processed foods, 95 per cent of the ingredients must be totally organic.

Free-range *Chickens that roam free, and are raised on organic feed, appeal to ever more consumers.*

Training slope In 1996 a slag heap at Noeux-les-Mines, in the Pas-de-Calais region of northern France, took on an entirely new life as a 350 yd (320 m) long artificial ski slope – an imaginative use for a notorious eyesore of the old coal-mining regions.

Mining museums

The last of the French coal mines, in the Massif Central, will operate until 2005. But already many old French mines have become part of industrial heritage. In the Nord-Pas-de-Calais, the Historic Mine Centre of Lewarde, near Douai, re-creates the great era of mining, and the lives of the *gueules noires* (literally, 'black faces'). Visitors are guided round the underground galleries by former miners. There is a comparable museum at Wakefield in West Yorkshire, where visitors are taken 460 ft (140 m) below ground.

Pit closure At the National Coal Mining Museum at Wakefield (inset), visitors learn about working life in mines such as the closed Pleasely Colliery.

The death of King Coal

One by one the coal mines closed. For generations the miners had provided the prime ingredient of industry, and fought for social justice through epic strikes. Now, in the Welsh valleys, the Scottish Lowlands, the Borinage in Belgium, the Nord-Pas-de-Calais in France they hung up their lamps for the last time and faced the dismal prospect of long-term unemployment.

In the 1930s, coal-mining was a major European industry, employing some 700 000 miners in the UK alone. But cheaper fuels, such as natural gas and oil, made the mines uncompetitive, and the old workings began to close down. In the UK this led to a bitter miners strike in 1984, but the die was cast, and when the last UK coal mine was privatised in 1995, there were just 13 500 coal miners left in the industry.

FOR ACCESS... TEL. 0623-812026

East meets West The Korean company Daewoo builds televisions at its plant at Fameck, in Lorraine, north-east France.

Enter the Japanese

Britain, founder of the Industrial Revolution, had to swallow its pride during the 1980s as it encouraged inward investment from foreign companies – notably Japanese. In 1986 Nissan opened its first car assembly plant in Sunderland, north-east England. Other Japanese manufacturers followed in its wake: Toyota, Sony, Hitachi, Toshiba. Soon other countries were wooing the Japanese. In 1997 Toyota promised to create up to 2000 jobs in an area of 20 per cent unemployment in north-east France.

Across Western Europe, the closure of coal mines, together with heavy industry in mining areas, has had repercussions on hundreds of thousands of people. Since the 1970s whole regions have suffered massive job losses, and been left with a degraded environment, and millions of acres of unsightly wasteland. Once the engine room of the world, these close-knit communities faced social and economic disintegration, and a devastating loss of self-worth.

Fortunately, many old mining areas have succeeded in attracting new industries – notably Wales, which has lured over 300 international companies to make use of its workforce.

Energy: nuclear versus fossil fuel

The sudden rise in oil prices, precipitated by the Arab-Israeli War of October 1973, plunged Western Europe into deep crisis. In an effort to meet their energy needs, many governments invested in nuclear energy – but it proved a troublesome option.

How clean? *The nuclear power station at Messe-Cruas, in Drôme, south-west France: the steam is clean, but what about the nuclear waste?*

In the 1960s, nuclear power seemed to be the energy source of the future. France took the lead in Western Europe, building 58 reactors that eventually contributed 75 per cent of the country's energy needs. Belgium, Switzerland, Germany and the United Kingdom all followed suit, though to a lesser degree.

In principle, nuclear power stations are efficient, economic and far less damaging to the atmosphere than those that burn fossil fuels. The problem is the lethal and insidious nature of radioactive fuel. The explosion at Chernobyl in the Ukraine in 1986 brought home the potential consequences of an accident. Nothing of this magnitude has occurred at any Western European nuclear power station; however, the disposal of nuclear waste poses serious questions. In the spring of 1998, it was discovered that a train taking radioactive material to the main French reprocessing plant at La Hague, on the Cherbourg peninsula, was contaminated, raising again the issue of nuclear safety.

No one feels comfortable with nuclear facilities close by, but all the alternatives also have their disadvantages. In Germany, the Green Party wants to abandon the country's nuclear programme in favour of coal, but coal-burning power stations produce greenhouse gases, which are known to be a potential cause of global warming – a serious threat in itself.

Energy resources

- Coal
- △ Gas
- Oil
- △ Nuclear power station

The Superphénix headache

France thought it had solved the energy problem: the fast-breeder Superphénix power station at Creys-Malville was designed to produce more nuclear fuel than it actually consumed. But throughout its ten-year history it was troubled by breakdowns and emergencies; it functioned for just 30 months, and was coupled to the grid for less than a year. In 1997 France announced that the reactor would be decommissioned. But this also poses many safety problems: the process will take several decades and will cost the French State over $1.5 billion.

The Ruhr: from coal to high-tech

Coal and steel are no longer the mainstays of the Ruhr valley, Europe's largest industrial zone. But since their decline in the 1970s, the Ruhr has refused to become a rustbelt. Instead it has succeeded in transforming its industrial base, and identity.

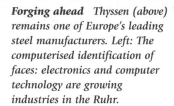

Forging ahead Thyssen (above) remains one of Europe's leading steel manufacturers. Left: The computerised identification of faces: electronics and computer technology are growing industries in the Ruhr.

When coal-mining began in the Ruhr valley in the 1820s, there were fewer than 275 000 people living in this region of north-west Germany, close to the Dutch and Belgian borders. Today the 2000 sq miles (5000 km²) south of the River Lippe, between Duisburg in the west and Dortmund in the east, are a vast conurbation, with 7.5 million inhabitants and one of the highest population densities in Europe.

Mending the landscape

The Ruhr was once famous for its industrial pollution. 'Between Dortmund and Duisburg', wrote the German author Heinrich Böll, 'white is just a dream.' In fact, beneath the grime, the Ruhr always retained some natural beauty, and since the 1970s major efforts have been made to clean up not just its environment but also its public image. Lakes, forests and areas of green belt now occupy nearly 60 per cent of the surface area of the Ruhr valley, and in the midst of many of the large cities, such as Duisburg or Dortmund, there are large public parks and open spaces. A major project has also been launched to clean up the Emscher Canal that runs across the north of the region.

The Golden Age of the Ruhr

Until the 1980s, the mines and steelworks of the Ruhrgebiet (Ruhr region) symbolised not just the industrial success of the area, but the power of the German economy. Several colossal industrial enterprises, such as Krupp and Thyssen, originated here. At its height earlier this century the Ruhr produced 110 million tons of coal a year, which was exported via Duisburg, the world's largest river port. But competition from oil, a steady rise in the costs of extraction, and a fall in demand for coal plunged the region into recession in the 1970s.

A successful conversion

Today there are fewer than 200 000 miners and steelworkers in the Ruhrgebiet, but this is still the powerhouse of Germany, with over 30 power stations; and steel is now used to supply new industries producing white goods (refrigerators, washing machines, dishwashers). As the large enterprises shrank, small and medium-sized businesses moved into the void: there are now some 450 000 of them, specialising in electronic or mechanical assembly and computer-based industries. Typical of these new industries is the groundbreaking research being done at Bochum into computerised identification of faces.

European industry: the big wheels

The countries of Europe have given birth to several giants of industry – Philips, Nestlé, Unilever – which are proud of their national origins, but now have global perspectives and multinational loyalties.

Philips has come a long way since the Dutch engineer Gerard Philips set up a small factory to manufacture light bulbs in April 1891. The company is now a world leader in electronics, lighting and household appliances, and communications equipment. Its pioneering work on the video recorder and the compact disc has had a major impact on modern life. Philips' headquarters and research laboratories may still be in Eindhoven, in the south-east of the Netherlands, but it has production plants all over the world, employing over 250 000 people to generate an annual turnover of some $30 billion.

State-of-the-art   Alcatel Alsthom is justly proud of its achievement in manufacturing the French TGV high-speed train.

Picture quality   Philips' research department has been working on high-definition TV.

Research and development

The electrical and engineering giant Alcatel Alsthom can trace its French roots back to the beginning of the century. It became a global enterprise when a joint venture was formed between the Compagnie Générale d'Électricité and the International Telephone and Telegraph Corporation (ITT) of the USA; it later joined forces with the Anglo-French electrical engineering company GEC-Alsthom, then fourth largest in the world in its sector.

Alcatel Alsthom devotes 9 per cent of its annual turnover to research and development, and has become a global leader in telecommunication systems and equipment. It now owns the world's largest network of terrestrial telephones – amounting to some 200 million lines.

Profitability and the workforce

Multinationals, by definition, operate in many countries at a time, buying, assembling and selling wherever conditions are most favourable. This has had an inevitable impact on their operations in Europe, where the workforce is skilled, but also expensive. In many cases, jobs have been lost to new factories abroad as companies have sought to maximise their profits.

Nestlé: many birds in the nest

These days there are rather more than three birds in the nest of Nestlé's famous logo. Henri Nestlé started the company in Vevey, Switzerland, way back in 1866 when he launched a milk-based baby food. The business grew and grew to become a world leader in food-processing. It began its chocolate range in 1904, invented instant coffee (Nescafé) in 1937, bought the Swiss soup manufacturer Maggi in 1947, and the international food company Crosse & Blackwell in 1960. The company now has 430 factories in over 100 countries around the world.

Oven-ready   Nestlé now also makes pizzas – here in its factory at Caudry, in north-east France.

Using the sea: containers and trawlers

Picturesque little fishing harbours, marinas crammed with pleasure boats, ferry terminals, sprawling commercial ports – all form part of the historic, multilayered interaction between the people of Western Europe and the five seas that lap their shores.

To see the greatest show of Christmas lights in the world, drive through the port area of Rotterdam on a dark December night. For mile after mile the ships, docks, cranes, refineries and warehouses are lit with millions of fairy lights, or at least that is how these industrial lights might be interpreted in the festive season. Rotterdam, the largest city in the Netherlands, has developed into the world's busiest port, employing 300 000 people to handle 350 million tons of goods a year, and 2.5 million containers. It stands at the cross-roads between the Atlantic and the network of motorways and inland waterways that leads to the heart of Europe. Location and communications are also essential factors for the other major ports of Western Europe, such as Antwerp in Belgium, Marseilles on the Mediterranean coast of France, and Hamburg in northern Germany.

European gateways Hamburg (right) is Germany's second largest city, and its largest commercial port. In the Netherlands, Rotterdam (below), is one of the largest ports in the world.

Fishing – large and small

The traditional fishing grounds of Europe are the Eastern Atlantic, the Baltic, the North Sea and the English Channel – a combination of cold and temperate seas over a vast continental shelf, where depths of no more than 660 ft (200 m) favour marine life. Mackerel, herring, cod, hake, tuna and sardines are the most commonly caught species.

Commercial fishing, however, is in crisis. There are a number of causes. Because of overfishing, stocks of many species have

become depleted, forcing the European Union to impose a quota system, and strict rules about net size. Reduced catches mean reduced incomes, so there is less money to invest in upgrading the fleets, and fewer prospects of profit. The larger enterprises tend to dominate in such straitened times. Even so, Europe still has numerous active fishing ports, large and small. The UK has the largest catch per annum, with 1 million tons, followed by France with 800 000 tons.

Farming the sea

Aquaculture – the farming of marine organisms – has become a growth industry. Mussels and oysters are cultivated on the shores of France, the Netherlands, Ireland and Britain. Salmon farming began in the 1960s, notably in Ireland, Scotland and Brittany. The fish develop in fresh water for a year, then are transferred to sea water, in large cages, where they are fattened. These salmon are largely reared for export, and Scotland in particular produces large volumes of smoked salmon.

Fishing in Brittany

The people of Brittany have a long and close association with the sea, and remain France's leading producers of fresh fish and shellfish. The courage and adventurousness of their sailors is legendary. Trawlers from St Malo, Concarneau, Lorient or Brest often head out into the ocean for several months at a time. Hence Concarneau has a reputation for tuna fished in the tropical waters of Africa, and is even twinned with the fishing port of Mbour in Senegal. The shellfish, on the other hand, comes mainly from the coasts of northern Brittany; Erquy, for instance, is famous for its scallops.

Not just pretty Fishing plays a key role in the life of Douarnenez.

Factory ships

The first factory ships belonged to whaling fleets: their job was to process whale carcasses during an expedition, avoiding the need to return to a shore station with each kill. Since the 1970s, factory ships (or 'mother ships') have become an integral part of fishing fleets on long missions. They take the catch from the trawlers and process it while still in mid-ocean – sorting, cleaning and filleting, so that the fish can go straight to markets.

Saving lives

One of the most popular charities in Britain is the Royal National Lifeboat Institution (RNLI), which is funded by public donations. It was founded in 1824 as a body to coordinate local life-saving operations. The crews manning the lifeboats have been mainly volunteers from the start. In the early days they rowed boats that had been specially adapted to remain buoyant even when virtually full of water. They now use a boat designed in 1958. RNLI crews still rescue on average three people each day of the year, and have saved 125 000 lives since the organisation was founded.

Fruits of the sea A fisherman sorts the catch on a Scottish trawler (above right). Draught horses are used to drag shrimp nets through the shallows off the Belgian coast (below).

The romance of the sea

Ports are essentially commercial places, but many smaller harbours are nonetheless spectacularly picturesque, such as Honfleur or Concarneau in France, Kinsale in Ireland, and Port Isaac in Cornwall. This gives them another economic resource: tourism. In recent decades sailing, windsurfing, water-skiing and diving have grown enormously in popularity, bringing more people to the sea and inspiring the development of marinas for pleasure craft. Fewer people may be making a living from the sea, but more than ever are enjoying it.

White gold in the mountains

Once the sport of the wealthy, skiing has now been democratised. With the massive growth in resorts since the 1950s, and the competitive pricing of package holidays, it has become a European passion accessible to large numbers of people. French schools even stagger their February half-term break by region, so that the slopes are not overwhelmed.

When, in January 1999, the French mayor of La Bresse, a ski resort in eastern France, suggested that gendarmes should be posted on the slopes, it seemed a sign of the times. The main bone of contention was the anarchic behaviour of snowboarders. The following month, a number of skiers and snowboarders died in avalanches that they caused by venturing off-piste – away from the prepared ski runs – against advice after heavy snowfalls. Winter sports in Europe have never been so popular, but the

Winter Olympics

The first Winter Olympics at Chamonix in 1924 included just two main events: cross-country skiing and ski-jumping. Downhill and slalom skiing, which play such a prominent role today, were not introduced into the Winter Olympics until 1936 at Garmisch-Partenkirchen in Germany. The participation of women has also been gradual: in 1924 women were permitted to take part in just one event: figure skating. Today, the games include a host of novel sports, including ice dance and acrobatic freestyle skiing (above), spread over 13 locations – and watched on television by 2000 million viewers.

pressure of the crowds is having a telling effect on safety in the resorts.

A new industry

Skiing is essentially a Nordic invention, dating back thousands of years. It began to be adopted as a sport around the turn of the century. The pioneers – usually wealthy people with time on their hands and an adventurous spirit – either stuck to the valleys or trails pursuing Nordic (cross-country) skiing, or had to be prepared to trudge laboriously up mountains for the thrill of a quick descent in Alpine skiing. The world's first Alpine skiing club was the Ski Club of Great Britain, founded in 1903.

Mountain railways and cable cars made Alpine skiing more attractive, and it really took off with the proliferation of lighter chair lifts, drag lifts and gondolas, which began to spread their web across the Alps in the 1930s. By the 1970s the ski industry was in full swing, with new resorts mushrooming in every suitable valley, notably in France. There are now over 100 ski resorts in France, 90 in Switzerland and 70 in Austria. In France alone, some 7 million skiers a year – 1.5 million of them foreigners – head down the hundreds of miles of prepared pistes at resorts operated by a staff totalling 14 500.

Flying high *Paragliding is a popular new sport in the Alps.*

The downside has been over-development: a rash of soulless resorts of high-rise apartments and hotels. Some resorts, such as La Plagne and Flaine in France, have been criticised as *usines à ski* – ski factories. They lack the romance that was so much a part of skiing's early appeal – the wooden chalets, log fires, icicle-bedecked barns. This has been addressed in more recent developments, and is reflected in the enduring success of the more authentic resorts, such as La Clusaz in Haute-Savoie, Saas-Fee in the Valais region of Switzerland, and Alpbach in Austria. There will always be nostalgia for the way that skiing once was before it became so popular.

French chic *Megève in Haute-Savoie is one of the most fashionable resorts in France.*

The value of good breeding

Horse-racing has become an industry worth billions. But its main inspiration is not so much money as a passion for horses. It is a tradition dating back to ancient times, reinforced by selective breeding, and a unique understanding between horses and humans.

Heavy brigade A pair of Clydesdales, one of Britain's traditional heavy draught-horses, at work on a farm. Originating in Lanarkshire, Scotland, the breed was improved by crossbreeding with other types.

Horses for courses Thoroughbred racehorses are the result of careful breeding over centuries. Only the best can compete in races like the Grand National at Aintree, Liverpool (left), the most famous steeplechase in the world. The course is 4 miles 4 furlongs (over 7 km) long and includes 30 fences.

A ll racehorses in Britain are thoroughbreds, and almost all of them can trace an ancestry that goes back to just three horses of the early 18th century. All have been meticulously recorded in the General Stud Book since 1791. That was not the beginning of the tradition, however. Thoroughbreds are believed to date back to the arrival of fine Arabian horses in England in the 3rd century AD, during Roman times.

Selective breeding

Horses have been vital to European civilisation for centuries – for transport, agricultural labour and national cavalries. Little wonder that so much effort was put into maintaining and improving the breeds. In 1665 Colbert, the controller of finances to King Louis XIV, began work on establishing a series of national studs in France. Apart from interruptions during the French Revolution and the reign of Napoleon III, the French national studs – such as Le Pin in Normandy and Pompadour in Limousin – have survived to this day, operated by the Ministry of Agriculture and funded by the Pari Mutuel, the official betting organisation in France.

The tradition is carried forward in other parts of Europe too: in 1967 a National Stud was opened in the horse-racing town of Newmarket, Suffolk, as a centre for breeding English horses.

The Spanish riding school of Vienna

It may seem odd to have a Spanish Riding School in the Austrian capital, Vienna, but the story goes back to about 1580, when the Habsburg family ruled both Austria and Spain. A breed of Spanish horses, mixed with Arabian and Berber stock, was fostered by the Austrian stud at Lipizza, near Trieste. These Lipizzaner were used at a new riding school in Vienna, founded in 1729 by the Holy Roman Emperor Charles VI to train horses for the imperial family. The Spanish Riding School adopted the disciplines of training called *haute école* ('high school') that was prevalent during the 18th century, and it has maintained the tradition ever since. It takes about 20 years for a rider to become fully trained: just as the older riders train the younger horses, so the older horses help to train apprentice riders, in a continuous cycle. The horses are all white-grey, but when they are born the foals have black or brown coats. Now the only riding school to use *haute école* methods exclusively, the Spanish Riding School has become a wonder of the equestrian world, and a major tourist attraction. Training sessions take place in a white neoclassical building inspired by the chapel at Versailles.

CHAPTER 3

LIVING IN WESTERN EUROPE

Europeans are proud of the historic structures that lie behind their complex and fascinating continent. Equally, they have never been short on innovation. Europe today is engaged in a process of homogenisation: the European Union is gradually centralising government, taxation, trade laws, even perhaps defence. Yet the Europeans remain fiercely protective of their national and regional identities. Western Europeans take life seriously, but they are also acutely aware of the importance of pleasure. Hard work is for security, family, progress: but it is also to ensure the rewards of leisure. 'Work hard, play hard' could perhaps be their motto. This is tempered by a strong inclination towards fairness, but not so strong that Europeans take it on trust. They have built institutions to police themselves and others, in which royalty, professional soldiers, priests, professors, customs and immigration officials, even football referees all play their part.

A market in Aix-en-Provence, France.

Royalty: public duty and public fascination

Whether they reign over a large country or a tiny territory less than the size of just one English county, the sovereigns of Western Europe represent an ancient system. These days the dignity of their ancestral lines has to be matched by a new ability to keep up with the times.

Defying evil
The British royal crest bears a motto in French dating back to 1348: **Honi soit qui mal y pense** *– 'Shamed be he who thinks evil of this'.*

The king reigns but does not govern – is how the monarchy is summed up in Belgium. It is a statement that holds true for all the royal heads of state in Western Europe, where the growth of democracy over the past two centuries has gradually whittled away their real power. It might be added, however, that although these constitutional monarchs wield little power, they nonetheless have an enormous amount of influence. They are also the object of international fascination, permanently in the public eye and under the constant pressure of media scrutiny.

No royal family has felt this pressure more acutely than the current British royal family. Queen Elizabeth II pronounced 1992 an

annus horribilis ('horrible year') following the breakdown of the marriages of her two eldest sons and a disastrous fire at Windsor Castle. But 1997 proved even more distressing when the tragic death of Diana, Princess of Wales, the divorced wife of Prince Charles, provoked a public outpouring of emotion – and much of it directed against the royal family, who

Head of state *The role of the British sovereign as constitutional monarch is most evident during the State Opening of Parliament. At the beginning of each new session of parliament, Queen Elizabeth and her consort, Prince Philip, travel in a procession to the House of Lords, where the Queen reads out a statement written by the government outlining its forthcoming programme of legislation.*

A royal tragedy

Visitors still come every day to the Pont de l'Alma in Paris, site of the underpass where Princess Diana and her companion Dodi Fayed died in a car crash in the early hours of August 31, 1997. Diana's beauty and humanity had captured the hearts of millions, and her death was mourned by much of the British nation in a spontaneous outpouring of grief.

A royal gathering
Members of several royal families of Europe joined the British royal family to celebrate the marriage of Prince Edward and Sophie Rhys Jones in June 1999.

Fairy-tale wedding In 1956 the beautiful American film star, Grace Kelly, famed for her roles in such films as **High Noon** and **Rear Window**, married Prince Rainier III of Monaco. She brought Hollywood glamour to the principality, but also a much-respected sense of integrity as she abandoned her film career to devote herself to her new royal responsibilities.

Modern prince Hans-Adam II, who has been Prince of Liechtenstein since 1984, rules over one of the smallest countries in Europe, with just 31 000 subjects.

did much to restore respect for the crown in Belgium, and made it a symbol of unity in a nation divided between two communities, the Flemings and the Walloons. The throne passed to his brother, Albert II, who has admirably maintained Baudouin's legacy.

The people of the Netherlands are similarly supportive of their queen, Beatrix, who came to the throne in 1980, when her mother, the popular Juliana, stepped down because of illness. Beatrix's marriage in 1966 – to a German, Claus von Amsberg – was controversial

had earlier distanced themselves from her. This was a pitiable turn of events for Queen Elizabeth. She had worked diligently to continue the good work of her father, the reluctant King George VI, to restore honour and stability to the British throne after the turmoil caused by the abdication of Edward VIII in 1936, over his marriage to an American divorcee.

In fact, public affection for Queen Elizabeth and the Queen Mother never really waned, and the storm soon began to abate. By the end of the century, Britain's royal family had demonstrated yet again the durability and flexibility of an institution that, in many ways, seems an unjustifiable anachronism in modern democracies – except that democratic people support it. The public seem to like having monarchs.

Leading by example

The other European monarchs are also held in high esteem by their subjects. When King Baudouin I of Belgium died suddenly in 1993, over 125 000 of his subjects queued patiently in the rain to pay their last respects. He had come to the throne aged just 20 in 1951, following the abdication of his father, Leopold III, in a constitutional crisis. Belgium was bitterly divided over Leopold's role during the Second World War, when he had elected to stay with his people during the German occupation – a decision seen by some as tantamount to collaboration. Pious, deeply concerned by social issues and family values, Baudouin and his Spanish wife Fabiola

Beloved Queen Astrid

Two tragedies struck the Belgian royal family in the 1930s. First King Albert I, a hero of the First World War, died in a climbing accident in 1934. Barely a year later, Queen Astrid, wife of the new King Leopold III, died in a motoring accident in Switzerland, at the age of 29. A princess of Sweden, she had married Leopold in 1926. She had won a devoted following in Belgium, for her elegance and beauty, her charity work, and as mother of the three royal children.

because the wounds of German wartime occupation were still fresh; but the couple won respect through hard work, modesty, and their common touch. It seems that they made the necessary adjustments to take monarchy comfortably into the 21st century.

The smallest monarchies

The three smallest states of the region are also constitutional monarchies. Luxembourg is a legacy of the post-Napoleonic carve-up of Europe at the Congress of Vienna in 1815. Its ruler, Grand Duke Jean, is a member of the House of Nassau. Liechtenstein was able to preserve its separate identity during German unification in the late 19th century, and is ruled by Prince Hans-Adam II. Finally, Monaco has been ruled by the Genoese Grimaldi family since the 15th century. Its current monarch is Prince Rainier III.

The people's monarch Queen Beatrix of the Netherlands is held in high regard by the vast majority of her nation, who appreciate her relaxed and informal approach. In Prince Willem-Alexander (pictured), she also produced the first male heir to the Orange-Nassau line since 1890.

The religions of Europe

*Church attendance figures may be down, but the fervour of the faithful remains.
Christianity has deep roots in Western Europe, and has played a central role in
shaping its civilisation. The sizable Jewish minority has suffered centuries of
persecution, but today the minority religions play an increasing role in national life.*

Asked about their religious allegiances, 40 per cent of the Dutch declared themselves to have no religion at all. Protestantism, which for centuries has been the dominant force in Dutch religion, now has fewer active participants than Catholicism.

Yet an important element of continuity remains in the form of tolerance – a national virtue in the Netherlands. Its origins can be traced to the 16th century, when the Dutch were striving for religious and national liberty, free from the dominance of Catholic Spain. Such tolerance was also inspired by the growth of Renaissance humanism, which questioned many of the old certainties of religion.

Throughout the 18th and 19th centuries, religious liberalism went hand in hand with economic development in all the Protestant lands – including Anglican England, Calvinist Switzerland, and Lutheran Germany. Catholic

countries, by contrast – France, Belgium, Luxembourg, Austria and Ireland – tended to move more slowly politically and economically. The economic consequences have become far less marked since the late 19th century, but the essential imprint still remains – as in the Republic of Ireland, where the Catholic Church

*With one voice   Erfurt in Germany,
where Martin Luther joined a
monastery early in his career,
organises an ecumenical celebration
every year on November 10. This is
Luther's birthday, but it is also
celebrated by Catholics as the feast
day of St Martin.*

Women priests

March 12, 1994, was a momentous day for the Anglican Church: it marked the ordination of the first women priests, and the end of a long battle for equal rights. In the USA, women priests had been ordained since 1981, but in England the issue was deeply divisive. Some 700 Anglican priests threatened to resign, and some converted to the Roman Catholic Church. The issue also threatened the rapprochement that had been built up with the Vatican as Pope John Paul II expressed his strong opposition. Most Anglican churchgoers, however, welcomed the change.

*New role   The first Anglican
women priests were ordained at
Bristol Cathedral in 1994.*

Age-old ceremony *The Bar Mitzvah, conducted in a synagogue, marks the religious coming-of-age for a 13-year-old Jewish boy.*

Cult following: the Solar Temple

On October 5, 1994, the bodies of 48 devotees of the Order of the Solar Temple, including its Belgian founder, Luc Jouret, were found dead in Switzerland and another five in Canada. Taught that the Apocalypse was imminent because of environmental pollution, they had all apparently committed suicide. A year later, on December 23, 1995, the remains of another 16 cult members, including three children, were found in France. Sects have proliferated in Europe, as elsewhere, since the 1960s, and some have clearly subjected their members to mental manipulation. The case of the Solar Temple graphically displays the dilemma that European democracies face in finding a balance between respecting religious beliefs and protecting the vulnerable.

continues to wield a significant influence on education and government, refusing to sanction any liberalisation of the law on issues such as divorce, abortion and contraception.

Religious allegiance still cements national and regional identities. It differentiates Protestant Switzerland from its close neighbour, Catholic Austria; and it separates the Catholic majority in southern and western Germany – in Bavaria and the Rhineland – from their Protestant compatriots elsewhere. Yet religion is only one aspect of identity among many. And although churches are now often emptier than before, there are growing ecumenical initiatives to unite the main branches of the Christian Church, or at least bring them closer together.

Catholic pilgrims

There is an ancient fervour at the heart of Roman Catholicism, which continues to manifest itself in a large number of processions across Western Europe. In Brittany these are known as *pardons*, and one of the largest takes place at Locronan (below), in the department of Finistère, every six years. The pilgrims, wearing traditional costume and carrying embroidered banners, walk over 7 miles (12 km) in the footsteps of St Ronan, who is said to have arrived from Ireland in the 5th century. Holy relics from each of the parishes are displayed at the 12 Stations of the Cross along the way.

Integration and assimilation

Christianity has been a major force in Western European civilisation. But there has always been a sizable Jewish minority. Persecuted in the Middle Ages, expelled from France, officially outlawed in England from 1290 to the 1650s, confined to ghettos elsewhere, the Jews have long been denied a place in European society. The violent manifestations of this age-old prejudice reached its terrible nadir in the Nazi extermination camps of the 1940s. Today there are around 1.5 million Jews in Western Europe, with 20 000 living in Switzerland, the birthplace of Zionism in the 1890s.

A latecomer to the region, Islam has grown rapidly since the 1950s through immigration from Turkey, North Africa and the Indian subcontinent. In France, Germany and Britain, Muslims now represent 2-3 per cent of the total population, and mosques are becoming a common feature of the urban European landscape.

Improvisation *Muslims pray at an open-air mosque in Marseille.*

Pilgrimage *Every year some 60 000 people gather to clamber to the top of Croag Patrick – a barren peak on which Ireland's patron saint, Patrick, is said to have spent 40 days in Lent.*

Football crazy: the sport of millions

Soccer, better known as football, has always been the sport of the people, and is now the premier sport of Europe. The reasons? Anyone can play, at any level; the rules are simple to understand; and the best games have a unique drama that is played out with balletic, instinctual skill by men at peak fitness.

Treble hero *Ryan Giggs was one of the stars of the Manchester United dream team of 1999.*

Hero *Franz Beckenbauer, a German legend.*

The tribal passions of football may have a medieval air about them, but football only became a properly organised sport in the 19th century, in England, where the first Football Association (FA) was created in 1863. From an informal street game, it was rapidly transformed into a major professional sport in the late 19th century, with huge crowds pressing into the new stadiums that were sprouting across the country. The FA Cup Final of 1893 drew 45 000 spectators, while over 100 000 attended in 1901, and some 160 000 in 1923.

Since then, football has become the number one sport across Europe. It has also been acknowledged as a key element of European culture. Its standing was officially recognised in Britain in 1965 when the veteran player Stanley Matthews, of Stoke City and Blackpool, became the first footballer to receive a knighthood. All nations have their national footballing heroes, such as Michel Platini of France and Johan Cruyff of the Netherlands. Franz Beckenbauer of Germany has even been jokingly called 'the last German emperor'.

Money, money, money

Football is now big business. Top players change hands for millions of pounds and earn tens of thousands every week. There are few other ways in which a boy can come from a very modest background and reach the top in the space of a few years. Players now think little of geographical boundaries: a wealthy Premier League team such as Chelsea, of London, can search the world market for players, and field a team with barely any British players at all.

Television has contributed hugely to the funding, and has also attracted a much wider audience to the sport. Families with children are now often seen at matches, where previously there would have been only men. In all respects, enthusiasm for football continues to grow apace.

Team loyalties *Scottish fans are known for their good behaviour, and are welcomed all over the world.*

Festival and drama

Anthropologists observing football fans have found all the marks of tribalism: the sense of fellowship, the shared ritual chants, warlike metaphors, and the badges of loyalty such as scarves, hats and even face-paint. Anyone who has attended a football match knows that the crowd has a major impact on the game: some call it the twelfth man. But a large and deeply partisan crowd imbued with passion, and perhaps alcohol as well, can create a volatile and threatening atmosphere. The sport has been marred by several serious incidents as some fans have taken rivalry to mean open warfare.

France triumphant *The French team exults after its victory over Brazil in the 1998 World Cup Final. Brazil got their revenge in 2002, winning the World Cup after beating Germany.*

In the scrum *France (in blue) and Ireland battle it out in the premier annual rugby tournament of the Northern Hemisphere – the Six Nations. England, France, Ireland, Scotland, Wales and Italy.*

Rugby: 30 men on a field

Rugby began in England, spread throughout the British Isles, then over the Channel to France and around the world. Today it has become a professional sport in which the human equivalents of ploughhorses and thoroughbreds line up to do battle.

It all started off as a gentleman's game, formulated by the sons of the British Empire at the exclusive public school of Rugby. But this gladiatorial clash of bodies clearly has a more universal appeal. After the 1870s, rugby spread rapidly, not only throughout the British Empire – to Australia, South Africa, New Zealand and Fiji – but also, through trading contacts, to France, Argentina and Japan.

Rugby Union has the advantage of serving all physiques. The heavily built forwards can put their weight into the scrum; the more fleet-footed line up as running backs behind the scrum. The role of scrum half is best served by someone short and nimble. The only common qualifications are fitness and physical courage. This is a contact sport of the first order, played with little bodily protection, and admired for its flow – in contrast to the heavy armour and stop-start of American football.

Professionalism

Rugby Union prided itself on being the sport of amateurs, in contrast to the rival professional game of Rugby League, played for money. By the 1990s this proved untenable. Top-level players needed to devote many hours each week to their sport, and could not survive without financial support.

In 1995, the International Rugby Football Association met in Paris to discuss the issue: it found that professionalism was already so widespread that it had no option but to abandon efforts to restrict the sport to amateurs. Rugby therefore became a professional sport.

France

Ireland

England

Full stretch *England win a line-out.*

Scotland

Wales

Italy

63

The greatest cycling race

Every July, 2 million spectators line roads in France to cheer on the select handful of some of the world's greatest and toughest athletes. With a worldwide television audience of more than a billion viewers, the Tour de France has become the third most widely followed sporting event after the Olympics and the football World Cup.

Standing out from the crowd *The Frenchman Bernard Hinault (inset, top), five times winner of the Tour, attempts to break away from the pack; the German Jan Ullrich enjoys being winner in 1997 (inset below).*

Some 120 professional cyclists take part in the Tour de France – a race held every July since 1903, barring interruption during the two World Wars. It is probably the greatest test of endurance of any sport. For 21 days, or stages, they race against the clock, sometimes on the flat, sometimes in the mountains, interspersed with sprint time trials. The pressure is relentless. In 1989, after covering 2030 miles (3267 km), Greg LeMond of the USA beat France's Laurent Fignon by a margin of just eight seconds to take the title. A single puncture, a fall, or one less-than-perfect performance can scotch a rider's chance of victory.

Climbing high *The Belgian Eddie Merckx won the Tour de France five times from 1969.*

A question of drugs

When the English cyclist Tommy Simpson collapsed and died during the Tour de France in 1967, it was rumoured that he might have been using amphetamines. But the subject remained taboo until 1998, when illegal performance-enhancing drugs were found in the car of a masseur from one of the leading teams, Festina. This brought in the full force of the law and more drugs were found, taking the shine off the race for that year.

A flash of colour

For the spectators, this is a grand day out, celebrated in a holiday atmosphere. Crowds gather early in the day, picnicking and listening for the approach of the peloton – the tight cluster of cyclists. First comes the publicity caravan, advertising the sponsors. Then come the cyclists, with cameramen mounted on motorbikes in close pursuit.

On the flat, unless the leading cyclists have broken away from the peloton, the passage of the Tour can be over in seconds. In the roar of cheering and applause, spectators hope to identify their favourite team from the insignia, and the race leaders from their distinctive jerseys: green for the leading sprinter, red polka dots for the leading climber or King of the Mountains, and yellow for the overall race leader on aggregate. Close behind, bringing up the rear, are all the back-up vehicles of the teams, with their doctors, mechanics and coaches.

Heroes of the Tour

Until the Second World War, the Tour de France was dominated by French and Belgian riders. In the 1950s the Italians, with Fausto Coppi above all, became the main challengers to French supremacy – and to Louis Bobet in particular. The 1960s belonged to Jacques Anquetil, the first to win five victories (1957, 1961-4). The Belgian Eddie Merckx repeated this achievement with five wins between 1969 and 1974. There have been two further five-fold victors: Bernard Hinault of France, and Miguel Indurain of Spain. Yet cyclists do not have to win to be popular: Raymond Polidor never got higher than second place, but has nevertheless earned his place in the pantheon of the Tour.

Place your bets

There are numerous casinos in Europe, but the well-established trio of Monte Carlo, Baden-Baden and Deauville have won a special place in the gambler's firmament. While the casino of Deauville has made concessions to modernism, the other two stick to the plush decor that recalls the pampered extravagance of the belle époque *before the First World War.*

Palace of games *The Casino of Monte Carlo was built at the height of the* belle époque, *between 1878 and 1910.*

Magic numbers *Casino staff lay out the chips and prepare the gambling tables ahead of a hard night's work.*

In 1939 Winston Churchill, on his way through the Riviera, stopped off at the casino at Monte Carlo and promptly lost a tidy sum of money. He announced that he would return the following day to win back what he had lost. As it happened, the start of the Second World War intervened, and he had to rush back to London before he could get even. Ten years later he returned to Monaco, sat down at the same table, and true to his promise, won back his bet several times over.

Gambling in style

Churchill was not, however, the man who broke the bank of Monte Carlo. This accolade went to Joseph Hobson Jagger, an expert on spindles, who perceived a fault in one of the roulette wheels in 1886, and won 2 million francs in eight days. He became a legendary figure, and although the casino had lost a lot of money to him, it too benefited from the episode: Jagger's stunt served to promote the casino's reputation.

François Blanc, who turned Monaco into the world's gambling capital during the 19th century, would be pleased to see how his legacy lives on. Royalty and aristocrats may have been replaced by jet-setters, but the numbers pressing around the tables have not diminished.

For over a century the casino-opera of Monte Carlo has been one of the principality's great architectural curiosities. Conceived in 1863 by Charles Garnier, architect of the Paris Opéra, it now stands in vivid contrast to the high-rise buildings that dominate the rest of central Monaco.

Also exuding an old-world charm is the casino of Baden-Baden, which forms an integral part of this famous German spa town. It is the largest casino in Germany, and the oldest in Europe: the first gambling concession here dates back to 1748.

Founded by the Duc de Morny in 1860, Deauville, on the Normandy coast, became one of the most fashionable resorts in France, offering golden beaches, golf, polo, a famous racetrack and luxury hotels. At its handsome casino, gambling enthusiasts of all nationalities spent, and still spend, millions. It was once the preserve of the wealthy, but the advent of gaming machines has democratised the casino's attractions, along with its clientele.

Lottery mania

The statistics do not add up: the chances of winning the top prize of any national lottery are infinitesimal, but that does not stop Europeans from indulging in a flutter with chance. Lotteries have ancient origins and have been used throughout history to raise funds. The first in Western Europe appeared in 15th-century Burgundy and Flanders, when towns would arrange lotteries to pay for fortifications, or to assist the poor. France's modern Loterie nationale dates back to 1933. Britain was the last country in the European Union to create a national lottery, in November 1994.

The Tyrol: folklore and tourism

The mountains are beautiful, the farms trimmed and manicured, the wines delicious, life peaceful. The most Catholic and unquestionably the most rural of the Austrian regions lives to the rhythm of the seasons, ever careful to preserve the quality of its environment, which thousands of visitors come to enjoy every year.

Grüß Gott! ('Greetings to God') is the familiar greeting of the Austrian Tyrol, as if in thanks to the Almighty for the gifts of nature that lie all around. In villages such as Alpbach and Reith – both of which have won the accolade of prettiest village in Europe – flower boxes and gardens overflow with colour beneath cheerfully painted gables on traditional wooden chalets. Beyond them the mountains soar into the bright, clear air.

The Austrian Tyrol is the most mountainous region of the country, occupying a narrow tongue of land between Germany and Italy. To the north are the Bavarian Alps, to the south the Ötzaler Alps, leading to the Brenner Pass and into Italy. (South Tyrol was ceded to Italy in 1919.) A population of 600 000 is spread over an area of 4883 sq miles (12 647 km²).

The peaceful Tyrol *Fields of vegetables, grass and hay (for winter cattle fodder) quilt the lower slopes, beneath the forested sides of the higher mountains.*

Costume parade *A squad of tirailleurs (sharpshooters) assembles for a traditional festivity.*

Beliefs and folklore

The Tyroleans have always been known for their joie de vivre, oompah bands and boisterous singing. They also have a deep respect for tradition. Driving their cattle up to summer pastures and then down again at the end of the season are eternal rituals, as are the carnivals celebrated by some 300 villages – notably Imst, Telfs, Thaur and Lans – with their medieval masked parades. The famous traditional Tyrolean costumes, with leather shorts and flower-bedecked hats, are brought out each year for such festivals. Religion is ever-present, as witnessed by the church spires that rise from every village, and the large number of tiny shrines that dot the fields and waysides. Corpus Christi (the second Sunday after Pentecost) is widely celebrated, marked in some parts by processions on horseback.

Transient tourism

There is of course far more to the Tyrol than old traditions, but these provide a reassuringly solid backdrop to the modern tourist activities that now underpin its economy. Traditions of centuries sustain the Tyroleans against the transient visitors that flood the area every summer and winter.

Focal point

Innsbruck, capital of the Tyrol, developed around a vital link on the medieval trading route between Austria and Italy – a bridge (Brücke) over the river Inn. Over the centuries it acquired a network of narrow streets, and grander avenues overlaid in the 18th century by baroque ornamentation. One of its most charming treasures is Goldenes Dachl ('Little Golden Roof'), a richly decorated stage box beneath a roof of 3000 gilt-copper roof plates, erected in 1500 by Emperor Maximilian I so that he could watch pageants in the town square below.

Perfect setting *High mountains tower over the city of Innsbruck.*

From conscripts to professionals

Since 1945, after centuries of confrontation, the countries of Western Europe have been working in unison towards a common peace. The reappraisal of defence priorities has brought a sea-change to their military traditions.

Military hardware *A helicopter of the Franco-German enterprise, Eurocoptor.*

Every July 14, France celebrates Bastille Day – the opening volley of the French Revolution – with a military parade. The Champs-Élysées, in the heart of Paris, resounds to the beat of martial music, beneath the roar of jets. In 1994, however, there was a significant difference: for the first time since the war, Germans marched down this sacred avenue, alongside their French colleagues in the new Franco-German Brigade.

Protecting the peace

Since the Second World War, the risk of conflict in Western Europe has steadily diminished. The Western European nations have reconciled age-old differences to present a united front, mainly under the umbrella of NATO and the Western European Union – the joint defence initiative formed by the Allies which helped to found NATO. Since 1989 these countries have no longer lived under the threat of nuclear attack from the Soviet bloc, and as a result they have had to re-think and re-orient their defence strategy.

Active duty for Western European soldiers these days is less likely to be the defence of national borders than a call to serve on humanitarian or peacekeeping missions abroad, such as in Bosnia. In the light of this, one of the top priorities for European armies is the ability to mount a rapid intervention force, armed with state-of-the-art equipment.

National Service

European armies have to reflect these revised priorities. Britain decided to create an entirely professional army by ending conscription, or National Service; the last batch of conscripts completed their service in 1962. Belgium decided to follow this path in 1995. Then, in 1996, the French president, Jacques Chirac, declared that France would phase out compulsory military service by 2002.

National Service, military or non-military, is still obligatory in the Netherlands, Germany, Austria and Switzerland. The Swiss have practised conscription since the 16th century, and all male citizens must practise with the reserves until the age of 50, or pay a hefty fine.

Defending neutrality *The Swiss army on manoeuvres.*

A European army?

Led alternately by a French general and a German general, the Franco-German Brigade forms part of a wider European army called the Eurocorps. Founded in 1994, the Eurocorps, with its headquarters in Strasbourg, is now a force of 45 000 personnel. It includes divisions from France, Germany, Belgium and Spain, as well as a small contingent from Luxembourg and a multinational battalion of 500 men.

Joint action *Soldiers of the Eurocorps.*

Regional identities: a powerful instinct

In Belgium, the quarrel between the country's two main linguistic communities, the Flemish and the French, has become ever more poisonous, and may even threaten the country's existence. Welsh, Scottish and Breton nationalists have shown that they too are deeply attached to their distinctive identities. It seems that while Europe unites, its constituent nations are prone to pull apart.

Local history *A girl from Alsace in traditional costume.*

Anthem to Scotland *With tartan kilts and bagpipes signalling their unmistakable Scottish identity, a military pipe band celebrates the annual Royal Highland Show in Edinburgh.*

Barely 4000 people live in a tiny area called Fourons (or Voeren), in eastern Belgium, but this enclave has become a symbol of the simmering dispute which pits the Dutch-speaking Flemish majority in the north (Flanders) against the French-speaking Walloon minority in the south (Wallonia). For Fourons, with a two-thirds majority of French-speakers, has been assigned administratively to Flanders, even though it is not actually attached to it.

Language is not the only source of contention between the Flemings and the Walloons. The two groups differ also in attitude and political affinities. The Flemings are traditionally more conservative and religious, while the Walloons are more liberal and more inclined to socialism. Flanders, with its North Sea ports and new microchip and light-engineering industries, is also considerably more prosperous than Wallonia; indeed it is one of the most prosperous regions of the European Union. Flemish nationalists resent having to subsidise their Walloon neighbours, who are struggling with a high level of unemployment as a legacy of defunct heavy industries – the very industries which, in the 19th century, had enabled them to dominate the Flemish.

As the differences between the two communities intensified from the 1960s on, Belgium – a unified state since 1830 – became increasingly devolved into two principal administrative regions, a process called federalisation. The last constitutional revision, in 1993, formalised this federal arrangement, but failed to allay the inter-communal tensions. The Flemish nationalists in the right-wing Vlaams Blok, supported by some 12 per cent of the Flemish electorate, see it only as a step towards total independence for Flanders.

Common humanity *Whatever their background, Belgians were united in horror at the murder of four children. In October 20, 1996, 300 000 people took to the streets of Brussels to protest at the failure of the justice system.*

Belgian compromise *Federal Belgium contains two main communities: Dutch-speaking Flemings (comprising 59.2 per cent of the population) and French-speaking Walloons (40.2 per cent); German-speakers make up the remaining 0.6 per cent. It has three administrative regions: Flanders, Wallonia and the capital, Brussels, which is bilingual.*

Language
- German
- French
- Dutch
- French and Dutch

Devolution in Great Britain

In September 1997 the voters of Scotland and Wales gave their approval to the idea of devolution. The Scottish were massively in favour; the Welsh approved by a small margin. In 1999, Scotland's parliament of 129 elected members and Wales' assembly of 60 elected members were officially opened. The assemblies can legislate in all matters, barring a few important areas of national concern such as defence. Some people worry that this taste of autonomy may lead to a desire for full independence.

Switzerland's model federalism

In contrast to France, which has kept a firm grip on centralised government, Switzerland has adopted administrative structures that preserve the regional, geographical and cultural differences of its regions. The 20 cantons (and six half cantons) of the Swiss Confederation have extensive political powers and elect their own representative assemblies. Ultimately, however, national issues are settled by the bicameral Federal Assembly: the National Council of 200 directly elected members, and the Council of States with 46 members elected from cantons (two for each canton and one for each half canton).

The British experiment

To a greater or lesser degree, all culturally distinctive regions of Europe are looking to reaffirm their identity – Bavarians, Bretons, the people of Alsace. They will be observing with interest events in the British Isles.

Scotland had its own separate parliament until it agreed to the Act of Union in 1707, which joined it formally to England and Wales, with government in London. The Scots nonetheless have always proudly worn their clan colours: they have kept their own judicial and educational system, their own bank notes, and independent Presbyterian Church of Scotland.

Yet there has long been an undercurrent of resentment towards the English. Some goes back to the distant past, such as the defeat and subsequent execution of Sir William Wallace (Braveheart), who led the rising against an English invasion in 1297. So when the Labour government offered the Scots a separate parliament again, they jumped at the opportunity. On September 11, 1997, three-quarters of those who voted in the referendum were in favour of a Scottish parliament – ironically, on the 700th anniversary of the Battle of Stirling Bridge, in which William Wallace routed the English army.

Wales proved somewhat less enthusiastic in its referendum on devolution, but voted by a slim margin to have its own assembly. One inhabitant in every five in Wales – annexed by England in the 13th century – is of English origin. Plaid Cymru, the Welsh nationalist party, has the support of only 10 per cent of the electorate.

Popular parade The Kinderzeche (children's festival) takes place in Dinkelsbühl in Bavaria in July.

Language
- German
- French
- Italian
- Romansch

Map of Switzerland showing: Lake Constance, Basle, Zurich, Rhine, Aare, Lucerne, Vierwaldstätter See, Bern, SWITZERLAND, Chur, Lausanne, St. Moritz, Rhône, Lake Geneva (Lac Léman), Geneva, Bellinzona

Celebrating the Federation August 1 is the Swiss national holiday, when people gather at the Vierwaldstätter See, near Lucerne. It was here that the Swiss Confederation had its beginnings in 1291, with a pact of mutual assistance between three forest cantons.

From nationalist fervour to armed struggle

Will Catholic and Protestant paramilitaries really lay down their arms in Northern Ireland? This British province has glimpsed a prospect of lasting peace; but in Corsica, separatists continue to wage a campaign of terror.

Hallowed traditions
Every summer, members of the Protestant Orange Order in Northern Ireland parade to celebrate past victories, such as that of William of Orange at the Battle of the Boyne in 1690.

Down the generations
Children in the Catholic areas of Belfast have grown up separated by barbed wire and walls from Protestant neighbours, believing that the British army is an army of occupation. It is the children, however, who will have to construct the peace.

Since 1969 the world has lived with disturbing images from Northern Ireland – soldiers in the streets, bombed-out pubs, the funerals of some 3300 victims. The six counties of Ulster have never been at ease since they were partitioned in 1921, so that Protestants loyal to Britain would not have to join the new Republic of Ireland to the south. During the 1960s the minority Catholics of Ulster demonstrated against the disadvantages they suffered, and the British army had to be sent in to protect them. Before long, extremists in the Irish Republican Army (IRA) began waging an armed campaign in pursuit of reunification with the south. They were countered by equally violent Protestant Loyalists who wished Ulster to remain part of the United Kingdom.

In April 1998 a potential solution was hammered out in the Good Friday Agreement, by which the two communities undertook to renounce violence and share power in the province. But the extremists, feeding off communal antagonisms stretching back centuries, have scant interest in peace, and little incentive to disarm. Northern Ireland remains on tenterhooks, fearing that the killings and bombings may start again.

Corsica: soured beauty

In February 1998 one out of every six Corsicans took to the streets in a silent march in protest at the assassination by nationalist extremists of the Prefect, Claude Erignac. It was the first time that the population had openly expressed their opposition to the violence that has ravaged the island for over 20 years. Since its foundation in 1976, the Corsican National Liberation Front (FLNC) has waged a campaign of bombing and assassination in pursuit of independence, targeting tourist complexes and public buildings. Over time, however, the nationalist cause has seen public sympathy ebb away, as the FLNC has been weakened by internal wrangling and become tarnished by involvement with crime, protection rackets and murder. Killing a representative of the state was the last straw. Corsicans want recognition for their distinctive culture, language and traditions, but they also want to live in peace.

Incognito *Masked members of the FLNC hold a press conference.*

The Euro: ending exchange rates

Say goodbye to marks, francs, schillings and guilders; wave farewell to pesetas, lire and drachma. On January 1, 2002, 12 member states of the European Union embarked on an historic transformation as they abandoned their old national forms of money in favour of a brand-new common currency – the Euro.

January 1, 1999, was the launch date, when most countries of the European Union (EU) had their currencies pegged to the new European currency – the Euro – and thus to each other. For three years from that date their national currencies remained valid, but citizens could also carry out non-cash bank transactions and purchases by cheque or banker's card in Euros. Then, on January 1, 2002, Euro notes and coins were introduced and the national currencies were progressively withdrawn over six months. Now, France, Germany, Italy, Belgium, Spain, Portugal, the Netherlands, Austria, Finland, Ireland, Luxembourg and Greece all share a common currency.

A rival to the dollar

Promoters of the Euro have long argued that it will hugely assist trade within Europe because the market will no longer be hampered by exchange-rate fluctuations and the costs of currency conversions. The Euro will also strengthen the bonds, both economic and political, of the 12 countries that are bound to it. In terms of population (300 million) and share of the world economy (18.6 per cent of world trade), these 12 countries add up to a fairly even match with the USA, and are well ahead of Japan. It is hoped that the Euro is destined to

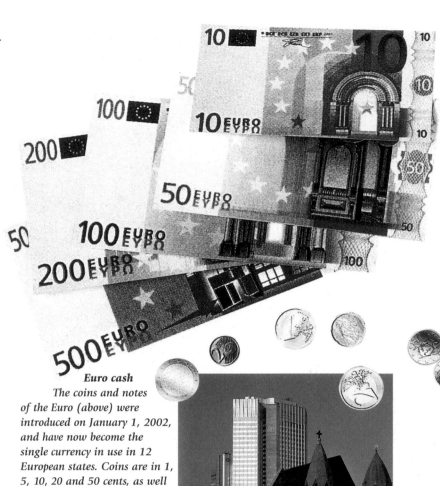

Euro cash
The coins and notes of the Euro (above) were introduced on January 1, 2002, and have now become the single currency in use in 12 European states. Coins are in 1, 5, 10, 20 and 50 cents, as well as 1 and 2 Euros. The European Central Bank in Frankfurt (right) defines the policies of the common currency.

rival the US dollar, and some 12 million unemployed also hope that it will bring economic growth and work.

Critics are not convinced. A single currency, they argue, lacks the flexibility to take account of regional needs, while uniform interest and exchange rates deprives nations of vital mechanisms for fine-tuning their national economies. For these reasons, three EU countries – Britain, Denmark and Sweden – have so far opted to stay out of the Euro conversion.

Seat of parliament *The Leopold Building in Brussels.*

European institutions

Brussels is home to the EU's most powerful bodies, including the Council of Ministers – the main decision-making body – and the European Commission, which is effectively the EU's civil service. There are 20 commissioners, appointed by the EU's 15 member governments, who implement decisions taken by the ministers of those states, and who also have regulatory powers. The Members of the European Parliament (MEPs) are based in Strasbourg, but the European Parliament also meets regularly in Brussels. The European Court of Justice, the Court of Auditors and the European Investment Bank are in Luxembourg, while the European Central Bank is in Frankfurt am Main, Germany.

From the Ecu to the Euro

In 1979, when the European Monetary System (EMS) was set up to limit fluctuations in exchange rates between the various European currencies, a common monetary unit was also created – the Ecu (European Currency Unit). It represented a basket of currencies, and was used only for transactions between the central banks of the EMS member countries in bond issues and trade – the Ecu was not a currency in the usual sense. When the European Monetary Union (EMU) was defined at the Maastricht summit in 1991, European leaders decided to abandon the Ecu; in 1995 they chose the name Euro for the new common currency.

Neutral ground   Two major UN agencies occupy this large complex in Vienna.

Switzerland and Austria: forever neutral?

Membership of NATO, the European Union and the UN raises important questions about the future of Switzerland's and Austria's neutrality.

World mission   The Red Cross, founded in Switzerland in 1863, helps victims of war and other crises.

Switzerland claims to have been neutral since 1516 – a status acknowledged by the Congress of Vienna of 1815. The country has remained unwavering in its neutrality ever since, even during the two World Wars. Austria owes its neutrality to Allied occupation after the Second World War: the guarantee of permanent neutrality, written into its State Treaty, was a condition for Soviet withdrawal in 1955.

The international stage

The Swiss are ardent defenders of their neutral status: they have never so much as entered a military alliance with a foreign power. The concept of neutrality, however, is always evolving, and the Swiss Confederation has allowed itself greater flexibility in recent years. Switzerland joined the UN on 10 September 2002 and it has sent unarmed observers to Bosnia, Iraq and other areas of conflict. In 1996 it joined the Partnership for Peace, an initiative launched by NATO in January 1994 to broaden the scope of its humanitarian and peacekeeping activities. Switzerland, does not aspire to join the military wing of NATO. EU Membership, on the other hand, may be possible: Sweden, Finland, Austria and Ireland have all maintained their neutral status within the EU. But EU membership for Switzerland would require it to surrender some of its banking autonomy, which it would be loath to do.

Secret banking   Safe-deposit boxes in a Swiss bank.

Austrian hesitation

Austria's neutrality played a vital role in the delicate political balance of central Europe during the Cold War; and its neutral status made it an obvious choice for the location of several key agencies of the United Nations: the headquarters of the International Atomic Energy Agency (IAEA), promoting peaceful uses of atomic energy, was established in Vienna in 1957; and the United Nations Industrial Development Organization (UNIDO) followed a decade later.

But the collapse of the Iron Curtain in 1989-90, and Austria's entry into the European Union in 1995, have altered the dynamics of the situation considerably. Like Sweden and Finland, which joined the EU at the same time, Austria has taken up observer status in the Western European Union. All three countries also participate in NATO's Partnership for Peace, though they do not wish to be full members of NATO.

This raises the difficult question about whether these neutral EU countries should benefit from the security of the EU's joint defence initiatives in perpetuity, without themselves contributing to them. Yet, as Switzerland can attest, resisting such pressures has always been a necessary part of actively maintaining one's neutrality.

The pleasure and pain of German reunification

On October 3, 1990, after 45 years of separation, East and West Germany were reunited. But disillusionment and bitterness followed on the heels of the euphoria.

One nation *The former West German flag flies in Berlin, new capital of a united Germany.*

It was at 6.57 pm precisely, on November 9, 1989, that Günther Schabowski, spokesman for the communist authorities in East Germany, announced on television that the borders would be open at midnight, and that East Germans would be free to leave the country without special permission. The Ossis (East Berliners) hurried to the control points along the

greater cost was incurred by the mountainous task of achieving parity of living standards between East and West: the sluggish economy and outdated industries of the East had to be converted to face the market forces of capitalism. The whole German economy slowed down, obliging the government of Helmut Kohl to increase income tax and cut welfare spending.

Unemployment across Germany reached record levels, peaking at 4.5 million at the start of 1998.

The East Germans, who were hit hard by the changes, became disillusioned, while the West Germans resented having to sacrifice their prosperity to support their ungrateful compatriots.

Bridging the gap *East Germans admire Western showrooms (left), a far cry from the shabby buildings they knew in East Berlin (above).*

infamous Berlin Wall: the Wessis (West Berliners) greeted them with champagne and open arms.

The Wall has come down!

The celebrations lasted several days. Bit by bit, the Wall was dismantled, along with the communist regime of the old and famously misnamed Democratic Republic of Germany (DDR). The East Germans thrilled at the wonders of the consumer society, and looked forward to becoming participants in it.

Monetary reunification took place on July 1, 1990, at huge cost to West Germany, which offered parity between the all-powerful Deutschmark and the almost worthless Ostmark. But

An apprenticeship in democracy

For some East Germans, the price of democracy has seemed very high. They lost many of the benefits offered by the old communist regime, such as free medical services and child care, holiday camps and guaranteed work. Now, with little income and low self-esteem, they felt excluded, and rapidly lost faith in the exercise of democracy, in which they had negligible experience. Since 1994, former communists, campaigning under the label of the Party of Democratic Socialism (PDS), have had members elected to the Bundestag (the German parliament). There has also been a rise in extreme right-wing groups, such as the nationalist Deutsche Volksunion (DVU).

Cafés, bars, brasseries and pubs

Drinking, exchanging gossip, sealing a business deal, celebrating with a toast – alcohol is part of the fabric of Western European culture, and bars, pubs, taverns, inns, brasseries and cafés play a central role in social life. Each aims to satisfy the needs of its clientele, from the gleaming, upholstered elegance of a city bar to the country pub that locals treat as a second home.

In Belgium there are city bars that have no keys: the door never closes. Twenty-four hours a day customers drift in and out, from the nightshift workers and market people at dawn, to the late-night revellers in the early hours. They are served by rosters of waiters and waitresses, capable of steering trays of drinks through the crowds at the busiest times, slowing down when things are quieter, quick to spot trouble and defuse it. Running a bar is an art form, developed over centuries.

Social life

Beer is commonly regarded as the drink of northern Europe. It is brewed from grain (usually barley, sometimes wheat). Belgium alone had 3223 breweries in 1900; nowadays, these have been amalgamated and 'rationalised' to 115. Wine is the drink of the warmer south, but the two cultures meet and intermingle across the central band of Western Europe. Gentle

Quintessential France In St Tropez, as all over France, bar terraces overlook a square where the game of boules can be played.

The Café de Flore and the Deux Magots

At the mid-point of Paris's Boulevard St Germain are two of the city's most celebrated cafés. Elegant locals and curious tourists alike gather to see and be seen in the Café de Flore, or its rival the Café des Deux Magots a few doors away. Both have a long tradition of intellectual and artistic patronage. The Deux Magots, founded in 1875, was the haunt of the *fin-de-siècle* symbolist poets Mallarmé, Verlaine and Rimbaud. The Flore opened in 1890 and attracted painters such as Picasso, and, after the Second World War, a circle of intellectuals and writers that included Boris Vian, Jean-Paul Sartre and Albert Camus.

After dark Vincent van Gogh's Night Café (1888) captures the atmosphere late at night when only a few solitary diehards, and one courting couple, remain.

intoxication has long been considered an acceptable oil for the wheels of social contact; excessive inebriation has always been mocked and condemned – as in the cartoons of the 18th-century English artist William Hogarth.

Coffee was considered an elegant and fashionable alternative to alcohol when it was first introduced into Europe in the 17th century, but there was some dispute as to whether its stimulant effects should be approved or condemned. The first coffee-houses appeared in England in about 1650, in Oxford and London. They soon became popular meeting places for businessmen. Lloyd's, the great insurance market of London, began as Edward Lloyd's coffee-house in the 1680s. The first coffee-house in Paris, the Café Procope, opened in 1689. By the 18th century several of the 500 cafés in Paris had become famous as

Vincent
le café de nuit

The *Heurigen*

A famous treat for the Viennese is to take the tram and head out to the city's hilly suburbs, such as Grinzing or Nussdorf, to visit one of the *Heurigen*. These are the new-wine taverns run by families who grow Grüner Veltliner grapes in vineyards within the city's

boundaries, and then convert them into a special *Heuriger* wine that is drunk young. The taverns are marked out by evergreen branches hanging over the entrance; inside there is often a small open-air courtyard, where platters of cold-meat and sliced sausage may also be served – all to the accompaniment of traditional *Schrammelmusik* played by a quartet of two violins, an accordion and a guitar or zither.

Viennese coffee

According to legend, when the Ottoman Turks retreated from besieging Vienna in 1683, they left behind them a sack of dark-brown beans – for which the Viennese soon developed a passion. Since then, coffee has become a Viennese speciality,

and the *Kaffeehaus* an essential part of life in Vienna. The most celebrated of these are redolent of their long history. Attentive staff, dressed soberly in black and white, glide through the polished interiors bearing cups of coffee, glasses of water and cream pastries. There is no sense of urgency: clients tarry over newspapers and magazines placed at their disposal, or while away the afternoon with games of cards. The Viennese have over 30 different ways to prepare and serve coffee, catering for every taste.

Diet begins tomorrow
Viennese cafés are famous for their excellent cakes and pastries.

meeting places for philosophers, but they then took on a sinister reputation as the places where the Revolutionary clubs gathered to choose the next victims of execution.

After the fall of Napoleon in 1815, Russian Cossacks entered Paris and would apparently call out impatiently to café staff *Bystro, bystro!* ('quickly, quickly!'), giving rise to the term *bistro* for a small French restaurant.

The brown cafés of Amsterdam

The atmosphere of Amsterdam is distilled in its famous brown cafés, so-named because their ceilings and walls have been stained by centuries of tobacco smoke. The dark wood of the floor, bar, tables and chairs, and the dingy light, enhance the effect. Many of these cafés have been in use for nearly 400 years. They are still very much a part of city life, and far from being museum pieces. At the other end of the spectrum are Amsterdam's new designer bars or white cafés – bright, spacious, and often substituting the throb of amplified music for the more traditional murmur of quiet chat. Amsterdam also has its coffee shops serving tea and coffee, cakes and pastries. Some, the so-called smoking coffee shops, openly sell marijuana. The pictures of marijuana leaves on the doors and windows, the psychedelic decor and general nostalgia for the hippie era tend to make it clear what kind of coffee house this is.

The local

In their brown cafés, Amsterdammers can feel *uit en thuis* ('out and at home') at the same time. This is the aim of all similar drinking places across Europe, from the German *Kneipe*, to the British pub and Irish bar. The Germans sometimes go one stage farther, by reserving tables (*Stammtische*) for their regular and favoured clients; it can be a major *faux pas* to sit down at one uninvited.

In Ireland, there are bars aplenty. What is unusual is the location of some of them: you are quite likely to find a well-stocked bar in the back of a grocery shop or a hardware store, or even at an undertakers – where selling alcohol could be seen as a logical diversification. Bars in Ireland, especially

Psychedelic scenery *Some coffee shops of Amsterdam declare loudly that they are designed by young people for young people.*

in rural areas, used to be considered more or less male preserves, and to some extent they still are. As the saying goes, if you see women in a bar, you won't see any men. But more egalitarian drinking has arrived with the spread of pubs and inns where there is more seating than just the stools at the bar.

To many British drinkers the local is virtually an extension of their home. They can join in the crush of the public bar, or retreat to the more upholstered zone of the lounge or saloon bar. As well as an increasing range of food, pubs serve a broad

The British and their darts

The first dart board is said to have been the end of a barrel, which is appropriate, given that this is the classic pub game, with some 5 million players in Britain. It became popular in the late 19th century when good-quality equipment could be made cheaply.

The principles are simple: players have to hit a round target, which is divided evenly into 20 segments, to score points (1 to 20). Hitting an outer ring earns double points, an inner ring triple points, with the outer and inner bull's-eyes scoring 25 and 50 points respectively.

The Dutch *proeflokaalen*

At the bar called De Drie Fleschjes ('The Three Little Flasks') in Amsterdam little seems to have changed since its opening in 1650. This is one of the most famous of the *proeflokaalen* bars serving *genever* (gin), and other spirits. Originally these were places where one could have a taste (*proef*) of a distillery's products before buying, but they evolved into bars in their own right. *Genever* means juniper, the main flavouring used in this spirit, which was developed in the Netherlands in the 17th century. It was corrupted into the English word *gin*, or even Geneva gin. Gin ranks as the third most popular drink in the Netherlands, after coffee and beer. It is drunk ice-cold in small glasses – often as a chaser with beer.

By the barrel *Hoecks – the oldest bar in Charlottenburg, Berlin.*

Picturesque pub *Holidaymakers and locals enjoy a drink in the sunshine outside the King's Arms pub at King's Saithe on the banks of the river Ouse in Yorkshire.*

Ireland's distinctive drinks

Everyone will tell you that Guinness tastes best in Dublin. Abroad, this famous velvet-black stout is rich and bitter; in Dublin it is creamy and subtle. Various explanations are put forward for this phenomenon: the Dublin water, the way the beer is kept, the temperature it is served at. Whatever the reason, Guinness has made its reputation internationally, to the extent that it is the best known Irish drink. Yet there are many others, including comparable stouts, such as Murphy's from Cork. Ireland also has its own fine whiskeys (spelled with the e), with a smooth flavour that sets them apart from Scottish whisky. Jameson's, Paddy's and Old Bushmill's are the leading brands.

variety of alcohol, from wine to spirits, as well as soft drinks; but beer is the staple. This was not always the case: in the 18th century Dutch *genever*, or gin, was the favoured tipple of the working classes, because it was cheap and relatively pure. But gin-drinking rapidly became a curse of the times. In the 35 years to 1735, gin consumption in London alone leapt from 600 000 gallons per year to 6.5 million, with disastrous social consequences. This trend was only reversed by government action; the Beer Act of 1830 abolished all duty on beer and reduced the cost of licences for beer sellers, thus returning beer to its central place in British drinking habits.

The one aspect of British drinking that confuses continentals and foreign visitors is the so-called licensing hours. Pubs have, by law, to stop serving drinks at 11 pm, usually after a bell has rung to sound last orders. Most Britons remember when pubs closed in mid-afternoon as well, but legislation in the 1980s permitted pubs to stay open from 11 am to 11 pm. In Britain there is still no such thing as a bar without keys.

The Gentlemen's clubs of London

London's famous gentlemen's clubs were intended to be home-away-from-home for gentlemen, an address in London where they could lodge, dine and drink, without being disturbed by women, children or business. Members were treated to a grand country-house style, with elegant dining rooms, a library and smoking room, and impeccable service. The clubs also became notoriously conservative and stuffy. More recently, economic necessity has caused many to close. There were about 120 clubs in the 1930s, but only about a third of that number survive.

Grand style *The Athenaeum Club in London was built in 1832.*

Wired to the world *A cybercafé demonstration at a fair in Nantes shows how bars and cafés can reinvent themselves to serve the needs of their times.*

New for old *Belgium's dispute over language (Dutch versus French) was the cause of a split in the university of Leuven in 1968. French-speakers created a new campus at Louvain-la-Neuve (above), south of Brussels.*

The old universities: pillars of learning

Founded mainly in the Middle Ages, the great universities of Europe were the cradle of new ideas, and often a crucible of cultural and political revolutions. These venerable institutions remain key transmitters of knowledge in the modern world.

Universities evolved out of the cathedral schools of the Middle Ages. In an effort to provide further education for monks and clerics, *studia generalia* were set up, teaching mainly theology to scholars from all over Europe. The very first universities were in Italy; the earliest in Western Europe was the University of Paris, founded in around 1150-70 and largely built on the foundations laid by Peter Abelard, who had attracted scores of international scholars to the Paris Left Bank a couple of decades before. Gradually colleges were set up around the university, essentially to provide lodgings for poor scholars. The most famous of these was founded in 1257 by a canon of Notre-Dame, Robert de Sorbon, whose name it still bears: the Sorbonne.

Oxford and Cambridge

A similar university was set up at Oxford at the end of the 12th century. As in Paris, teaching took place in rented halls and churches, until the residential colleges developed. University College was the first, founded in 1249. It was followed by Balliol and Merton before the end of the 13th century. Cambridge claims to be even older than Oxford, although its first college – Peterhouse – was founded in 1284.

During the late Middle Ages and Renaissance, the university movement spread across Western Europe: new universities were established in France at Montpellier (1220) and Aix-en-Provence (1409); in Germany at Heidelberg (1386), Leipzig (1409) and Freiberg (1457); in

Seats of learning and rebellion *The Grand Amphithéâtre of the Sorbonne (above) reflects the university's eminent past. In fact, the Sorbonne is just one part of a restructured University of Paris, spread over 13 campuses across the city and beyond. This reorganisation came about in the wake of the student revolt of May 1968, which began at the faculty at Nanterre (right), built in the early 1960s just to the west of Paris.*

Oldest in Germany *Heidelberg University was founded on the Sorbonne model in 1386. The town later became a centre for the German Romantics.*

Belgium at Leuven (1425); in Scotland at St Andrews (1411) and Glasgow (1451). They were always closely tied to religious education. Roger Bacon, for example, who taught at Oxford from 1247 to 1257 and helped to found the tradition of experimental scientific research, was a Franciscan friar. Because all universities taught in Latin, there was considerable movement among them across Europe. The great humanist Desiderius Erasmus was born in Rotterdam, ordained as a priest near Gouda, studied at the University of Paris, taught in Bologna in Italy, lectured at Cambridge, helped to develop the Trilingual

College (Latin, Greek, and Hebrew) at Leuven in 1517-21, and spent the latter years of his life in Basel in Switzerland and Freiburg in Germany, fleeing persecution.

It was religion that brought a crisis to the older universities. During the Protestant Reformation, many of them stood doggedly by Catholic orthodoxy. The intellectual impetus shifted towards the Protestant universities, such as Leiden in the Netherlands, founded in 1575. After 1540, Cambridge became the largest Protestant university in England. The international fame of Isaac Newton, who was professor of mathematics there from 1669, played a major role in rebuilding its reputation.

Later, in the 18th century, the Enlightenment began to shake off the bonds of religion: the first modern university free of religious interference, and championing rational thought and scientific analysis, was at Halle, in Germany; it had been founded in 1694. At Halle, teaching was no longer in Latin, but in German. The University of Paris, by contrast, was a symbol of Catholic-dominated education, and when the French Revolution came it was closed – except for its fine, domed chapel, which was designated a Temple of Reason. Napoleon turned the other buildings into artists' studios. After the defeat of Napoleon in 1815, the restored Bourbon monarchy reopened the Sorbonne.

The power of books *Trinity College, Dublin, was founded in 1592 by Elizabeth I to reinforce the Reformation in Ireland. The Long Room of its famous library is 210 ft (64 m) in length, and was completed in 1732.*

Old traditions

In the 19th century intellectual freedom and scientific research blossomed, notably in Germany. Universities began to admit women students: the first women's college at Oxford, Lady Margaret Hall, opened in 1878. During the past hundred years the number of universities has grown dramatically. Today, going to university has become almost a rite of passage, a stage in life when young people leave home to begin an independent existence.

For some, going to one of the older universities means a chance to join in a community with traditions going back centuries – such as attending evensong in a college chapel, or taking part in the boat race between Oxford and Cambridge, which has been held annually since 1836.

At Heidelberg, some old traditions live on. Members of student drinking clubs, wearing their special caps, gather in old pubs such as Zum Seppl (founded 1634) to elect the *Bierkönig* ('Beer King') who can down the most beer in an evening. But students are no longer locked up for misdemeanours in the old *Studentenkarzer* ('Students' Prison'), an experience no serious student would wish to miss before it was closed down in 1914.

Undergraduates, tutors and colleges

The universities of Oxford and Cambridge offer their students a high degree of personal attention. Undergraduates are admitted to one of the colleges on the basis of their final school exams and interviews, and are expected to live in the college for at least their first year. Within the college, they come under the care of an individual tutor for each subject they study. They attend lectures organised by the university faculties, as well as tutorials with their tutors. These are conducted on a one-to-one basis, or in small groups, guaranteeing that each student is closely supervised.

Dressing the part *An Oxford undergraduate, accompanied by his proud mother, wears the compulsory bow tie, gown and mortar board to attend the matriculation or enrolment ceremony.*

Lazy days *Punts glide gently past a parade of magnificent Cambridge colleges.*

The French Riviera

From Toulon to Menton on the Italian border, the Côte d'Azur unfurls in miles of beaches, dotted with romantic towns and cities such as Cannes and Nice. The allure of the French Riviera includes Mediterranean sunlight and colour, as well as a backdrop of flashy villas and an undercurrent of sleaze.

In 1763 the English novelist and travel writer Tobias Smollett fell in love with Nice and the surrounding coast. His enchantment filtered through to his readers, and before long the English were heading south to the Riviera, to catch an early spring in a region where the almond trees blossom in January. The fashion for the Côte d'Azur was launched.

Ever the adventurers, the English were the first to make something of the charms of Hyères, Nice, Cannes, and Menton. By 1820 there were already some 100 English families living in Nice: the famous palm-lined Promenade des Anglais, overlooking the Baie des Anges (Bay of Angels), was named in their honour in 1822. Royalty, wealthy aristocrats, industrialists and bankers from France, England, Russia and the USA headed for this coast, building extravagant palaces, such as the Villa Massena at Nice, the Palais Carnolès at Menton, and the Rothschilds' Villa Ephrussi at Cap-Ferrat, still the scene of spectacular parties. In 1880 the coast was baptised the Côte d'Azur (the azure-blue coast), a term invented by the writer Stephen Liégeard, who spent the final years of his life in Cannes and used the term to name one of his guidebooks to the coast. The gilt became somewhat tarnished after the Second World War, however, with the advent of universal paid holidays in France, and a rash of property development and road-links that have disfigured a large part of the coastline.

Unspoilt corners

Every day a tide of visitors arrives by boat at the quays of the Îles d'Hyères Porquerolles, Port-Cros and Le Levant. Here, they can glimpse what the Côte d'Azur used to be like before the scourge of real estate took hold. The Île de Port-Cros has been

St Tropez

If the car parks and the luxury shops can be ignored, the old St Tropez, beloved of the 19th-century painters, is still there to be found: the charming old fishing port bordered by red-tiled roofs clustered around the pretty baroque church. With her film *And God Created Woman* (1956), set in St Tropez, Brigitte Bardot helped to turn this into a centre for show-business people, and hence also for star-spotters. Every summer about 100 000 visitors invade its streets and beaches, but these days the stars of screen and fashion hide behind the walls of heavily guarded villas outside the town. Traders put up their prices in June, as the painters arrive and begin jostling for a place at the port. Few have the talent of the pointillist Paul Signac, who lived here in the opening years of the century, and whose paintings can now be seen at the town's Musée de L'Annonciade.

The Eagles Nest The village of Èze, set on a hilltop between Nice and the Italian border, offers one of the most spectacular views of the Côte d'Azur.

Monaco

'I am Monaco built on rocks, I sow no crops nor do I harvest, yet I want to live.' The motto of the Princes of Monaco is just as valid today as when the family took over in 1297. Covering just 0.75 sq miles (1.95 km²), this tiny independent state knows that its only means of surviving and developing is as an important financial centre. Thus major businesses around the world have bases in this fiscal paradise, where the per capita income is one of the highest in the world. A full calendar of glittering cultural and social events – including the Monte Carlo Rally – ensures that the tiny principality is never out of the public eye for long.

designated a *parc naturel*, France's smallest, with just 2.7 sq miles (7 km²) of land, plus the surrounding sea. Nature takes on a different meaning on the Île du Levant: half the island has been set aside as a nudist colony.

One can always escape the packed beaches and soulless marinas by travelling inland to the area's hilltop villages, known as *villages perchés*. The winding streets and old stone houses absorb the Mediterranean sun, and resonate with the hum of cicadas, the wind in the pine trees, the tapping of metal balls as a game of boules takes place in the village square. The air is heavy with the aromatic oils of lavender, rosemary, wild thyme and cultivated roses, scents that are distilled in the famous perfumeries of Grasse. Many of the houses in the *villages perchés* have been converted into holiday homes; others have become studios for artists, potters, weavers and silversmiths.

The *calanques* of Cassis

Oppressed by the heat, eyes dazzled by white rocks, walkers make slow progress over limestone tracks leading from the interior. But their pains are well rewarded. All along the Côte de Cassis, just east of Marseille, high white cliffs plunge down to the turquoise sea and carve out deep indentations. These *calanques* (rocky inlets) are breathtakingly beautiful, particularly at sunset, when the sky, sea and rocks merge into a soft golden haze. Designated a protected natural site, they are accessible only on foot or by boat, with the exception of the Calanque de Port-Miou, close to Cassis, which can be reached by car.

Star hotel *Film stars often stay at the luxurious Hotel Carlton at Cannes.*

A mosaic of immigration

Postcolonial immigration has brought new riches to Western European cultures, symbolised by the bright colours of African robes, the heady flavours of Indian spices and the uplifting beat of reggae music. But immigrants, often living in depressed inner-city areas, have found themselves at the forefront of economic and political tensions, and their resentment at acts of open racism erupts intermittently in riots.

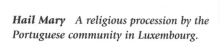

'We are all foreigners!' declared a banner paraded through the streets of French cities in June 1997, as protesters marched against a proposed tightening of laws affecting immigrants. Like all slogans, it was an exaggeration, but not much of one. One French person in four has foreign parents or grandparents.

During the 20th century, the countries of Western Europe, with growing economies and declining populations, have actively encouraged a foreign labour force. The arrival on the Thames of the old troopship *Empire Windrush* in 1948, carrying 510 smartly dressed Jamaicans, marked the start of the postwar phase of immigration in Britain. By 1961, 120 000 immigrants a year were arriving in Britain, mainly from former colonies in the Caribbean, and from Africa and South Asia. Meanwhile, North Africans were heading for France and Belgium, and Indonesians for the Netherlands. Recruitment from abroad remained at a high level across Europe until the world recession that began in the mid-1970s.

Victims of economic crisis

As industries began laying off workers, machines started to replace human labour on the assembly lines. Thus a combination of recession and structural changes to industry transformed the market for jobs, and exacerbated the tensions between immigrants and native inhabitants. Immigrants are often casually accused of stealing jobs from the nationals, and of taking too much from the welfare state. Nationalism revives in times of stress, and is easily exploited by political extremists.

Hail Mary *A religious procession by the Portuguese community in Luxembourg.*

Stick together *Minority communities reinforce their identity by ensuring a supply of familiar provisions, as at this Turkish shop in Germany.*

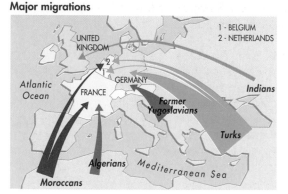

Major migrations

1 - BELGIUM
2 - NETHERLANDS

UNITED KINGDOM
Atlantic Ocean
FRANCE
GERMANY
Former Yugoslavians
Indians
Turks
Algerians
Mediterranean Sea
Moroccans

Carnival
The West Indian community of London holds its massive carnival in Notting Hill Gate each August. The atmosphere is predominantly one of fun, exuberance and goodwill.

Since the early 1970s, European governments have begun to restrict the right to political asylum, while also limiting quotas for immigrant workers. The movement of non-European migrants is now closely regulated. But stricter entry requirements also increase the recourse to illegal or clandestine immigration, often arranged by criminal organisations exploiting the gullible and vulnerable. The economic and political pressures in the former communist countries of Eastern Europe, and in Yugoslavia and Albania, have resulted in a tide of refugees, asylum seekers, and illegal immigrants from these countries, principally to Germany, Austria, Switzerland and Italy, though increasing numbers have arrived in Britain.

Assimilation

Italians, Poles, Russians, Spanish and Portuguese were the first immigrants in Western Europe, from the 19th century on. They were not always well-received, but being European and mainly Christian their assimilation was comparatively smooth. For more recent immigrants of Asian and African origin, the greater cultural divides have often made integration more difficult, to the extent that many have begun to ask whether assimilation is a desirable goal at all.

After studying in European schools, second and third generation immigrants have a perfect understanding of the culture and language that surrounds them, yet they may still feel excluded by prejudice and discrimination. Often living in depressed suburbs of big cities, they forge a spirit of solidarity for self-protection, and to re-assert their own cultural identity.

Virtually all Western European countries have to contend with the issues of immigration: the most successful will be those that provide a constructive framework in which to develop the talents of their people across the board, regardless of their ethnic origins or background.

Vigilance   Border posts, as at Menton on the French-Italian border (above), deal with many desperate people trying to enter Europe. Most are prepared to work long hours in small businesses (below) in order to stay.

CHAPTER 4
CITIES OF WESTERN EUROPE

The capitals of Western Europe are rich in symbolism. These cities are the seats of power, which historically centred on grand palaces designed to impress. They are cultural, intellectual and economic hubs, home to a nation's key institutions. They are also cosmopolitan, with foreign embassies, headquarters of multinational companies, immigrant communities, and the swarms of tourists who help to keep the city economy oiled. The cities have to balance their legacy from the past with the need to ensure a vibrant future.

On the one hand, there is the ongoing restoration and preservation of historic buildings; on the other, there is a new trend for grand projects – eye-catching, futuristic, often deeply controversial buildings intended to evoke a sense of innovation and dynamism. Cities inspire love-hate relationships, but while the city dwellers dream of the gentle pace of village life, they also find it hard to relinquish the energy of urban life.

The old town of Salzburg, Austria.

Paris today

Paris is the heartbeat of France and always has been. Its mansions, churches and public squares were the settings for the nation's key historical events. It cradles an artistic and cultural heritage of exceptional richness. But Paris is very much a lived-in city, characterised by the urgent bustle of its people. They remain loyal to their quartiers, *which over time have evolved distinct characteristics, and help to give the city a human scale and the charms of diversity.*

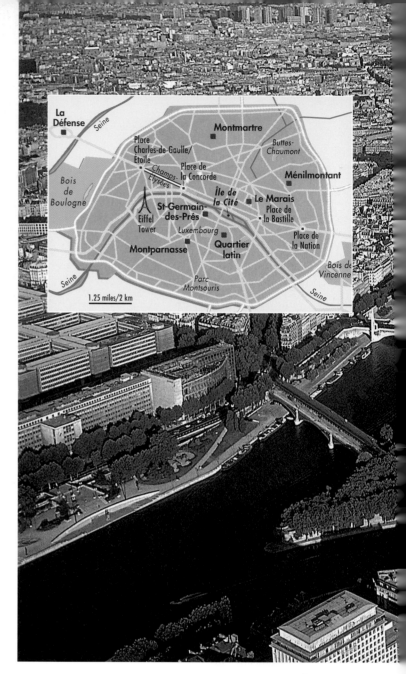

The best time to arrive in Paris is at night. The grand avenues and boulevards, the mansions and museums, the bridges over the Seine, the government offices, the world-famous Eiffel Tower, are all floodlit. Like a theatre set, central Paris was built to make a visual impact. Most of this was the work of Baron Georges Haussmann, who drew up his plans for the city under Napoleon III in the 1860s, though they were not implemented until the 1880s, after the Franco-Prussian War.

While London is sprawling and essentially low-rise, Paris is stacked high. Most Parisians live in apartments several floors up, but centrally located. This forces them out into the streets, bringing constant animation to the cafés, bars and shops, the Métro and the cinemas. Consequently, they have their finger on the city's heartbeat, which remains vibrant 24 hours a day. Arrive at 3 am and restaurants in the popular areas for eating, drinking and being entertained are still humming; as diners leave, fresh oysters are arriving for the next busy day.

Islands in the stream   The River Seine divides to pass the Île St Louis and the Île de la Cité at the heart of the capital. This is where Paris was founded, as a settlement in the lands of a Celtic tribe called the Parisii.

The Latin Quarter

The essential character of Paris's *quartiers* goes back much farther than Haussmann's time. The Latin Quarter of the Left Bank, for example, was known as a centre for radical intellectual activity in the 12th century, a reputation earned afresh during the 1950s and 1960s. The area earned its name from the fact that Latin, the language of scholarship, was spoken around the university precincts until Napoleonic times. This *quartier* is still home to

Rural Paris   Although close to the heart of Montmartre, the Cabaret du Lapin Agile has a country air to it, occupying the same street as a vineyard. It has been a famous venue for singers and performers since 1860.

publishers, bookshops, art cinemas and bohemian cafés, but these days they increasingly rub shoulders with fashion boutiques, and evidence of rampant, commercial tourism.

There is Paris for the Parisians, and Paris for the tourists, although the two intermingle. Tourism is nowhere more apparent than at the *butte* ('hilltop') of Montmartre, beneath the domes of the Basilique du Sacré Coeur. In the decades around the turn of the 20th century, Montmartre was the hub of bohemian Europe, a honeypot for painters, poets and writers including Baudelaire, Verlaine and Picasso. Even today hidden secrets await discovery off the well-beaten track – alleys lined with quaint shuttered houses and flower gardens, and even a vineyard.

Art and order The extensive fountains and gardens give a sense of order that extends outwards from the vast palace.

Versailles

Louis XIV wanted nothing but the best for his magnificent chateau at Versailles, to the south-west of Paris, and above all he wanted it to be huge. Built by 30 000 workers, the rooms alone cover 125 acres (50 ha). There is also a 250 acre (100 ha) park and gardens, with 1400 fountains supplied by water from a man-made Grand Canal. Today Versailles receives some 3 million tourists a year, but public intrusion is nothing new. Louis opened the gardens to anyone who could dress presentably, and the public could also watch him dine.

City markets Paris has some 80 street markets, of which Rue Mouffetard is one of the most picturesque. Many of the stall-holders are here to sell their own produce – not only fruit, vegetables and wild mushrooms, but also bread, pâtés, cheese, sausages and ready-made meals.

Parisian's Paris

Beyond the city centre Paris marches to a different tune – in the residential *quartiers* such as Barbès near Montmartre, or Belleville farther to the east. Barbès is famous for its sprawling Tati store, which attracts the immigrant populations of the *quartier*, as well as keen shoppers from elsewhere in search of bargain prices. In the 19th century, working-class Belleville was notorious as the stronghold of the Paris Commune, which defied the authorities. Despite much demolition, Belleville retains something of its traditional atmosphere.

Noble grandeur The Place des Vosges lies at the heart the Marais, the city's most aristocratic quarter during the 17th century.

Paris on the Seine

The Tuileries Gardens stretch between the Louvre and the Place de la Concorde. They were originally the gardens of the Tuileries royal palace, built in 1560, and redesigned in the 1660s by the great landscape gardener and architect André Le Nôtre.

The Eiffel Tower was erected in under 18 months, in time for the centenary of the French Revolution in 1889. It was designed by the engineer Gustave Eiffel, and built almost entirely of wrought iron. At 984 ft (300 m), it was the world's tallest structure for 40 years. It was not universally approved at the time: a protest by artists and writers called it a gigantic black factory chimney and a dishonour to the city. It has since been accepted as a wonder of the modern world.

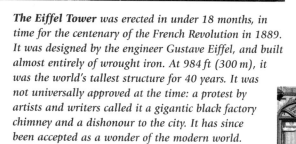

The Paris Métro was inaugurated in 1900, during the Art Nouveau era.

The Louvre was once a royal palace, which also provided lodgings for artists under royal patronage. In 1793, after the Revolution, the royal art collections were opened to the public. The buildings received a dramatic face-lift in the 1980s, when the controversial glass pyramid designed by the Chinese-American architect I.M. Pei was built to solve the problem of access to the galleries.

Galeries Lafayette, a fine department store, was founded in 1895.

The François Mitterrand Library, in the Bercy district in the south-east of the city, is designed to look like four open books on the corners of a rectangle, but has been widely criticised for being unsuitable for storing books.

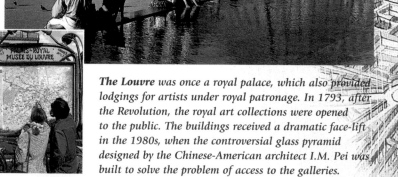

The Parc de la Villette, the site of the old slaughterhouses of Paris, is now the setting for the Cité des Sciences et de l'Industrie, a futuristic science museum and exhibition centre.

1. Eiffel Tower
2. Grande Arche at La Défense
3. Arc de Triomphe
4. Palais de Chaillot
5. Grand Palais
6. Petit Palais
7. Place de la Concorde
8. The Tuileries
9. The Louvre
10. Opéra Garnier
11. Opéra Bastille
12. Pompidou Centre
13. Hôtel de Ville
14. Tour St Jacques
15. Île St Louis
16. Notre-Dame Cathedral, Île de la Cité
17. Hôtel des Invalides
18. National Assembly
19. Musée d'Orsay
20. Montparnasse Tower
21. Palais de Justice
22. Church of St Sulpice
23. Palais du Luxembourg
24. Panthéon
25. François Mitterrand Library
26. Jardin des Plantes

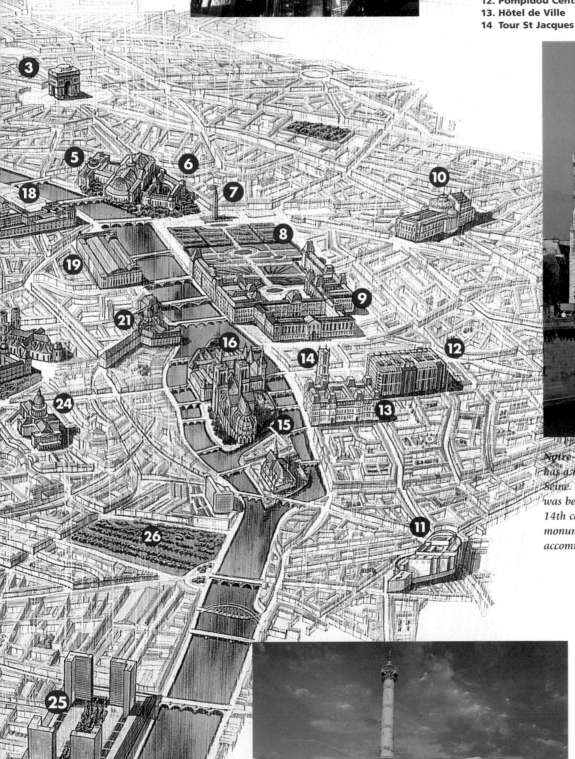

Notre-Dame Cathedral, on the Île de la Cité, has a magnificent position overlooking the River Seine. A masterpiece of Gothic architecture, it was begun in 1163, but not completed until the 14th century. The cathedral was planned on a monumental scale, and is capable of accommodating 9000 worshippers.

Old family run stores keep alive the tradition of the small shopkeeper.

The Place de la Bastille is the site of the old Bastille prison. At the centre of the square rises a column surmounted by the Genius of Liberty, today somewhat upstaged by the gleaming façade of the new Opéra Bastille, which opened in 1990.

City of seafarers *The canals of Amsterdam are a constant reminder of the city's maritime heritage, as is the plaque (above) on the Tower of Currency, built around 1490.*

Amsterdam: canals and bicycles

It was an Italian, in 1582, who first called Amsterdam the Venice of the North. The two cities have much in common: canals and bridges, seafaring and trading traditions. In Amsterdam, it is the people's ability to work hard and then relax and enjoy themselves with equal gusto that creates the city's unique character.

Its name alone reflects the challenge of Amsterdam: Amsteldam – 'the dam on the River Amstel'. Founded by Friesian fishermen in the 13th century at the confluence of the rivers IJssel and Amstel, the city was forged out of a struggle with nature. It was built on a hundred or more sandy islands around a web-like network of canals linked together by 400 bridges. A large part of the city lies below sea level.

Through trading skills, the seafaring people of Amsterdam turned their city into one of the grain centres of Europe. The 17th century was the city's Golden Age, when the powerful Dutch East India Company, founded in 1602, took control of some of the world's most valuable exotic products, notably spices from the East.

The tradition of liberty

Converted to Protestantism in 1578, the city has always prided itself on its tolerance. Banned authors came here to publish; Jews fleeing persecution sought refuge here in the 16th and 17th centuries; Huguenots arrived from France after the Revocation of the Edict of Nantes in 1685. All contributed to the prosperity of the city, and fostered local industries,

such as silk weaving and the diamond trade. One of Amsterdam's most visited sights is the house of Anne Frank, where the young Jewish girl and her family hid from the Nazis from 1942 to 1944. She died in a concentration camp after being captured, but her *Diary* survived, a moving testament to humanity amid the barbarity of the Nazi occupation.

For some, the Amsterdammers' tolerance is synonymous with permissiveness, which is often associated with the red light district, where legalised prostitution has become something of a tourist attraction, and the coffee shops, where the sale of soft drugs is tolerated.

Art in Amsterdam

Dutch painting stood at the forefront of European art in the 17th century. Its reputation was rekindled in the present century through the work of Van Gogh, Piet Mondrian and the De Stijl group. This heritage can be seen in Amsterdam's three great art galleries. The Rijksmuseum, founded in 1816, offers a panorama of Dutch art from the medieval period to the 19th century. The Stedelijk Museum houses contemporary art, while the airy Rijksmuseum Vincent van Gogh is dedicated to 700 works by the troubled man who is perhaps the most famous Dutch painter of all.

Transports of colour
Trams crisscross the city on a network of routes, linking the centre with the suburbs.

Brussels, at the heart of Europe

Thanks to its central location, Brussels has become the administrative capital of Europe. The Flemish cities of Bruges, Ghent and Antwerp have also carved out roles in the modern world, just as they did in medieval times.

In medieval times the walled city of Brussels benefited from trading links between the rich Flemish cities to the north – Bruges, Ghent and Antwerp – and inland Germany and France. The craftsmen's guilds wielded considerable power, and surrounded the Grand Place with magnificent guildhouses, creating a focus at the heart of the city. After independence in 1830, Brussels had a lively arts scene that fostered the first manifestations of Art Nouveau architecture. In the 1950s and 1960s Brussels gradually became home to more and more institutions of the Common Market. By the end of the 20th century, it had the headquarters of the European Commission, the Council of Ministers and a branch of the European parliament.

Restored grandeur   The square known as Grand Place is the centrepiece of Brussels. It is surrounded by magnificent gothic and baroque buildings, many of them built after war devastated the city in 1695.

Prosperous Antwerp

Trade route   The broad River Schelde (or Scheldt) passes beneath the spire of Antwerp's splendid Gothic cathedral (on the left).

Founded in the 8th century, Antwerp owes its prosperity to its location on the broad estuary of the River Schelde. As Bruges' fortunes ebbed away with the silting up of its port, Antwerp's star rose. It had its Golden Age in the early 17th century, when it served as a gateway to the European hinterland for burgeoning trade with Asia and the Americas. Later, the city fell on hard times as a result of religious wars, which led to a formal split with the Netherlands in 1648. After that the Schelde was blocked for trade for around 150 years. Antwerp has since revived to become one of the world's busiest ports and a centre of the diamond trade.

Bruges – held in a time warp

Flanders has many proud and historic cities, built on a rich trading past, but none has been better preserved than Bruges. Founded in the 9th century, it was an inland port, linked to the sea by rivers and canals. On the back of a lucrative wool and textile trade, it developed in medieval times into one of the richest cities in northern Europe. Its heyday was in the 14th and 15th centuries when the Dukes of Burgundy held their court there. Bruges' streets thronged with merchants and bankers from Britain, France, Germany, Scandinavia, Spain and Italy. It became a centre for some of the greatest artists of the late medieval period, such Jan van Eyck and Hans Memling. But the river silted up, and Bruges' development ceased. The slumbering city was rediscovered by 19th-century romantics, who gloried in its atmospheric decay and restored its buildings. Today tourism has become the chief industry. The city is cherished for its winding roads, canals and an all-pervading sense of history.

Tranquil refuge   The Begijnhof in Bruges was founded in 1245 as a settlement for women called béguines, who adopted a simple religious life of good works.

91

Berlin: rebuilding the past

As the capital of the kings of Prussia, Berlin was ridiculed for its militarism and pomposity. Then it earned a reputation for bohemian depravity in the 1920s, before becoming the capital of the Third Reich. It was flattened in the Second World War, then split in two by the Wall. The city now enjoys calmer times in which to revive and flourish.

Salute *The Statue of Victory is located in central Berlin.*

Berlin was once the site of the only crossing point on the River Spree for miles around. It began to prosper with the rise of Prussia as a major European power. Friedrich-Wilhelm, the Great Elector, undertook a massive reconstruction programme in the 17th century, following widespread destruction in the Thirty Years' War. Later, Friedrich II, 'the Great', who reigned from 1740 to 1786, brought the Enlightenment to Berlin, installing Voltaire at his Sanssouci palace at Potsdam to the south-west. He began reshaping the city around the impressive central avenue Unter den Linden ('Beneath the Lime Trees') which, after 1791, led up to the Brandenburg Gate.

During the 19th century, Berlin grew rapidly as an industrial centre. Leafy suburbs spread, but so did insanitary tenement blocks crammed with millions of workers and their families. The city became a hotbed of social discontent, exacerbated by defeat in the First World War. The yawning gap between rich and poor in interwar Germany was nowhere more vivid than in Berlin. The communist-inspired Spartacus Revolt was savagely crushed in 1919, and thereafter capital status was transferred to Weimar. During the 1920s, while the well-to-do dabbled in cocktails, jazz and drugs in decadent cabaret clubs, the communists and

socialists fought street battles against the Nazi brownshirts, who were intent on converting this most liberal-minded city to their own illiberal way of thinking.

When Hitler became chancellor in 1933, he moved the seat of government back to Berlin and set about reshaping the city with a vast building programme. By making Berlin his base, he also brought upon it the full wrath of Allied bombing during the Second World War.

Palatial charm *Schloss Charlottenburg (below) is considered one of the best examples of Prussian baroque architecture. Built in the early 18th century, it contains a notable collection of porcelain and paintings.*

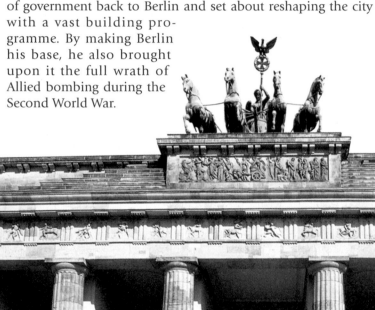

Museum Island

In the 1820s, when the British Museum and the Louvre had already existed for several decades, the Prussian authorities

decided that they too needed a museum in which to show off the treasures of their kingdom. A major complex was built on the northern tip of Cölln Island, in the River Spree, which became known as the Museuminsel (Museum Island). For over four decades during the Cold War this lay in East Berlin, and West Berlin had to make do with its own

parallel collections. Since 1989 the collections across the city have been undergoing comprehensive reorganisation, with the Museuminsel once again the prime focus. The Altes Museum (Old Museum), founded in 1829, contains contemporary art. The Alte Nationalgalerie, completed in 1876, is devoted to 19th and 20th century painting and sculpture. Inaugurated in 1904, the Bodemuseum (named after the first director of the royal museums) contains a rich collection of Egyptian antiquities. The Neues Museum (New Museum) is due to reopen as a new home for Egyptian antiquities. The real star is the Pergamonmuseum, completed in 1930. This contains one of the world's great collections of archaeological treasures, including the monumental Pergamon Altar removed wholesale from the Aegean coast, and the tiled Ishtar Gate dug up at Babylon.

Different moods Berliners relax beside the Wannsee, a large lake in south-west Berlin (above). There are extensive lakes and woodlands around the city. A more bustling atmosphere reigns among tourists and pavement artists (right) at the Kurfürstendamm (or Kudamm), formerly the premier shopping street of West Berlin.

Divided city

After the war, Berlin was little more than ruins. It was split into sectors governed by each of the Allies: the British, Americans and French in the West, and the Soviets in the East, reflecting the division of Germany as a whole. This divided city itself lay deep inside Soviet-controlled East Germany. For years, people were allowed to move between East and West Berlin, but so many East Germans used this as an opportunity to flee communist rule that the Soviets erected the Berlin Wall in 1961. This stood as a visible symbol of communist repression until the government of East Germany collapsed in 1989, allowing the Wall to be breached, then demolished.

Berlin had a huge task ahead of it, repairing the arteries between the two halves of the city that had been severed by the Wall for nearly 30 years. It was a question not just of rebuilding but also of amalgamating Berlin's municipal organisations, its public transport, and its rich heritage of museums and galleries.

For many years after *die Wende* ('the turn' or 'the change') of 1989, Berlin remained effectively split into East and West by a psychological barrier – *die Mauer in den Köpfen* ('the Wall in the minds') – reinforced by unequal living standards and deep ingrained attitudes. The healing process could not happen overnight, but it was helped when the government decreed in 1991 that Berlin would again become the capital of a reunited Germany. As politicians, diplomats, the Press and business chiefs gravitated towards it, the city began to come to terms with its renewed status and the opportunities this implied: it began to redefine itself with a new vigour.

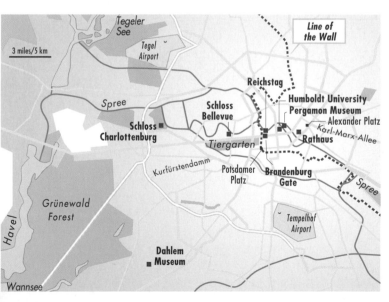

Triumphant again The Brandenburg Gate, built in 1791, was loosely based on the entrance, or Propylaeum, of the Acropolis in Athens. Until 1918, only the royal family could pass through the central arch. It has always stood as a symbol of Prussian power and German grandeur, but was long isolated by the Berlin Wall that passed close beside it.

Bridges and tunnels: building links across divides

What would Paris be without its 38 bridges, or London without Tower Bridge? Bridges are often places of romance, but they are also vital strategic and economic links, as well as symbols of technical and design prowess on a grand scale.

Up and over   *The Pont de Normandie, spanning the Seine Estuary at Le Havre, is supported by 184 cables anchored to towers 702 ft (214 m) high.*

After defeating the Germanic tribes in Gaul, Julius Caesar wanted to ram home his advantage on the far side of the River Rhine. So he constructed a bridge across it in just ten days. Some 2000 years later the Pont de l'Europe over the Rhine symbolises a different aspect of bridges: no longer an instrument of conquest, it is a gesture of friendship between two nations – Germany and France. Rivers were, and still are, major barriers, and often represent cultural and political frontiers as well. As a result, the bridges that span them represent far more than the mere materials of which they are made.

From stone to iron

Much water flowed beneath the bridges of Europe between the construction of the Pont du Gard in southern France 2000 years ago and the bridge over the River Severn in England at

High flier   *A raised motorway, completed in 1975, rises smoothly from the city of Innsbruck towards the Brenner Pass in the Tyrol. This is one of Europe's most ancient trade routes, linking Austria and Italy.*

The Delta Project

The floods of 1953 were among the most serious in Dutch history: a combination of very high tides and swollen rivers caused massive floods in which nearly 2000 people died and vast areas of land were swamped. To prevent this from happening again, the Delta Project was devised to construct a series of dams and barriers, including the Oosterscheldedam (Eastern Schelde Dam). At 5¹/₂ miles (9 km) long, it is the longest tidal barrier in the world.

Defences *A vast array of tidal barriers protect the Netherlands.*

Lasting connection *The Forth Railway Bridge was one of the first cantilever bridges, and for several years had the world's longest span.*

Coalbrookdale, completed in 1779. The first is a splendid triple-tiered Roman aqueduct, built of stone (some blocks weighing as much as 5 tons), with a 900 ft (275 m) long channel carrying 700 000 cu ft (20 000 m³) of water a day 160 ft (49 m) above the valley floor. The second was the world's first bridge made entirely of cast iron. Its span is 100 ft (30 m), elegantly poised on its semicircular supports. It launched a rash of ever more ambitious bridge-building endeavours, spurred on by the age of steel. One of the finest achievements of 19th-century bridge-building was the magnificent Forth Railway Bridge near Edinburgh, a cantilever bridge 8295 ft (2528 m) long, completed in 1890.

Majestic bridges

The 20th century saw even more daring projects, made possible by reinforced concrete. One of the first steel-and-concrete bridges, the Pont Adolphe, was built across the Pétrusse in Luxembourg in 1904. Once an outward sign of the prosperity of a town or country, bridges also became important symbols of technological progress. In 1994, France took the record for the longest cable-stayed bridge, when the Pont de Normandie, 7024 ft (2141 m) long, linked Honfleur to Le Havre over the Seine. Not only did these bridges fulfil an important function in the infrastructure and economy of their regions; they also attracted visitors who came to admire the sheer beauty of the projects – a beauty that easily matches London's Tower Bridge or Paris's Pont Neuf.

Tunnelling through the Alps

Tunnels had a similar inspiration: to provide a link through a natural obstacle. Being buried, they do not attract the admiring gaze of sightseers in the way that bridges do. Yet they represent equally formidable engineering skills. Tunnelling projects have saved miles of winding road or railway track, and cut hours off journey times. The Alps were the first great barrier to be breached. The Fréjus Tunnel, linking France to Italy, was opened in 1871. At 12¹/₂ miles (20 km) long, the Simplon Tunnel in Switzerland, completed in 1906, held the record as the longest rail tunnel in the world for 76 years.

The Channel Tunnel

The idea of linking France to Britain across the Strait of Dover, just 21 miles (34 km) across at its narrowest, had been the dream of engineers since the beginning of the 19th century. Finally in 1994, after seven years' work, the dream became reality when Queen Elizabeth II and President François Mitterrand of France officially opened the Channel Tunnel. The result of an Anglo-French joint venture, it was a remarkable feat of engineering, with a length of over 30 miles (nearly 50 km). Of this, 23¹/₂ miles (37.5 km) are under the seabed, making this the longest undersea tunnel in the world. In fact, the Channel Tunnel consists of three separate tunnels: two rail tunnels and a smaller service tunnel. Eurostar trains now provide a direct non-stop link between London and Paris or Brussels, while the Shuttle ferries cars, coaches and lorries between the ports of Folkestone and Calais. Eight million travellers pass through the tunnel each year.

Tunnel-cutter *Huge tunnel-boring machines were used to dig the Channel Tunnel.*

The power of dams

High water *The Vinça Dam lies in France's eastern Pyrenees.*

Built at a height of 7875 ft (2400 m) on a small but fast-flowing river in the Swiss Alps, the Grande Dixence Dam is one of the most impressive in Europe. It fills a 5528 ft (1685 m) wide valley with a concrete wall rising 935 ft (285 m), and was the tallest dam in the world for nearly 20 years after its completion in 1961. Water from its reservoir generates enough energy to supply three power stations. Switzerland, Austria and France all exploit mountain rivers for power, but dams also help to regulate the flow of water in rivers, and supply water to cities. Reservoirs can also provide important watersports amenities, as at Kielder Water in Northumberland, England, the largest reservoir in Europe.

A 'capital' of the European Union

In 1952, when the seeds of the European Union were sown, Luxembourg was the first city to provide a home for the new European institutions. It now ranks alongside Brussels and Strasbourg as one of the three 'capitals' of the EU. The main institutions are clustered together on the Kirchberg Plateau, to the north-east of the city centre. They include the European Court of Justice and the European Investment Bank.

City centre *The easy-going atmosphere of Luxembourg-Ville is evident in the Place des Armes, a popular gathering place lined with cafés and restaurants.*

Luxembourg: capital of the grand duchy

The capital of a small state with a 1000-year-old history, Luxembourg-Ville packs plenty of surprises. Behind its historic stone façades and disarmingly gentle pace of life is a cosmopolitan city that has carved out a niche as a major business centre.

In AD 963 Sigefroi, Count of the Ardennes, chose a rocky promontory overlooking the ravines of the rivers Alzette and Pétrusse to build a castle. From this beginning developed a city with one of the most dramatic settings in Europe. The old town, classified as a UNESCO World Heritage Site, has a mix of Spanish lookout turrets, French-style ramparts and Austrian casemates – legacies of the Duchy's tortuous history. The upmarket shopping streets tell another story, for this city of just 76 000 inhabitants and 100 nationalities is the headquarters of some 300 banks and insurance companies – the highest concentration of financial institutions in the European Union.

Water views *Covering 225 sq miles (582 km^2), Lake Geneva – also known as Lac Léman – is the largest lake in Western Europe.*

Geneva: international city

It is its superb location that makes Geneva what it is: built on the banks of Lake Geneva, it straddles the River Rhône and is framed by mountains. One of its most famous landmarks is the Jet d'Eau, a giant fountain which propels 110 gallons (500 litres) of lake water a second skyward in a single jet to a height of 460 ft (140 m). Geneva is a city of banks and a centre of clock-making, as well as being the capital of French-speaking Switzerland. It is a haven of peace, with its richly appointed apartment blocks, well-kept parks and picturesque medieval buildings. Since the foundation of the Red Cross here in 1863, Geneva has broadened its international role. It was the headquarters of the League of Nations from 1920 to 1946, and is now home to a number of key UN agencies, among them the World Health Organization.

London

1. **Buckingham Palace** is guarded by soldiers who are usually from one of the regiments of élite infantry Foot Guards. They wear full dress uniform and bearskin hats (popularly known as busbies), a style dating back to 1815.

2. **Regent's Canal,** winds through an elegant residential district between Camden Lock and Little Venice, skirting the northern edge of Regent's Park.

3. **Hyde Park** opened for public use during the reign of Charles I (1625-49). On Sunday mornings, anyone can come to Speakers' Corner in the north-east of the park to sound off their views before whatever audience gathers to experience this somewhat haphazard exercise in free speech.

4. **Oxford Street** is the longest shopping street in London and throngs with traffic and pedestrians throughout the day.

5. **Canary Wharf** is the centrepiece of the Docklands development, an initiative of the 1980s to breathe new commercial life into the dilapidated riverside area to the east of the City, the capital's main financial district.

6. **Tower Bridge** is one of the most instantly recognisable symbols of London. Its neo-Gothic towers contain lifting gear which raises the road deck to allow large ships to pass.

7. **Portobello Road,** in Notting Hill, west London, is a centre of the antiques trade, with a huge antiques and bric-à-brac market every weekend.

In the shadow of Big Ben

London, Western Europe's largest metropolis, is the sum of its parts – a sprawling, diverse place with countless points of interest and village-like clusters, woven into a composite whole. There has never been much of a grand plan in the building of the city, just spontaneous growth, and histories of accretion, along with localised prosperity and decline. Space has never been a great problem and Londoners have always tended to build outwards rather than upwards, with the result that suburbs spread out into the surrounding hills for miles around. By the same token, there are huge green spaces even in the very centre, where moorhens nest on lakes and office workers can sun themselves on the grass during a summer lunch break. Cosmopolitan, innovative, rejoicing in their eccentricities, and wedded to understatement, Londoners seldom enthuse about their city, but they cannot imagine living anywhere else.

The Palace of Westminster, or Houses of Parliament, is on the site of a former royal residence, dating back to the 11th century, and has been the main seat of government since that time. The clock tower is generally known as Big Ben, but strictly the name refers to the largest bell inside.

The Royal Albert Hall was named as a memorial to Albert, Prince Consort to Queen Victoria, who died in 1861. Completed in 1871, it is a remarkably versatile building, capable of staging classical concerts, rock concerts, boxing matches, circus performances and fashion shows.

1. Hyde Park
2. The Serpentine
3. Harrods
4. Royal Albert Hall
5. Victoria and Albert Museum
6. Westminster Cathedral
7. Buckingham Palace
8. Tate Gallery
9. Madame Tussaud's Waxwork Museum
10. Regent's Park
11. National Gallery
12. Trafalgar Square
13. Piccadilly Circus
14. Covent Garden
15. St Paul's Cathedral
16. Houses of Parliament
17. Westminster Abbey
18. 10 Downing Street
19. Charing Cross
20. British Museum
21. Barbican
22. Royal Exchange
23. Stock Exchange
24. Lloyd's
25. Tower of London
26. St Katharine's Dock
27. Tower Bridge
28. Waterloo Station

Kew Gardens, the Royal Botanic Gardens, has more species of plants than any other botanical garden in the world: over 40 000. Founded in 1759, the royal gardens were given to the nation in 1841 to become a national centre of horticulture and botany. The glass Palm House was opened in 1848.

Harrods was just a small grocery shop when it first opened in 1849 on Brompton Road. It has since become perhaps the world's best-known department store, and is certainly one of the most sumptuous. Products of the highest quality are found in all its departments, from perfumes to pianos, toys to televisions.

Westminster Abbey is virtually a national shrine. It is here that Britain's monarchs are crowned, and where many of them are interred. The abbey is also the resting place of many national heroes. The current building dates mainly from the 13th and 14th centuries, but there may have been a church here since the 7th century.

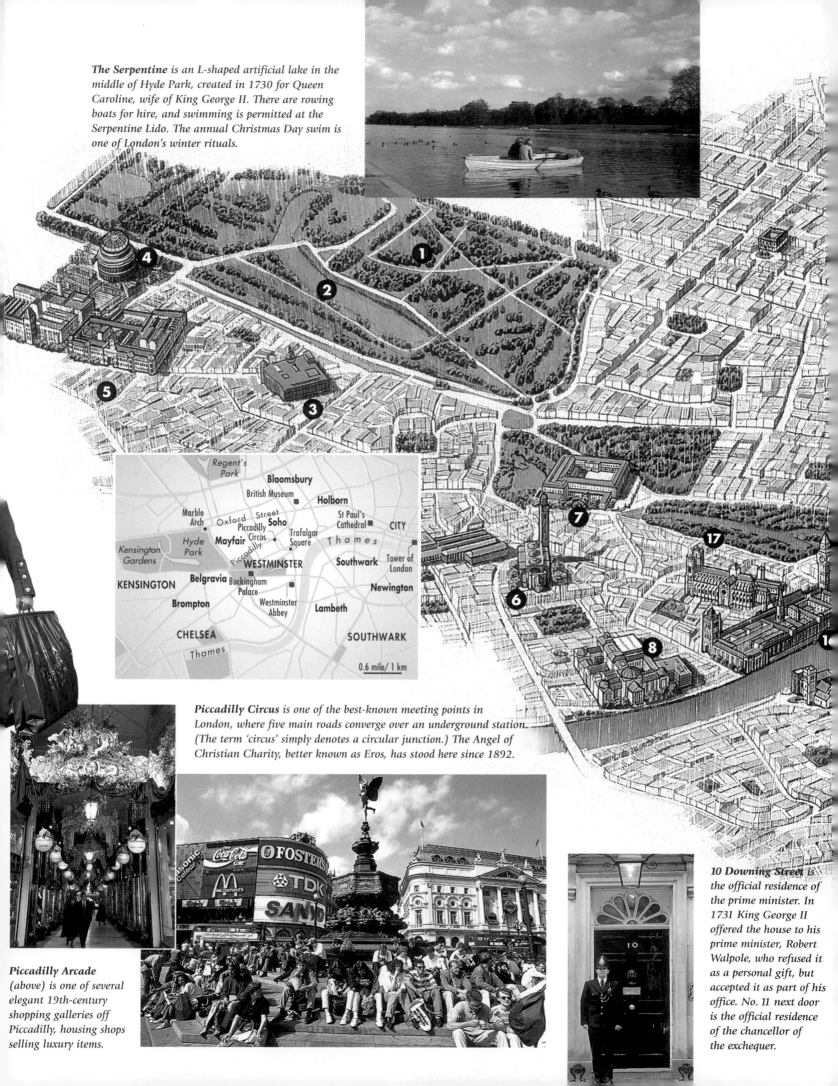

The Serpentine is an L-shaped artificial lake in the middle of Hyde Park, created in 1730 for Queen Caroline, wife of King George II. There are rowing boats for hire, and swimming is permitted at the Serpentine Lido. The annual Christmas Day swim is one of London's winter rituals.

Piccadilly Circus is one of the best-known meeting points in London, where five main roads converge over an underground station. (The term 'circus' simply denotes a circular junction.) The Angel of Christian Charity, better known as Eros, has stood here since 1892.

Piccadilly Arcade (above) is one of several elegant 19th-century shopping galleries off Piccadilly, housing shops selling luxury items.

10 Downing Street is the official residence of the prime minister. In 1731 King George II offered the house to his prime minister, Robert Walpole, who refused it as a personal gift, but accepted it as part of his office. No. 11 next door is the official residence of the chancellor of the exchequer.

Map labels:
Regent's Park · Bloomsbury · British Museum · Holborn · Marble Arch · Oxford Street · Soho · St Paul's Cathedral · CITY · Piccadilly Circus · Mayfair · Trafalgar Square · Thames · Kensington Gardens · Hyde Park · Piccadilly · WESTMINSTER · Southwark · Tower of London · Belgravia · Buckingham Palace · Newington · KENSINGTON · Brompton · Westminster Abbey · Lambeth · CHELSEA · Thames · SOUTHWARK

0.6 mile/ 1 km

Vienna: still waltzing

Built as the imperial centre of the vast Habsburg domains, Vienna now seems disproportionately imposing as the capital of one of the smaller states in Europe. Its stately grandeur, coupled with its roots in high European culture, give the city a distinctive and aristocratic air.

**Waltz king
Johann Strauss**

The founding of Vienna was no chance event: the Roman town of Vindobona was at the heart of the continent and at the junction of two key highways – one linking the Adriatic Sea to the Baltic, the other following the River Danube westwards from the Balkans.

From the 13th century onwards, Vienna's history shadowed that of the ruling Habsburg family, many of whom also held sway over the Holy Roman Empire. Despite its declining power in the 20th century, Vienna has retained the trappings of its former prestige, in the grandeur of the imperial palace, the Hofburg, in the emperors' summer residence at Schönbrunn, and in the stately disciplines of the Spanish Riding School. Vienna was also Europe's music capital in the 18th and 19th centuries, being the birthplace of Schubert and of the master of the waltz, Johann Strauss the

Modern Vienna *A block of flats designed in 1985 by the painter Friedensreich Hundertwasser.*

Younger. Haydn, Mozart, Beethoven, Brahms and Mahler all worked here. The pride and culture of the city is distilled in two famous traditions: the annual Opera Ball at the Vienna State Opera, and the famous New Year's Day Concert when the Vienna Philharmonic Orchestra plays in the new year with a series of vigorous waltzes.

The Blue Danube

Many visitors to Vienna are disappointed by the colour of the Danube. Athough one of Johann Strauss's most famous waltzes is called *The Blue Danube*, the river usually looks murky and grey. But some stretches do turn a deep, cobalt blue, especially on a bright summer's day with the reflection from a cloudless sky.

Vienna 1900

At the start of the 20th century Vienna was a cultural and intellectual centre, drawing gifted people from far afield. Despite the stuffy reputation of the imperial court, there was a strong avant-garde movement in the city. In around 1898 a group of artists, designers and architects broke away from the official arts academy to create the Vienna Secession. Architects such as Joseph Olbrich and Josef Hoffmann built some of the most radical buildings of the time, while Adolf Loos stripped design to its bare minimum, foreshadowing the Bauhaus style of the 1920s. The artist Gustav Klimt produced sublime paintings and mosaics combining sensuality with an intense decorative effect. Meanwhile, Sigmund Freud laid the basis of psychoanalysis with *The Interpretation of Dreams* (1900), and the composer Arnold Schoenberg revolutionised music with his 12 tone scale.

Reflected glory *The Belvédère Palace, built in 1714-22, overlooks Vienna and houses a collection of Austrian art from the Middle Ages to the modern era.*

Dublin: Ireland's fair city

As the capital city of one of the fastest-developing countries of the European Union, Dublin has a cosmopolitan air. It now looks more to its neighbours in Europe than to Britain, the former ruler. It differs in character, tone and history from Belfast, capital of Northern Ireland, which has been scarred by conflict between Protestants and Catholics.

Georgian elegance   *Dublin's O'Connell Street is the city's main thoroughfare.*

Dublin was originally a Viking settlement. Then it was a Norman one, from which the English spread their rule 'beyond the Pale' – the defensive boundary of the city – and across the island as a whole. Dublin's most impressive architecture dates from the Georgian era, between 1714 and 1820, combining stately elegance with a human scale.

The General Post Office (1818), in O'Connell Street, was the focus of the doomed 1916 Easter Rising against the British, and still bears the scars of British shelling. But Dubliners wear their past lightly, weaving it into literature and myth. They balance the weight of their history with an irrepressible sociability that underpins their reputation as bon viveurs in a city with some 600 pubs.

James Joyce's Dubliners

One of the most influential authors of the 20th century was James Joyce, born in Dublin in 1882. Among his first successful writings was *Dubliners,* a collection of evocative short stories published in 1914. Joyce declared that when he died he would be found to have 'Dublin' written on his heart. In fact, he had a love-hate relationship with Ireland and spent almost all his adult life after 1904 in exile in Austria-Hungary, Italy and France. He died in Switzerland in 1941.

Belfast: divided world

For 30 years, if not 300, Belfast has been riven by sectarian divisions and violence. An industrial city, specialising in shipbuilding and engineering, it never had quite the elegance of Dublin. Despite many fine buildings, a gritty grimness predominates, contrasting startlingly with its magnificent backdrop of hills. With high unemployment, and an undercurrent of deep communal antipathy, Belfast seems a city ill at ease with itself. And yet it remains engaging, sociable, friendly and optimistic.

The Beatles appear in wax at Madame Tussaud's, one of Britain's top tourist attractions. Madame Tussaud (1761-1850) was a French sculptor of wax portraits, and had the grisly task of making death masks of victims of the guillotine during the French Revolution. After emigrating to England, she founded this museum in 1835.

Camden Market, around Camden Lock in north London, attracts huge crowds every weekend. The market sports a bohemian range of bric-a-brac, jewellery, Third-World craft products and international food.

Trafalgar Square pays homage to a popular hero in British history, Admiral Horatio Nelson, victor at the battle of Trafalgar in 1805. His statue rises to 185 ft (56 m) on Nelson's Column. The square is the traditional focus of rallies, public demonstrations and New Year's Eve celebrations. The north-eastern corner is flanked by the temple-like, neo-classical façades of the church of St Martin in the Fields (centre) and the National Gallery (left), which contains one of the world's great collections of European art.

Waterloo Station in 1848 as a termi serving the south-u In 1993 a new ext for the Eurostar se

Covent Garden, once the kitchen garden for the monks of Westminster Abbey ('convent garden'), later became the site of London's great flower and vegetable market. In 1974 the market moved to modern buildings south of the River Thames, with better transport access. The old covered marketplace was transformed into a shopping arcade, enlivened by cafés, market stalls and street entertainers.

The Cutty Sark is an old clipper sailing ship, built for speed in 1869 to bring fresh tea from China to London. She remained in service until 1922, and since 1954 has been preserved as a museum piece in dry dock beside the Thames at Greenwich, and next to the old Royal Naval College.

St Paul's Cathedral, built at the end of the 17th century to replace a Norman church destroyed by the Great Fire of London of 1666, is the masterpiece of the architect Sir Christopher Wren. The dome rises to 365 ft (111 m), and affords visitors a magnificent view of London and the Thames.

The Lloyd's Building, designed by Richard Rogers and completed in 1986, remains one of London's most controversial office blocks. It houses the august international insurance market, Lloyd's of London. As with the Centre Pompidou in Paris, also designed by Rogers, all the service elements of the building are on the outside, which frees the interior space for business.

The Royal Exchange was the centre of commerce and banking in the City of London until it ceased to function as an exchange in 1939. The present Greek-revival building dates from 1844. The statue of the Duke of Wellington that stands before it was made from melted-down French cannons captured in the Napoleonic wars.

The Tower of London was begun shortly after the Norman Conquest of 1066, and for centuries remained a symbol of royal authority. It served as a royal residence and stronghold as well as a prison, and earned a fearsome reputation as a place of execution and murder. The royal crown jewels can be seen in a heavily secured vault, and the whole of the castle is watched over by yeomen warders, popularly known as Beefeaters, wearing costumes dating back to Tudor times.

was completed
us for trains
est of England.
nsion was built
vice to Europe.

Cities: juggling the past with the future

Back to the future Classical shapes form part of this housing project at Montpellier, France.

In the international urban beauty contest, big cities invest in eye-catching showpieces of contemporary architecture, while carefully preserving the valuable heirlooms from the past.

Monument to private enterprise

Docklands, to the east of the City of London, underwent a spectacular conversion after 1981. With massive investment and financial concessions from the government of Margaret Thatcher, 8 ½ sq miles (22 km²) of derelict docks were transformed into a vast business centre. It was not universally applauded, especially by office workers who resented moving from the centre of London. But Docklands has become a part of London life, gradually shifting the focus of the capital downriver.

During the 1980s many companies moved their offices out of capital cities to outlying towns to benefit from lower costs. But the trend slowed down, and now town planners talk less about building new towns from scratch and more about regeneration – bringing life back to undervalued urban areas which have lost their original industrial *raison d'être*. Despite predictions to the contrary, the city is far from dead. Indeed, the 21st century is likely to be increasingly urban.

London invested massively in its Docklands development during the 1980s and 1990s, to provide acres of new offices with river views. Prestige also comes into it: France is a world leader in the grand architectural gesture, such as the Grande Arche at La Défense, just to the west of Paris, and the new pyramid entrance to the Louvre art collection.

Blending old and new

Since the reunification of Germany and the restoration of Berlin's status as the country's capital, the city has been the scene of frantic new building work. Many of Europe's finest architects are involved,

Greeting a new age London's Millennium Dome was built to welcome in the year 2000.

such as Renzo Piano and Norman Foster. There are two focuses for this rebuilding: one is economic and commercial, with offices and skyscrapers around Potsdamer Platz and Alexanderplatz; the other is political and cultural, around the Brandenburg Gate and Reichstag, where new development seeks to blend with the design and layout of the 19th-century architecture and urban planning.

European cities are at once ambitious and nostalgic. Modern architects and town planners know that architectural heritage is ferociously protected, but cities have to respond to modern needs, or die. The grand projects that lack human scale are the least loved, such as the Nanterre development to the west of Paris, and Birmingham's Bull Ring, described as an enormous doughnut. City planning is a fine balancing act, and never without its critics, but the ultimate judgment comes from the inhabitants, who vote with their feet.

105

CHAPTER 5

THE TREASURES OF HERITAGE

Every Western European country has its annual Heritage Open Day – called a Journée du Patrimoine in France and Belgium. The doors of historic buildings are thrown open to the public, allowing glimpses of interiors that are normally hidden from view. They include not just castles, stately homes and manor houses, but industrial workshops, old railway stations, Victorian government offices, even the studios of leading contemporary architects. The gradual expansion of Heritage Day activities is evidence of the growing appreciation Europeans have for their common heritage. The treasures of this heritage are spread far and wide across the region, many of them carefully conserved and open permanently to the public, and include architectural gems of international fame. They are monuments to wealth, power and privilege, but also to imagination and a sense of place, and have become inseparable elements of the landscapes that surround them.

The Louvre pyramid, Paris.

Fantasy and romanticism in Bavaria

Bavaria, the southernmost state of Germany, likes to see itself as a place apart. Its mountains and forests, exuberant baroque churches and palaces, and King Ludwig II's fairy-tale castles have made it one of Germany's most treasured tourist destinations.

Sharing its southern border with Austria, Bavaria is Germany's biggest state. It is predominantly agricultural and Catholic, and is known for its conservative bent. One of the favourite local sayings is *Mir san mir*, meaning literally 'We are us' or 'Take us as we are'. The capital, Munich, is the main business hub of southern Germany; its setting, against a backdrop of snow-capped mountains, expresses perfectly the mixture of hard-headedness and romanticism that is characteristic of

Baroque fantasy *Linderhof Castle, located in a wild alpine valley, was the first of Ludwig II's palaces.*

Bavarians. This is the city that King Ludwig I of Bavaria (reigned 1825-48) wanted to develop as the Athens of the North. Passionate about all things Greek, he engaged one of the great German neoclassical architects, Leo von Klenze, to adorn his capital, creating most notably the imposing Glypothek to house his collection of classical antiquities.

Castles in the sky

The first half of the 19th century was a good time for Bavaria, under a succession of enlightened kings. However, their dynasty headed down an eccentric branch line when Ludwig II came to the throne aged 19, in 1864. He led a solitary, detached existence, dressing up as the heroes of German legends, living by

Dream castles *Ludwig II was brought up at Hohenschwangau (left), near Füssen. A theatrical designer helped Ludwig to draw up plans for his most famous creation, at Neuschwanstein (right), a fantasy castle that inspired Walt Disney.*

Empress of Austria Ludwig's friend and cousin Elizabeth ('Sisi'), painted in 1854.

The end of the Wittelsbachs

From the middle of the 19th century, bad luck seemed to surround the Wittelsbach family, who had ruled Bavaria since 1180. King Ludwig I was forced to abdicate in the revolutionary year of 1848, mainly on account of his affair with the dancer Lola Montez. His grandson, Ludwig II, became known as 'the mad king' because of his irresponsible behaviour. Another tragic figure was Ludwig II's beautiful cousin Elizabeth, better known as Sisi. She endured a loveless marriage with Emperor Franz Joseph of Austria, in the shadow of her mother-in-law, the Archduchess Sophie. Their son and heir Rudolf died in a double suicide with his mistress in 1889, and Sisi was assassinated by an Italian anarchist in 1898. The rule of the Wittelsbachs in Bavaria finally came to an end in 1918 when Ludwig III was deposed in the upheavals that followed the end of the First World War.

Frozen in time Rothenburg ob der Tauber is one of several beautifully conserved medieval towns on the Romantic Road. It was lovingly restored after suffering severe damage in the Second World War.

night and dreaming of the absolute monarchy of his hero Louis XIV of France. He was obsessed by the music of Richard Wagner, and became his most important patron. Ludwig II is remembered above all for his fantasy palaces: a baroque extravaganza at Linderhof, a neo-medieval fortress at Neuschwanstein, and a replica of Versailles at Herrenchiemsee. Work on the last of these stopped when Ludwig ran out of money. To the despair of his ministerial cabinet, Ludwig was not only extravagant, he also had little patience with affairs of state. The cabinet attempted to have him certified insane, but

Twin spires The Frauenkirche in Munich.

he drowned in mysterious circumstances in 1886. The Bavarians, however, have never accepted the label 'Mad King Ludwig' for one of their popular heroes, preferring the verdict of his only close woman friend, 'Sisi', the Empress Elizabeth of Austria: 'The king was not mad; he was just an eccentric living in a dream world.'

The Romantic Road

That dream is still on display in Ludwig's castle at Neuschwanstein, one of Germany's top tourist attractions and the culmination of a famous route southwards known as the Romantic Road. Tracing the line of an old trade route, the road stretches over 200 miles (320 km) from Würzburg past a remarkable collection of medieval towns, baroque palaces and rococo churches. It passes through Augsburg, a 2000-year-old town named after Emperor Augustus, before reaching its crescendo in the Bavarian Alps and the fantasy world of King Ludwig.

Reflections of the past   Azay-le-Rideau looks out over a still pool drawn from the River Indre.

The chateaux of the Loire

East of Angers, the Loire and its tributaries provide a glorious setting for the world's most impressive array of country houses. The chateaux of the Loire were built as showpieces, symbols of the greatness, wealth, style and taste of their owners and builders. The effect remains undiminished today.

By the end of the 15th century, gunpowder had rendered the medieval fortress obsolete. So when the French kings Charles VIII (1483-98), Louis XII (1498-1515) and François I (1515-47) built new palaces for themselves in the Loire valley, they could indulge in the most fashionable style of the day – from Renaissance Italy. These monarchs expressed their power in buildings of magnificent architectural proportions, with exquisite detailing in the doors and windows, and long, light-filled galleries. Nobles and financiers followed the royal example, and over the next two centuries the Loire valley acquired its dazzling collection of chateaux, as well as more modest manor houses.

Water palace   The long gallery of the Chateau de Chenonceau straddles the River Cher.

François I and the Renaissance

In 1520 Henry VIII of England and François I of France met near Calais to discuss an alliance. They also took the opportunity to display their wealth and power, and the event went down in history as the Field of the Cloth of Gold. Like Henry, François I was hailed as an elegant Renaissance prince. His career was patchy, however, overshadowed by the Holy Roman Emperor, Charles V, against whom he fought an unsuccessful war. He was also vastly extravagant, continuing to employ 1800 workmen at Chambord when deeply in debt. Nonetheless, he was a generous and influential patron of both the arts and the sciences.

Chateau-museums

Many of these buildings are now open to the public. Each has its own charms. Some are dream homes, surrounded by moats, lakes, gardens and parkland. The chateau at Villandry has an extensive Renaissance garden: rows of flowers and vegetables are neatly ordered and patterned behind box-hedges. The Chateau d'Ussé is believed to have inspired Charles Perrault, the 17th-century author of *The Tales of Mother Goose*, providing him with the setting for his story 'Sleeping Beauty'.

The chateaux are rich in tales of intrigue, violence and romance. The King's Chamber at Blois, for example, was the scene of a notorious piece of treachery during the 16th-century Wars of Religion. The Duc de Guise, head of the Catholic League, was murdered here in 1588 at the behest of King Henri III, who hid behind the tapestry as his guards carried out the

A royal life in the Loire valley

King Charles VIII was so taken by the ornamental gardens of Italy that he had one built at Amboise on his return to France in 1495. The Loire landscape provided the perfect setting for the new chateaux, built by Charles and his successors. There was ample space for hunting, a royal sport involving hundreds of participants; François I employed 125 men just to look after his hounds, and 50 for his hawks. The green pastures, orchards and vineyards, the farms, pigeon lofts, mills and beehives of the Loire valley also sustained the region's reputation for gastronomy and fine wine. At Chinon,

stone was excavated from the riverside cliffs in the 12th century to build the castle, creating deep caves that proved perfect for storing wine and have been used for that purpose ever since. Under the patronage of François I, writers such as Rabelais and Ronsard sang the praises of this region, calling it *douce France* ('sweet France').

Reflections *The chateau of Amboise overlooks the Loire.*

Renaissance extravagance *Chambord's rooftop is composed of a variety of ornamented bell towers, turrets, belvederes, chimneys and dormer windows.*

deed. The Chateau de Chenonceau belonged to Diane de Poitiers, the beautiful mistress of Henri II, but after his death in 1559 his vengeful widow Catherine de Médici humiliated Diane by forcing her to hand over Chenonceau in exchange for the simpler Chateau de Chaumont.

The royal chateau of Chambord is perhaps the greatest of them all, a vast pile built by François I after

Stylish staircase
The François I wing at Blois has a spiral staircase on the outside.

1519 – as a mere hunting lodge. At its centre is a double-helix staircase, possibly designed by Leonardo da Vinci, who spent the last three years of his life at Amboise as the guest of the king. In subsequent eras various noble inhabitants have vainly attempted to make Chambord more cosy, but they could do little more than make a small number of the 440 rooms comfortable.

Many of the chateaux have lost their original furnishings, largely as a result of the French Revolution: what is seen in them today often consists of relatively recent acquisitions. This matters little in the context of such fine buildings.

Son et lumière

The kings of France used every means at their disposal to display their power and glory, from massive hunting parties to balls and grand festivals. Something of the lively times of the great chateaux can be relived today in the summer season of *son et lumière* performances. Sound-recordings and lights are used to give audiences seated outside a chateau an atmospheric sense of the key events that took place at that very site. At Amboise, Blois and Chenonceau costumed actors breathe life into dramatic reconstructions. Most of the participants are local people, stepping into the roles that their own ancestors may have played.

Le Plessis-Macé

ORLÉANS

Chambord

Amboise

Blois   BLOIS   CHAMBORD

CHEVERNY

ANGERS

Chinon

AMBOISE

TOURS

Cheverny

Saumur

SAUMUR

AZAY-LE-RIDEAU

CHENONCEAU

Chenonceau

Valençay

CHINON

Azay-le-Rideau

VALENÇAY

The bay of Mont-Saint-Michel

The rising tide in the Bay of Mont-Saint-Michel is said to advance at the speed of a galloping horse. At low tide the sea drops back 10 miles (16 km), then surges across the sands as it rises by as much as 50 ft (15 m) in six hours. The island itself nestles fairly close to the south-eastern shore, but the shallow bay stretches for 20 miles (32 km) between Cancale and Avranches. This area is popular with both food enthusiasts and nature-lovers. Cancale is particularly renowned for its oysters.

Mont-Saint-Michel: shrine to the Archangel

In misty weather, the church seems to float on a cloud. In full sunlight, the sparkling bay throws a halo of light around the island. Mont-Saint-Michel is a place of dreams, majestic even under the pressure of hundreds of thousands of visitors every year.

The Celts believed that the huge granite outcrop in what is now called the Bay of Mont-Saint-Michel, in south-west Normandy, was a place where human souls were taken after death. But in AD 708 Archbishop Aubert of Avranches dreamed that St Michael – the protector of Christians, guardian of the sick, and worker of miracles – called him to build a shrine on the summit of this rock. Aubert's chapel soon became a site of pilgrimage, then expanded into a Benedictine abbey which was enlarged and enhanced, notably in the early 13th century.

Pilgrims would make their way to the island at low tide, guided by locals to avoid the quicksands. The abbey declined in the

18th century, and had only three monks when it was dissolved during the French Revolution. It then became a prison, but was restored as a historic site after 1863. A 3000 ft (915 m) causeway, connecting the island to the mainland, was built by the French government in 1879, and in 1897 a gilded statue of St Michael slaying the dragon was carefully hoisted onto the tip of the church spire that rises 515 ft (157 m) above the sands. The abbey was returned to the Benedictine Order in 1966, and today it receives over 700 000 visitors a year.

Sanctuary The abbey cloister offered a quiet space where Benedictine monks could walk and meditate.

Churches and cathedrals: foundations of faith

Europe's great cathedrals are the embodiment of the religious feeling of the Middle Ages. The progression from the solid mass of romanesque architecture to the filigree of high Gothic represents one of the greatest leaps ever in creative imagination.

Heavenly vision
The interior of the Church of the Virgin's Birth at Rottenbuch in Bavaria shows the baroque style merging into rococo.

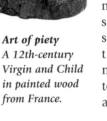

Art of piety
A 12th-century Virgin and Child in painted wood from France.

Christianity inspired the most concerted artistic effort in medieval Europe – the building of churches and cathedrals to the glory of God. The end of the 10th century saw the emergence of a new style of architecture that soon spread across all Europe. On the continent it is called romanesque; in Britain it is called Norman, because it was introduced by the Normans following their conquest of England in 1066.

Romanesque churches broadly followed the pattern of Roman basilicas, with a nave extending into a choir and flanked by aisles. (The cruciform ground plan, formed by the addition of transepts, was a later development.) Romanesque churches have a massive, solid look, with heavy pillars supporting semicircular arches: they reflect the fact that this was an insecure age when the other major constructions were fortresses. High bell towers signalled the presence of Christianity across the land for miles around.

The Gothic adventure

Romanesque architecture was always constrained by the problem of vaulting: bulky semicircular arches required massive columns to support them. Architects then found that by crossing two semicircles they created an arch that was both stronger and lighter; the arch could also be made higher and more pointed. As a result, interior columns could be more delicate. Gradually, architects refined the load-bearing in their structures, with the result that increasing areas of wall could be filled with glass, supported by delicate tracery.

The style is called Gothic – in fact, a term of abuse coined by Renaissance architects, who lamented the fact that their medieval predecessors had turned their backs on Roman and Greek models. By Gothic, they implied the Gothic barbarians who had destroyed the Roman Empire; but the term stuck.

Gothic architecture evolved in northern France in the second half of the 12th century. It permitted builders to work on an ever-grander scale, with soaring roofs, and ever-higher towers and spires. The interiors of these buildings were decorated with stone sculptures and often brightly painted, but much of this decoration later fell victim to Protestant zealots and then to French armies during the Revolutionary and Napoleonic wars.

Baroque and Rococo

Baroque architecture takes neoclassicism as its starting point, borrowing the pillars, pediments and domes of Roman temples. It then improvises, adding curves, breaking up the pediments, giving barley-sugar twists to columns, punching oval windows through the walls. At its best, baroque architecture strikes a delicate balance between solemn grandeur and opulent ornamentation, as in St Paul's Cathedral in London. The Rococo style came next with an approach that was even more frothy. Buildings were often asymmetrical and encrusted with stucco ornament, carving and gilding. When successful it coupled lightness of touch with a joyous, virtuoso swagger.

One of the greatest examples of early Gothic architecture is Chartres Cathedral in northern France, which was consecrated in 1260. Its 28 000 sq ft (2600 m^2) of stained glass – enough to cover ten tennis courts – creates a breathtaking interior that lights up like a giant magic lantern in bright weather.

It is clear that medieval architects reaching for the heavens were working at the limits of their understanding of engineering. The spire of St Rombout's Cathedral in Mechelen, Belgium, rises to 318 ft (97 m), but was originally planned to rise almost twice as high. Work mysteriously petered out in the 1520s, leaving Lincoln Cathedral in England with Europe's highest tower – 525 ft (160 m) – until it fell down in a storm in 1548.

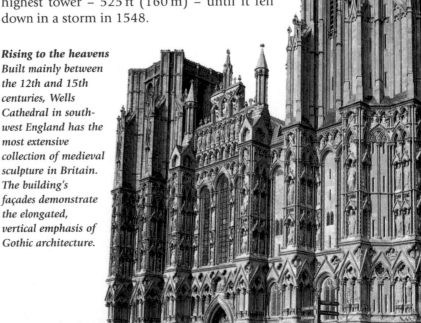

Rising to the heavens
Built mainly between the 12th and 15th centuries, Wells Cathedral in southwest England has the most extensive collection of medieval sculpture in Britain. The building's façades demonstrate the elongated, vertical emphasis of Gothic architecture.

The castles of Britain: relics of a turbulent past

As fortresses, centres of power and scenes of battles, Britain's many castles have had an unequal share in the bloodstained aspects of the nation's history. But they have also been the residences of monarchs and noble families, places where the civilised pursuits of music, art and poetry found patronage and encouragement. Some remain inhabited today, but the vast majority are in the care of national heritage agencies.

Royal home *Windsor Castle (left) is the largest castle in England, and one that remains in use as a royal residence. Established by William the Conqueror, it has been expanded by numerous monarchs.*

Guarding the lochs *Eilean Donan Castle (right), in western Scotland, was a stronghold of the MacRae clan. Its walls are up to 14 ft (4.2 m) thick.*

Armoury *A fine collection of arms and armour is preserved at Warwick Castle (below).*

The British countryside has been largely peaceful since the end of the Civil War in 1648. And no foreign army has invaded the island since the Norman Conquest of 1066. Yet conflict and bloodshed were once common enough, as competing families and dynasties strove for power in a land composed of several rival nations – English, Welsh, Cornish, Scots and Normans. The most visible reminder of these years of discord are the castles that dot the landscape, many of them fortified strongholds that are at once symbols of puissance and evidence of dangerous and uncertain times.

The age of castles

William the Conqueror, Duke of Normandy and vassal of the king of France, initiated an age of castle-building as he sought to bring England under his control. The first Norman castles were simple wooden structures perched atop man-made mounds in a straightforward motte and bailey design. They were little more than fortified enclosures for noblemen and their militias, and were soon replaced by more permanent stone constructions. These were considerably more elaborate, comprising outer defensive walls that could be over 10 ft

(3 m) thick, a courtyard with stables and accommodation for armed men and servants, a hall with apartments for the nobleman and his family, and sometimes a heavily fortified keep, or tower, in case the castle's outer walls were breached.

The first castles marked the spread of Norman lords across the land once held by Anglo-Saxon thanes. They also sprang up in Wales, as the Normans pushed back the frontier between

Mark of the conqueror   Conwy Castle, in northern Wales, was built by Edward I in 1283-92.

perhaps also on Skenfrith and the White Castle, which were all greatly extended by later English lords.

Variation and decline

The English also pushed their way into Scotland, especially under Edward I. The castles they built there are very similar to others in England, though the native style of the region is quite different. Looking more like overgrown houses, Scottish castles often have high, straight walls, with windows at the top, and arrow-slits lower down. A good example is Eilean Donan Castle at the junction of Loch Duich and Loch Alsh in the west. Built in the 13th century, it offered protection against marauding Scandinavian pirates.

By the end of the 17th century the great age of castles was over. Gunpowder and canons had rendered them obsolete, with the result that many were abandoned, to be dismantled stone by stone by villagers looking for building material. This was the fate of Berkhamsted Castle in Buckinghamshire. Having once imprisoned the king of France after his capture at Poitiers in 1356, most of the castle's stones now live on in the older houses of the town.

A few castles have survived intact, usually to become tourist attractions. Some remain as residences of royalty or titled families, but even these are often at least partly open to the public.

A touch of mystery

It is easy to be romantic about castles and their supposed inhabitants – courtly knights and noble ladies. They certainly existed, but it is also important to remember that castles were military fortresses in an often violent age, and were therefore the settings for many violent acts. Conspiracies, murders, executions, torture and cruel imprisonment took place in castles – and some people believe that such events have left their mark on the buildings themselves. Even in our sceptical age, strange rumours persist of hauntings in historic buildings. Perhaps the most famous is Lady Jane Grey, queen for only nine days, who was executed in 1554 by Queen Mary, and whose ghost is said to haunt the Tower of London. Similarly, the library of Windsor Castle is claimed to be haunted by Queen Elizabeth I, still troubled by weighty affairs of state.

King Edward I and his castles

During the reign of Edward I, castles were built, extended or improved with feverish intensity. From 1277 to 1283 Edward commissioned work on 15 castles in Wales, most of them in the north, to ensure that his conquest of the region was secure. The counties of England, from Kent to Northumberland, provided an army of workmen, including 150 masons, 400 carpenters, 1000 labourers and 8000 woodcutters, whose contribution to posterity includes some of the finest medieval castles in Britain. They include Conwy, Caernarfon, Flint and Harlech. It was at Caernarfon in 1301 that Edward I invested his son, the future King Edward II, as the first English Prince of Wales. And in 1969, 668 years later, Prince Charles received this same honour from his mother, Queen Elizabeth II, in the castle's courtyard. Caernarfon survived into the 19th century largely unscathed, and is now immensely popular with visitors to Wales.

England and its neighbour. For example, William FitzOsbern, Lord of Breteuil in Normandy, was made Earl of Hereford in 1066. He immediately set about building castles at Chepstow and Monmouth, from which he successfully overran parts of eastern Wales. There he began work on Grosmont Castle, and

CHAPTER 6

6 CULTURE AND TRADITIONS

Western Europe has given birth to countless movements in art and music, some espousing the attitudes of their age, some in reaction against them. For centuries, society maintained a segregation between the art of the upper classes, which adorned fashionable houses and was later collected in museums, and the culture of the masses, which the evangelists of good taste ignored or scorned. Today, art has been democratised and popular culture revalued. European culture is always searching for new means of expression, and over the past 150 years it has been increasingly open to ideas from other continents. The influence of the USA in particular has been pronounced, and many people feared that it would inundate European culture. In fact, it has had the effect of reinforcing Western European art and giving it new vigour – seen, for example, in British pop music or French cinema.

The Dunkirk carnival (France).

National and local festivals

In Europe, it seems that any pretext will do for holding a festival. Anniversaries, beer, wine, sausages, pancakes, oysters, cheese, cats – there are festivals in honour of all these. The common element is having fun, with gaudy processions, funfairs, games, the blare of local bands, often accompanied by the hearty consumption of food and drink.

In late July and August every year, the Foire du Midi takes over part of southern Brussels, packing the area with fair-ground attractions and stalls serving beer, wine and seafood. It is a summer celebration, one of many across Europe that help to mark the rhythm of the passing year.

Historic roots

Some of Europe's folk festivals date back thousands of years and retain their pagan undertones. At the Puck Fair in Killorglin in County Kerry, Ireland, a wild goat is crowned and enthroned as the centrepiece of a livestock fair, and as a signal for boisterous merrymaking. Christian celebrations were often grafted onto pagan traditions that celebrated the seasons, Christmas being the most obvious example. Across much of

St Patrick's Day

On March 17 all of Ireland's diaspora – in Britain, France, Germany and around the world – celebrates the Irish national festival honouring the nation's patron saint, St Patrick. Green is the colour of the day, and its emblem is the three-leaved shamrock – in memory of the tradition that St Patrick used this plant to explain the notion of the Holy Trinity to converts in AD 432. His teachings led to the foundation of a number of monasteries, the basis of the Irish Church that had a fundamental influence across northern Europe in the 6th to 9th centuries. St Patrick is a popular folk-figure, the subject of numerous endearing legends. For example, he is said to have rid Ireland of all poisonous reptiles by ringing his bell on Croagh Patrick, St Patrick's Mount. His Saint's Day is marked in Ireland as a public holiday, and the surrounding week is celebrated with parades, concerts and partying.

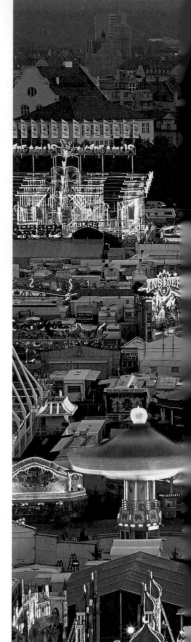

Beer, food and skittles
The epicentre of Munich's Oktoberfest is the fairground on the Teresienwiese, known colloquially as the Wies'n.

Floral parade *Nice is awash with flowers and confetti during its pre-Lenten carnival: ten days of processions ('corsos') with flower-bedecked floats, fancy-dress balls and civic entertainment, all accompanied by local bands and orchestras. On the evening of Shrove Tuesday 'His Majesty Carnival' is ceremoniously burned and the festival ends in a blaze of fireworks. The carnival dates back to at least the 13th century.*

Europe, Britain excepted, Christmas is heralded by the Feast of St Nicholas on December 6, when children are visited by the saint dressed as the Bishop of Myra and given presents.

The religious roots of several celebrations have often been obscured. August 15 used to be the Festival of the Virgin Mary in France and Austria, but nowadays it is marked by summer balls and fireworks rather than sacred rites. However, many festivals retain their religious content. On the eve of Good Friday, the people of Sartène in Corsica perform the Procession du Catenacciu, in which a penitent carries a large cross through the town, dragging a heavy chain by his ankle.

Carnival

In origin, carnivals combined a pagan celebration of the end of winter with a feast prior to the 40 days of fasting in Lent. The word derives from Italian-Latin *carnelevare*: 'to remove meat'.

More power to his elbow

The Oktoberfest is not only Munich's most famous festival, but also the world's biggest beer festival. Local breweries prepare a special beer called Wiesnbier: 5 million one-litre tankards of this are consumed, as well as half a million sausages, 650 000 chickens, 70 000 knuckles of pork, and 70 or so oxen. Strength and endurance are required of the waiters and waitresses who carry armfuls of heavy glasses to cheerful revellers during the 16 days of the festival.

Although now most famously celebrated in Rio de Janeiro and New Orleans, European cities also have their share of pre-Lenten madness and fun. One of the biggest and wildest European carnivals takes place in the German city of Cologne. After four months of preparations, the *Drei tollen Tage* ('Three crazy days') erupt with parades, feasts, costume balls and mad-cap antics. The motto is: 'Anyone who is not foolish at carnival is foolish for the rest of the year'.

Many cities in Europe hold an annual arts festival. The Edinburgh International Festival claims to be the largest arts festival in the world, and the Brighton Festival is the largest in England. Avignon in France holds a theatre festival each year.

Carnival in Belgium

A number of pre-Lenten carnivals take place in Belgian towns, but by far the most famous is the one held at Binche, between Charleroi and Mons. On Shrove Tuesday, after two days of processions and dances, the *Gilles* (clowns) appear, wearing colourful jester-like outfits decorated with heraldic lions, with bells at their waists and frilled cuffs, anklets and rosettes on their clogs, and bizarre bespectacled masks on their heads. They dance slowly around the streets to the sound of drums, brandishing bundles of twigs to ward off evil. In the afternoon they exchange the masks for towering headdresses of ostrich feathers and throw oranges at their friends. The day ends with fireworks and a dance.

Spring madness The origin of the Gilles de Binche is obscure; some historians believe their costumes imitate Aztec or Inca dress.

Happy birthday Amsterdam, along with all the Netherlands, is in holiday mood on Koninginnedag, the Queen's Birthday, celebrated on April 30.

A passion for museums

Western Europe has a host of museums of international standing. They are monuments to the passion and vision that drove so many of the collections' founders to track down such a rich legacy of the world's treasures.

Grand trophy *The Altar of Zeus (c.175 BC) from Pergamon gives its name to the Pergamonmuseum in Berlin.*

The museums of Europe contain and preserve many of the greatest and most valued articles of European heritage. But their collections go farther than that, including treasures from all over the globe.

The oldest public museum in the world is the Ashmolean in Oxford, founded in 1679 to house a collection given to Oxford University by the antiquarian Elias Ashmole. He in his turn had inherited most of the collection from his friend, the naturalist John Tradescant, which is why the majority of its original exhibits related to natural history.

Cultural competition

The wider passion for public museums began in the 18th century. The British Museum was founded in 1753, and acquired its first ancient Egyptian exhibits three years later. By the 1820s its collections were large enough to require the construction of the massive building in Bloomsbury, London, which is still its home.

The Louvre in Paris was a royal palace until Louis XIV abandoned it for Versailles, and it became a centre for various royal academies and for artists under royal patronage. It later became a public museum in 1793, after the Revolution, and was given a major boost by Napoleon, who broadened its collections with

booty gathered through imperial conquests. Before long, other countries were building their own museums so as not to be left behind in this new expression of national pride.

The Great Exhibition of 1851 in London's Hyde Park provided the incentive and funding for a trio of London museums: the Natural History Museum (1881), the Victoria and Albert Museum (1909), and the Science Museum (1913). In Brussels, the Royal Collection of Art and History was founded in 1835, but was renamed the Musée du Cinquantenaire in 1880 to mark the 50th anniversary of an independent Belgium. It is smaller by far than, say, the British Museum, but has an impressive collection of treasures across

Timeless victory *Visitors to the Louvre (below) throng the stairs built in 1937 to highlight the ancient Greek masterpiece the Victory of Samothrace, which dates from the 2nd century BC.*

The Kröller-Müller Museum

Situated 43 miles (70 km) east of Amsterdam, in the midst of De Hoge Veluwe National Park, the Kröller-Müller Museum is the perfect combination of art and nature. This was the intention of its founders, industrial heiress Hélène Kröller-Müller, an avid collector of modern art, and her husband Anton, a lover of nature. In the years leading up to the First World War they purchased large tracts of land and built a lodge to live in and a museum. The collection, now state-owned and still growing, has paintings by Renoir, Monet, Cézanne, Van Gogh, Picasso and many others. In the sculpture park outside are works by Rodin, Henry Moore and Barbara Hepworth, among others. Beyond lie paths through the extensive woodlands, and hides (blinds) from which to observe the park's rich wild life, which includes boar and red deer.

Exploring art *The Jardin d'émail ('Enamel Garden' – 1973) by Jean Dubuffet is in the Kröller-Müller's sculpture park.*

120

The Rijksmuseum

The Netherlands' premier art collection is housed in the Rijksmuseum (National Museum), Amsterdam, in a building completed in 1885. It contains mainly Dutch paintings from the 15th to the 17th centuries, including numerous works by Rembrandt, as well as such well-known works as *The Merry Drinker* by Franz Hals and Vermeer's *Woman Reading a Letter*. The museum also has notable collections of sculpture, Delftware and Asiatic art. Its most famous possession is undoubtedly Rembrandt's *The Night Watch*, a large group-portrait of militiamen painted in 1642. The painting has had a chequered history: it lost some of its outer edges when installed in the Town Hall in 1715, and was hidden in a cave near Maastricht during the Second World War. Twice the victim of vandalism, *The Night Watch* has acquired a legendary status to match the fame of its creator.

almost as wide a range. The Musée Royale des Beaux Arts (Fine Arts Museum) in Brussels was built around the same time to house a collection recovered from France after looting during the Napoleonic wars, as well as later acquisitions. It contains outstanding examples of Rubens' larger canvases and a fine collection of paintings by the late 19th-century Symbolists.

Labyrinth of art Vienna's main art museum, the Kunsthistorisches Museum, was built in 1891 to house the great imperial collection of the ruling Habsburgs, which was begun in the 16th century. Its galleries lead off from an elaborately decorated atrium.

Renewal and expansion

All galleries have to keep up to date in their design, lighting, presentation and security. Ninety years after it first opened in 1897, the Tate Gallery in London added the new Clore Gallery to house its Turner collection. It is also refurbishing the defunct Southwark Power Station on the River Thames as a new home for its collection of modern art.

By the 1980s the chaotic presentation of the Louvre collections had become an embarrassment. This was solved by the ingenious glass pyramid entrance completed in 1989. It provides much easier access to the Louvre, which is visited by 5.2 million people a year. Only one museum has a higher attendance record: the British Museum, with 5.75 million visitors a year.

Misnamed Rembrandt's painting The Shooting Company of Captain Frans Banning Cocq *became known as* The Night Watch *because it was darkened by old layers of varnish. Cleaning in 1947 revealed a day scene.*

Transformed Paris's Musée d'Orsay, which opened in 1986, was once a railway station. It houses the nation's collection of French art produced between 1848 and 1914.

London's National Gallery

The National Gallery was founded in 1824 to house 38 paintings bought by the British Government from the Russian-born financier John Julius Angerstein. It is thus the fruit of both private passion and state intervention. Housed in its present buildings in Trafalgar Square since 1838, it has grown through purchase and bequests into one of the world's great collections, with major and representative paintings from just about all the key movements of European art from the 14th century to the early 20th. Among its famous works are Jan van Eyck's *Arnolfini Marriage*, Hans Holbein's *The Ambassadors* and Leonardo da Vinci's cartoon for the Virgin and Child with St Anne and St John. The Sainsbury Wing, which houses the Renaissance collection, was opened in 1991.

121

Festivals of film

France and Germany host two major film festivals: the Cannes Film Festival is the more famous; Berlin's may be less star-spangled, but is more committed to discovering new directions in cinema.

The Berlin International Film Festival

February 2001 marks the 50th anniversary of the Berlinale – Berlin's film festival. Born in postwar Germany, under a joint initiative by the Western Allies, the Berlinale has followed all the twists of the Cold War, from the rise of the Berlin Wall to reunification. The first Soviet film at the festival was shown in 1974. Each year the coveted Golden Bear is awarded to the best film in the competition, but the public and the media are equally interested in the International Forum of New Cinema and the Children's Film Festival.

Army of fans *The gaping entrance of the Palais des Festivals at Cannes explains its nickname – 'The Bunker'.*

Star-gazing *Gina Lollobrigida arrives at Cannes in 1961, to the delight of thronging fans and photographers.*

The world's first film festival was launched in Venice in 1932, and it remained unique until after the Second World War, when it was joined by a handful of others. International cinema provided a suitable forum for reconciliation in the shattered postwar world. Founded in 1946, the International Film Festival at Cannes, in the South of France, soon emerged as the most dynamic cinema gathering in Europe. In fact, plans had been laid to hold a film festival at Cannes in 1939, overseen by none other than Louis Lumière, the creator of the first film images in 1895. But war intervened.

In the 1950s and 1960s the Cannes Film Festival forged its reputation for glamour with the help of stars such as Rita Hayworth, Grace Kelly, Elizabeth Taylor, Sophia Loren, Tyrone Power and Errol Flynn. At the same time, there was a serious commercial side to the festival: while the crowds came to gaze at the stars, and cinema enthusiasts queued for the screenings of new films, producers and distributors were busy discussing projects, negotiating deals and signing contracts.

Double winner *British director Mike Leigh's* Secrets and Lies *won the Palme d'Or at the 1996 Cannes Film Festival and Brenda Blethyn won Best Actress award.*

The New Wave

Film-makers and critics use Cannes as a forum in which to argue about their medium – and often they do so with passion. Unlike the Oscars ceremony at Hollywood, Cannes has managed to maintain a challenging, controversial and unpredictable edge. During the 1960s the big bone of contention was the merits of 'La Nouvelle Vague' ('The New Wave') of film-making, led by French directors such as François Truffaut and Jean-Luc Godard.

Each year one film is selected from the rest for the award of the *Palme d'Or* ('Golden Palm'), Cannes' top accolade. This is a much-cherished prize, not least because it often goes to films that are not part of the main commercial circuit. At Cannes – and also at Berlin and the smaller London Film Festival, held in November – film-makers take satisfaction from the fact that their work is seen by knowledgeable enthusiasts, who appreciate artistic risk.

The joy of reading

Each year, twice as many new books are published in Europe as in the USA. Books are big business and Europeans obviously enjoy reading them, whether for entertainment, relaxation, information or intellectual challenge.

Tricky choice   The jury of the Prix Goncourt deliberates at Drouant, a celebrated Paris restaurant.

Thousands of publishers from around the world bring their books to Frankfurt-am-Main every October to take part in the world's largest book fair. Strangely, this event is not about selling books to the public: it is about selling books to other publishers, giving them translation and distribution rights in foreign markets. The atmosphere is usually intense, the bidding can be hectic, and millions of dollars' worth of business is transacted.

The end of the book?

Until the 20th century, newspapers, journals and books were the primary channels for the dissemination of information. Radio and then television have since taken up that baton, and are now joined by the Internet. Because of these and other factors, the death of the book has long been predicted. But the book has shown strong powers of endurance, and the number of new books published increases every year. Britain holds the European record: some 95 000 new titles annually. Britain is particularly well known for the high quality of its illustrated children's books, both fiction and non-fiction, which are widely translated abroad.

Books are now available from a wider range of outlets than ever before, including book clubs, which have millions of members in France, Germany, the Netherlands, Belgium and the UK. High-street booksellers are also fighting their corner, offering a vast range of titles in increasingly comfortable surroundings. Many now provide a café-like setting in which shoppers can sit and read while drinking coffee, echoing the old literary cafés of London, Vienna, Paris and Amsterdam. The European love affair with books looks set to continue with vigour into the 21st century.

Tip of the iceberg   Small traders put up their stalls outside the Frankfurt Book Fair (left).

Shrine to books   A reader browses in the Paris bookshop, L'Arbre à Lettres.

Literary prizes

Christmas is the busiest time of year for French bookshops, when sales of fiction, biography and other literary works are boosted by annual awards such as the Prix Goncourt and Prix Fémina. These prizes help to raise the profile of books generally, and to project French literature onto the world stage. The British equivalent of the Prix Goncourt is the Booker Prize, which has created an annual brouhaha since it was first introduced in 1969. The whole process stimulates lively literary debate, and winning authors see their sales multiply many times over.

Secondhand books

In Paris they are part of the landscape: the *bouquinistes* who line the Seine. Some occupy shops that have served this function for decades – and seemingly with the same stock of old books. In England, Hay-on-Wye in Herefordshire provides a picturesque centre for the antiquarian book trade, and an alternative to London's Charing Cross Road. In both cases, shops are often run by experts who know the location of every volume of their stock.

Flemish colour

Sacred vision *Rogier van der Weyden's* Last Judgement *(c.1445) at the Hôtel-Dieu in Beaune, France, exemplifies the close observation of detail that is typical of Flemish painting.*

Jan van Eyck, Rogier van der Weyden and Robert Campin – three masters of early Flemish painting – were innovators in a time of change who took Western European traditions of art to new heights.

Italy may have been the source of the Renaissance, but it was not the wellspring of all innovation. The Flemish painters of the 15th century had a major impact on European art through oil painting, a new technique developed in the north-west. One of its great pioneers was Jan van Eyck (1390-1441).

Tradition and innovation

The Flemish painters inherited the skills of the illuminators of medieval manuscripts. Oil paint allowed them to pursue, on a larger scale, the illuminators' tradition of painting precise detail. It also gave them rich colours – far richer than the fresco pigments and tempera that Italians were using at the time. Van Eyck's *Adoration of the Mystic Lamb* (1426-32), a 12 panel work in Ghent cathedral, is one of the supreme achievements of early Flemish oil painting.

Similar precision, inspired by a deep spirituality, is seen in the work of van Eyck's contemporaries Rogier van der Weyden (*c.*1399-1464) and the Master of Flémalle (identified as Robert Campin). Most of their paintings were of Biblical scenes, though these were increasingly given contemporary settings.

In the next century many artists from the Low Countries went to Italy and came back with a taste for classical subjects. But they lost some of the human qualities of the earlier masters. It took Rubens to create a successful fusion of the two traditions.

Trick of the eye The Conjuror *by the Dutch painter Hieronymus Bosch (c.1450-1516) shows his peculiar vision of the world around him. He applied this to contemporary scenes, but also used it to produce purely imaginative images, showing the tortured psyche of a world caught between guilt and redemption.*

Rubens' Descent from the Cross *(1612) is in Antwerp Cathedral.*

Pieter Bruegel the Elder (1530-69)

The Reformation in the Low Countries permitted painters to take a more liberal attitude towards religious subjects. None did so with more charming effect than Pieter Bruegel the Elder, the father of a dynasty of painters based in Brussels. Bruegel took religious subjects, such as *The Census in Bethlehem*, and placed them in peasant settings of his day, giving Biblical stories a contemporary poignancy. His love of detail and humour infuse his work with an endearing humanity.

Rubens (1577–1640)

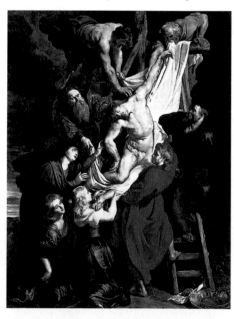

As a young man, Peter Paul Rubens left home to study in Italy. During his eight years there, he learned the techniques of large-scale painting, but managed to avoid becoming hemmed in by the dogmas of Italian art. Instead he used his supreme technical gifts to produce works of great emotional power, sensuality and verve.

Impressionism: capturing the moment

In the early 1870s a group of young French artists came together to explore a new, spontaneous way of painting the world around them. At their first, much-derided exhibition in Paris in 1874, Claude Monet showed his sketchy Impression: Sunrise, *which gave the movement its name – Impressionism.*

From 1874 to 1886 there were eight impressionist exhibitions, all of them challenging the prevailing taste in painting, as represented by the official 'Salons'. Among the exhibitors were the four key impressionists – Claude Monet, Auguste Renoir, Alfred Sisley and Camille Pissarro – as well as numerous influential associates such as Edouard Manet, Paul Cézanne and Edgar Degas. Many critics raged against them, saying that they could not paint and that they made a mockery of the art establishment. But gradually their integrity, dynamism and talent began to be appreciated. By the 1880s Monet, for example, had become a successful artist. From highly controversial beginnings, Impressionism went on to become one of the most popular, influential and best-loved movements of Western painting.

New dawn *Monet's* Impression: Sunrise *hangs in the Marmottan Museum, Paris.*

Poised for fame *Degas was fascinated by dancers; his sensitivity can be seen in the sculpture* Young Dancer, Aged 14.

Innovation

What made Impressionism new was not just the use of rapid brushstrokes to create a spontaneous image of mood, weather and light conditions; it was also the subject matter. The impressionists liked to paint out of doors, not in the studio. And they painted the world around them as they saw it. Renoir painted Parisians at leisure, and Monet painted impressions of the Paris railway station, the Gare St-Lazare – scenes that had never before been considered suitable for art.

Van Gogh and Gauguin

Impressionism was a key source of inspiration for both Vincent van Gogh and Paul Gauguin, who became friends in 1886. Van Gogh's subject matter broadly conformed to Impressionism, but his passionate use of paint and colour communicated a feverish spiritual anxiety, which paved the way for the development of Expressionism. Gauguin was in contact with the impressionists from 1874 and was encouraged by Pissarro, but he later adopted his distinctive style using large patches of vivid colour.

Cézanne and modern art

Paul Cézanne (1839-1906) was a close friend of the impressionists, but soon began to pursue his own path. He extrapolated shapes from nature, exploring new ways to create satisfactory compositions. He introduced geometric forms – an approach that had a major influence on Picasso and Braque when they developed Cubism in 1907-8, and on abstract art in the next decade.

Distilled life *Cézanne's* Apples and Oranges *(c.1900) shows his concern with structure and composition.*

125

Techno, house and garage

Young bodies pulsate beneath the lasers and strobe lights of the megaclubs, or at 'raves' – massive illegal parties – in disused warehouses or forest clearings. The music is loud, throbbing and insistent.

In the early 1990s, raves were all the rage in Britain. They sprang up in abandoned industrial sites, barns and fields, their location signalled only at the last minute to evade police intervention. The music, propelled by massive mobile speaker systems, sent rhythmic shudders through the surrounding landscape, bombarding the frenetic dancers, many of them fuelled by drugs such as Ecstasy. But after the biggest illegal rave drove residents of the quiet English village of Castlemorton to distraction in 1992, legislation was tightened and the key perpetrators were hounded into silence, or abroad. Raves continue, but without their original spark of anarchy.

Family connections

The ravers preferred music that was essentially electronically generated, such as 'house', a form of dance music developed in the USA in the mid 1980s, with a driving beat from electronic drum machines and synthesised base lines, sampled sounds and minimal lyrics. By the 1990s house had spawned the more rhythmic acid-house, and consorted with the acceptable face of muzak to form the mellow ambient-house. A more soul-influenced kind of house was baptised 'garage'. In the late 1980s, experiments in electronic music in Germany led to the thumping, fast-beat rhythms of computer-assisted techno. An electronically enhanced form of rap called hip-hop had arrived in Europe from the USA in the mid 1980s, and it now combined with West Indian reggae to form ragga (or ragamuffin), and with techno to form jungle or drumbass. Techno also grew into the more hypnotic style called trance. Punjabi-based bhangra, Algerian rai, classical music, even clichéed dance anthems of the past – all have been drawn on to feed the thirst for new, beat-driven dance music.

Serious business The DJ of Crash Crew at the Rex Club in Paris creates his desired mix. Dance clubs are careful to delineate the precise genre they are presenting, be it techno, house, garage, techno-funk, ambient-techno, hip-house or drumbass.

Berlin's Love Parade

Over a long, usually hot weekend in July every year, a million fans from across Europe congregate in Berlin for the Love Parade, the world's biggest techno festival. They dance their way through the streets, accompanying a caravan of some 50 elaborately decorated floats, from which DJs unleash floods of ground-juddering sound. It ends with a massive party: spotlights and lasers intensify the bond between music and dance, sending the crowds, gathered from the four corners of Europe and beyond, into an ecstatic frenzy of liberated energy.

Victorious The Love Parade reaches the Victory Column in Berlin.

Rebel rock

It may have been born in the USA, but Europeans quickly took rock 'n' roll to their hearts. Over the years, in the hands of European musicians, it has metamorphosed into new forms, such as glamrock, heavy metal and folk rock. The music's long-lasting popularity is personified by the Rolling Stones – still rebellious, still able to rock a stadium of 80 000 fans, and still able to claim, with some justification, to be 'the greatest rock 'n' roll band in the world'.

Going strong The Stones have been popular for over 35 years.

Festivals of music

Salzburg in Austria, Bayreuth in Bavaria, Montreux in Switzerland: three European cities which host music festivals of worldwide renown, attracting leading performers in the worlds of classical music, opera and jazz.

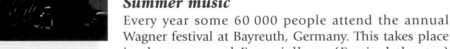

Bayreuth The lovers meet in Wagner's opera Siegfried in 1994.

In 1917, the great Austrian theatre director Max Reinhardt wrote of Salzburg: 'Here where the eye delights everywhere it looks, where every glimpse encounters exquisite harmony, where an entire city reveals beauty in its innermost being, here is the right place to celebrate a festival.' He was true to his word. Three years later the first Salzburger Festspiele (Salzburg Festival) took place, steered by an artistic committee that included Reinhardt, the composer Richard Strauss and the poet Hugo von Hofmannsthal. Now numerous musical events are crowded into five weeks starting in late July, with the main attractions, notably operas, staged in halls specially built for the festival.

But this is just one highlight of Salzburg's rich musical life. Throughout the year concerts takes place in the city's array of palaces and churches, such as the Marble Hall of the 18th-century Mirabell Palace, and the state rooms of the medieval castle that looms over the city. The main focus is the music of Salzburg's most famous son, Mozart, who spent much of his childhood and early career here.

Music at Montreux

Every year in July, Montreux in Switzerland hosts one of the world's most celebrated jazz festivals. Since its founding in 1968, it has attracted many of the greatest names in jazz, blues, soul and pop, including B.B. King, Herbie Hancock, Miles Davis, John McLaughlin, Stevie Wonder and Van Morrison. This sedate town on the eastern shore of Lake Geneva may seem an unlikely setting for such an event, but Montreux has welcomed many controversial artists over the years, including the writers Byron, Shelley and Tolstoy, and the composer Stravinsky.

Jazz gold Miles Davis at Montreux in 1991.

Summer music

Every year some 60 000 people attend the annual Wagner festival at Bayreuth, Germany. This takes place in the renowned Festspielhaus (Festival theatre) designed by Wagner himself for the staging of his own works. The building opened in 1876 with a performance of Wagner's gigantic four-part opera *The Ring of the Nibelung*, and this remains the centrepiece of the festival. The demand for tickets is so high that they are granted only to people who have renewed their request for several years running.

Across Western Europe, scores of music festivals, great and small, provide platforms for performances of the highest calibre. Aix-en-Provence in France holds a festival of opera, classical music and dance every June. A private theatre at Glyndebourne, a country house in southern England, has been the enchanted setting for a summer opera festival since 1934. In Ireland, the opera festival of Wexford in October is celebrated not only for the charm of its small scale, but for the originality of its productions, through which many singing careers have been launched.

Ever young Mozart's The Magic Flute *is a perennial favourite at Salzburg.*

CHAPTER 7

LANDS OF INDUSTRY AND INVENTION

The Industrial Revolution got off the ground with breakthroughs made by British inventors such as James Hargreaves, Richard Arkwright and Edmund Cartwright, whose spinning and weaving machines revolutionised the textile industry. It gathered momentum with help from James Watt's improved steam engine. Later still, electricity was converted into a formidable power source by scientists such as the Frenchman André-Marie Ampère, the German Georg Simon Ohm and the British Humphry Davy and Michael Faraday. The motor car took shape in the hands of German and French engineers such as Karl Benz, Gottlieb Daimler, René Panhard and Émile Levassor. The tradition of scientific and technical research continues in the pursuit of improvements in vehicle performance and safety, machinery design, and space technology. Traditional industries, such as watchmaking in Switzerland, meanwhile, have changed to meet the increasingly aggressive world market.

The Mercedes production line, at Sindelfingen, near Stuttgart.

Keeping time

When manufacturers in the Far East began to produce high-quality, cheap watches in the 1970s, the Swiss watchmaking industry looked doomed. But investment, skilled promotion and design flare produced a dramatic turnaround.

By the mid 17th century, European clockmakers were demonstrating great feats of precision and artistry, especially in France, Switzerland and Britain. The British clock-maker John Harrison (1673-1776) devoted much of his life to the creation of an accurate marine chronometer. In 1762, he produced a clock so accurate that it could keep time to within a few seconds for the duration of long sea voyages.

Call of the past The cuckoo clock demonstrates the Swiss talent for mechanical inventiveness.

Swiss watches

The Swiss learnt clock and watchmaking from French and Italian refugees in the 16th century. The main centres of the industry were Geneva and La Chaux-de-Fonds, between Neuchâtel and the French border. Watches were expensive luxuries until 1868, when Georges Frédéric Rosskopf invented a reliable but simple version that could be mass-produced at an affordable price. Switzerland became the world's leading producer of watches for the next century.

Precision engineering Technology is allied to skill at the Patek Phillippe workshop in Switzerland.

Abraham-Louis Breguet

Abraham-Louis Breguet (1747-1823) was one of the great masters of watchmaking. He was born in Switzerland, but spent most of his working life in Paris. His main contribution was the tourbillon, an improvement that meant watches could weather the jolts and knocks incurred when carried around. He also transformed the watch from a sphere in a double-sided case into a flat shape that could be slipped into a pocket. He became France's official nautical horologist after 1807, but was best known for his exquisite and precise luxury watches.

The threat

Switzerland became the byword for quality, but the revolution in quartz and digital watches in the 1970s caught Swiss manufacturers off-guard. By 1980, Japan and Hong Kong had cornered 85 per cent of the digital watch market, dominating the huge middle and lower price bands in North America, Europe and Asia. Swiss watch manufacturers such as Rolex, Breitling, Longines, Patek Phillippe and Vacheron

The Swatch story

Swiss watchmaking was in the doldrums when SMH, the Swiss Corporation for Microelectronics and Watchmaking Industries, launched the Swatch in 1983. It was a brilliant marketing coup: a plastic watch of just 51 components that was fashionable, affordable and reliable. Two collections of 30-60 new models are usually produced every year, many designed by top artists. So any one person might own several Swatches. Their plastic finish suggests a throwaway culture, but enthusiastic collectors go to great lengths to acquire the rarer models.

Constantin were left with only the luxury market, until the Swatch phenomenon of the 1980s reasserted Switzerland's reputation as one of the world's leading watch manufacturers.

Porsche: speed on an open road

Part of the reputation of Western Europe's car manufacturers rests on prestigious brand names such as Mercedes, Rolls-Royce, Jaguar and Porsche. But cult followings have also grown up around more modest vehicles, such as the Volkswagen Beetle, the Citroën Deux Chevaux, the Renault 4 and the Mini.

The Austrian-born engineer Ferdinand Porsche (1875-1951) worked for Daimler in Stuttgart before setting up his own company specialising in racing cars in 1931. With his son Ferry, he was also involved in the development of the Volkswagen in prewar Germany.

In 1951, the Porsche 356 Coupé won its class at Le Mans: 25 000 of this model were sold over the next seven years. In 1963, Porsche produced a six-cylinder version of the 356, with a leaner body. It was named the 911.

The Porsche 911 has remained in production ever since. Through improvements and upgradings over the years, it has become one of the world's best-engineered cars. Porsche introduced other models, but it was the 911 that the public coveted – an instantly recognisable symbol of success.

The Goddess

Another European car that fired people's imagination was the Citroën DS saloon, which caused a sensation when it was introduced in 1957. DS was a play on words: from the French *déesse*, meaning goddess.

Onwards and upwards *The Porsche 911 continues its career in its 1997 guise.*

'I think that cars today are almost the exact equivalent of the great Gothic cathedrals', commented the French writer Roland Barthes. 'I mean the supreme creation of an era, conceived with passion by unknown artists.' With its gliding hydropneumatic suspension and luxury interior, the Citroën DS stood for French style in the 1960s.

Britain, meanwhile, had its Mini. Launched by Austin and Morris in 1959, it was the car to be seen in during the Swinging Sixties, and its timeless design looks as fresh 40 years later. Renault replaced its successful postwar car, the 4 CV, produced from 1947 to 1961, with the equally popular Renault 4, which was eventually phased out in the 1980s. All inspired devotion, but for style and swagger nothing could surpass the Porsche 911 – let alone overtake it.

The Beetle: cult insect

The Volkswagen (the People's Car) was designed in the 1930s by Ferdinand Porsche as a low-cost car. It did not go into production until after the Second World War, when it was part of Allied efforts to rebuild the German economy. By 1972 the Beetle – so nicknamed for its carapace-like shape – was the world's most popular car. Production ended in Europe in the 1980s, but it is still made in Brazil and Mexico, and has been reintroduced in the USA. The total sold exceeds 21 million.

The *Deux Chevaux*

The Citroën 2 CV (*Deux Chevaux*, two horsepower) was intended as a runabout for French farmers in the postwar era. The specifications in 1948 stated that it could carry four people and 110 lb (50 kg) of potatoes or a wine cask at a speed of 37 mph (60 km/h) with a fuel consumption of 0.65 gallons (3 litres) per 62 miles (100 km). The car became a style statement for the 1970s alternative culture. After 7 million had been made over 42 years, Citroën ceased production.

Pleasure and luxury

Haute couture, precious scents, jewellery, fine foods – these are the luxury items that lie beyond the reach of 99 per cent of the planet's population. Western Europe excels in producing them.

Once when Marilyn Monroe was asked what she wore to bed, she replied: 'Nothing but Chanel No 5.' It was a gift to the publicists, neatly encapsulating all the glamour, sensuality and mystique that the French perfume industry strives to promote. Perfume has always been a luxury commodity, distilled from flowers, spices and herbs and mixed to secret formulae for consistency and lasting fragrance. Gabrielle (Coco) Chanel triggered the vogue for designer perfumes with Chanel No 5 in 1921, so-named not because it succeeded Nos 1-4, but because it was launched on the fifth day of the fifth month, May.

The combination of high prices, haute-couture brand names and gem-like bottles reinforced the air of exclusivity. Now these products are within the reach of a much broader public, sold through high-street stores and duty-free shops. Nonetheless, the associated dream of luxury is carefully nurtured through the suggestion of rarity, a price that bears little relation to the quantity bought, and

Dream traders
A theatrical offering from John Galliano's Spring 1998 collection for Christian Dior.

Counterfeits: appearance without substance

The huge turnover of the luxury-goods industry has proved a tempting target for counterfeiters. Perfumes, clothes, watches, fine leather bags and belts – few luxury goods with prestige labels are immune. French products, such as Cartier watches and Lacoste shirts, have been particularly hard-hit: 70 per cent of targeted products are French. Customers are often aware that they are buying fakes, but are happy to pay much lower prices for lookalike items. This trade does significant damage to the luxury-goods industry.

Window shopping *Cartier's shopfront in the Rue du Faubourg-St-Honoré, one of the smartest shopping streets in Paris.*

high-profile publicity that emphasises desirability. The products are good, but would be valued less highly if they were markedly cheaper.

King of diamonds

Perfume has a parallel in jewellery, spanning a chain of production from the raw materials via the craftworkers to the exclusive retail outlets. Antwerp, a centre

Time bandits *Vast numbers of counterfeit watches are produced.*

for diamond polishing since the 15th century, handles 85 per cent of world trade in uncut diamonds. This multi-million-dollar business is conducted in the quiet streets of the city's diamond district – a far cry from the luxurious premises of the European jewellery houses where the diamonds may eventually be sold, places such as Asprey of London (founded in 1781) and Cartier of Paris (founded in 1847).

The catwalks

It was an Englishman, Charles Worth (1825-95), who propelled Paris dressmaking into the art form known as haute couture. His House of Worth, founded in 1858, was built on the distinction between designer-led fashion and dressmaking to order.

Haute couture took off during the first three decades of the 20th century, with designers such as Paul Poiret, Coco Chanel and Robert Piguet. Christian Dior relaunched feminine elegance after the Second World War, when his New Look rolled back wartime austerity. He in turn trained the 17-year-old Yves Saint Laurent, who later extended the haute-couture range to ready-to-wear and accessories.

Since the start of the 1960s, the ready-to-wear world has become more daring and trendy. This has allowed young designers to find a niche between high-street chain stores and haute couture. In the 1960s, the British designer Mary Quant revolutionised popular fashion by promoting the mini-skirt.

Exclusive street Newcomers jostle with long-established names in New Bond Street, London, home of some of the world's leading fashion stores.

Belgian chocolates

At the turn of the century, the Belgian chocolatier Jean Neuhaus perfected a method for inserting delicately flavoured fillings into *pralines*. Neuhaus is still a leading brand, now joined by others, such as Godiva, Leonidas and Corné de la Toison d'Or. Godiva, founded in 1929, was named after Lady Godiva, who in the 11th century rode naked through the streets of Coventry – an image of romance, daring and sensuality that was considered appropriate to luxury chocolates. These companies produce top-quality, fresh-cream chocolates, and have forged an international market. But not all the chocolates go abroad: the average Belgian eats 18 lb (8.4 kg) of chocolate a year.

Today, this more populist, youth-orientated approach is echoed in the work of the Belgian designers, such as Dries van Noten, Ann Demeulemeester and Walter van Beirendonck (founder of Wild and Lethal Trash) – all graduates of the Antwerp Academy of Arts.

The great labels have responded to this changing market without compromising their cachet. The young and unconventional British designers John Galliano (at Dior) and Alexander McQueen (at Givenchy) have made a dramatic impact in Paris. Outlandish though the collections of Paris or London may seem, their influence filters down, and ends up in fashionable off-the-peg clothing a few years later.

Needlework Lesage of Paris provides embroidery accessories for the haute-couture fashion industry.

Traditional service Fortnum & Mason's horse-drawn carriage is a reminder of the shop's long tradition of quality.

Fortnum & Mason: a taste of luxury

Every hour, in Piccadilly, the clock strikes above the entrance to one of London's most famous shops, and models of the shop's founders bow to each other. William Fortnum was a footman to Queen Anne in the early 18th century, and Hugh Mason was a shopkeeper. They went into business, supplying high-quality foods to the nobility. Today, Fortnum & Mason is a department store, but its primary focus remains food, elegantly displayed beneath the chandeliers of its food hall.

Airbus: Europe reaches for the sky

Over the past three decades the skies have witnessed two major European adventures in civil aviation: Concorde and Airbus. The first was a feat of engineering prowess, but a commercial failure; the second heralded Europe's return to the forefront of airline technology.

First flight   In 1890, Clément Ader made the first powered flight.

In the 1960s, the future of air flight seemed to lie in speed. France and Britain joined forces to take up the challenge, and produced the Concorde, which entered service in 1976. Unfortunately, the predictions had been wrong. The future lay in bulk, and the Boeing 747 jumbo jet, introduced in 1970, ruled the air. Orders for Concorde fell flat: instead of a projected 1370, just 16 were built.

Airbus takes off

The European air industry had received a body blow. But other developments were stirring. In 1970, Airbus, a Franco-German consortium, completed the A300, a twin-engine plane with 270 seats. At the outset it was bought only by Air France and Lufthansa, who had imposed stringent financial and technical specifications. The result was a plane with astonishingly low running costs – the lowest passenger-mile costs in aviation history. It entered the market at a time when airlines were competing for volume sales through cost-cutting – an era when the concept of using aeroplanes almost as buses became current. But despite its clear advantages, the A300 took a while to catch on.

The transatlantic battle

When the American company Eastern Airlines started ordering Airbus planes, the market began to shift, and suddenly the US manufacturers had lost their monopoly over their home territory. Airbus succeeded in winning an ever-larger client base. Before long, the A300 had begun transatlantic flights: Boeing responded by introducing its 767 and 757 range.

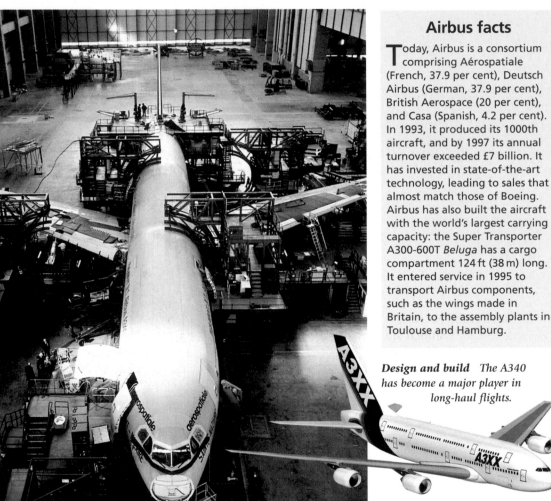

Airbus facts

Today, Airbus is a consortium comprising Aérospatiale (French, 37.9 per cent), Deutsch Airbus (German, 37.9 per cent), British Aerospace (20 per cent), and Casa (Spanish, 4.2 per cent). In 1993, it produced its 1000th aircraft, and by 1997 its annual turnover exceeded £7 billion. It has invested in state-of-the-art technology, leading to sales that almost match those of Boeing. Airbus has also built the aircraft with the world's largest carrying capacity: the Super Transporter A300-600T *Beluga* has a cargo compartment 124 ft (38 m) long. It entered service in 1995 to transport Airbus components, such as the wings made in Britain, to the assembly plants in Toulouse and Hamburg.

Design and build   The A340 has become a major player in long-haul flights.

Into the future   The A3XX is set to challenge the Boeing 747.

This tussle for market-share took a new turn in 1988 when Airbus produced the A320, a plane for which the American manufacturers had no match. Although comparatively small, with just 150 seats, its cockpit was completely computerised – a first in civil aviation. Airbus next developed a shorter version, the A319 (120 seats), and a longer version, the A321 (180 seats). Then, with its A340, Airbus made a serious bid to take on the long-haul planes of Boeing. Still out in front, however, was the Boeing 747, the world's largest passenger plane. But Airbus plans to challenge this supremacy with its A3XX, a jumbo capable of carrying 600 passengers on two decks.

Ariane: putting Europe into space

The success of the Ariane programme helps to place European technology on a world stage, while accruing notable commercial benefits.

Blastoff *The second test launch of Ariane 5, in 1996. It is built by a European consortium (above).*

A luminous cloud rises into the sky at Kourou, the European Space Agency's launch site in French Guiana: an Ariane 5 has just blasted off. The three-stage rocket will power into space at 17 400 mph (28 000 km/h) to place two 3 ton satellites in geostationary orbit.

Economic star wars

The success of Ariane is the result of the collaboration of European aerospace engineers. Twenty years ago the countries of Europe, well aware of the huge strategic and commercial implications of space, created a partnership to finance the programme. Ariane 1 was launched in 1979.

There are now 14 launchers of satellites in the world. It is a lucrative business: telecommunications satellites have become indispensable to television, radio and multimedia broadcasting. For example, the five Eutelsat Hot Bird satellites, launched by Ariane rockets from June 1996 on, carry 320 television channels to more than 70 million homes.

In cooperation with the European Space Agency, Arianespace – the world's first commercial space transportation company – has developed into a leading launcher of satellites, with an unsurpassed reliability record of 98.5 per cent. Ariane 4, developed in the 1980s and still operating for 4.5 ton payloads, has been the most commercially successful of all satellite launchers. There are now over 250 satellites orbiting the Earth, excluding military ones: Arianespace has launched more than 150 of them.

Ariane 5, first test-launched in 1996, belongs to the next generation: it can carry a heavier payload, and can also make low Earth orbits for missions to space structures, such as the International Space Station, Alpha. At the dawn of the new millennium, Europe is poised to make a major contribution to space research.

Destination Mars

In 2003-4, Mars passes at its closest to Earth for 17 years, and a series of missions are planned. Among them will be the European Space Agency's Mars Express, to be launched in June 2003. It will reach Mars in December, with a lander, called Beagle 2, designed to search for evidence of sub-surface water.

The line-up Ariane matches its main rivals for power and scope.

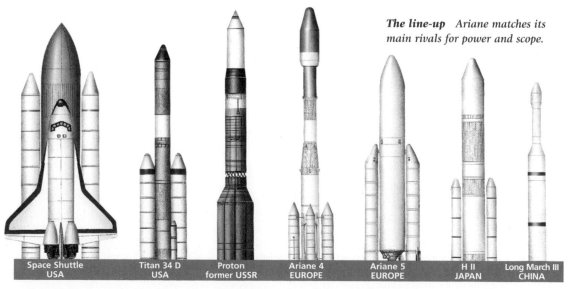

Space Shuttle USA   Titan 34 D USA   Proton former USSR   Ariane 4 EUROPE   Ariane 5 EUROPE   H II JAPAN   Long March III CHINA

MAPS, FACTS AND FIGURES

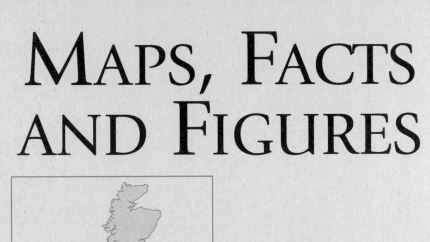

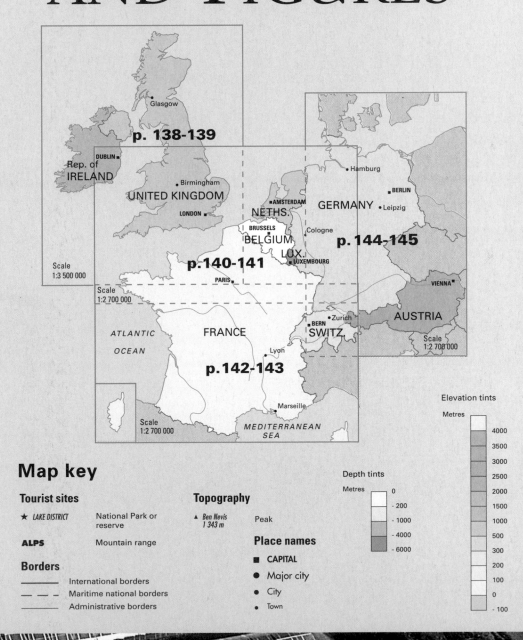

p. 138-139

p.140-141

p. 144-145

p.142-143

Rep. of
IRELAND

DUBLIN

UNITED KINGDOM

Glasgow

Birmingham

LONDON

Scale
1:3 500 000

NETHS.

AMSTERDAM

BELGIUM

BRUSSELS

LUX.

LUXEMBOURG

PARIS

Scale
1:2 700 000

Hamburg

GERMANY

BERLIN

Leipzig

Cologne

VIENNA

AUSTRIA

BERN

Zurich

SWITZ.

Scale
1:2 700 000

ATLANTIC

OCEAN

FRANCE

Lyon

Marseille

Scale
1:2 700 000

MEDITERRANEAN
SEA

Map key

Tourist sites

★ *LAKE DISTRICT* National Park or reserve

ALPS Mountain range

Borders

International borders

Maritime national borders

Administrative borders

Topography

▲ *Ben Nevis*
  1 343 m Peak

Place names

■ CAPITAL

● Major city

• City

· Town

Elevation tints

Metres

4000
3500
3000
2500
2000
1500
1000
500
300
200
100
0
- 100

Depth tints

Metres 0

- 200
- 1000
- 4000
- 6000

United Kingdom • Ireland

NORTH SEA

ATLANTIC OCEAN

SCOTLAND

HIGHLANDS

HEBRIDES

SEA OF THE HEBRIDES

FAROE ISLANDS

SHETLAND ISLANDS

ORKNEY ISLANDS

GRAMPIAN MTS

CAIRNGORM MTS

MONADHLIATH MTS

Glen More

UNST
FETLAR
YELL
WHALSAY
BRESSAY
Lerwick
St Magnus Bay
MUCKLE ROE
PAPA STOUR
FOULA
MAINLAND
Sumburgh Head

FAIR ISLE

NORTH RONALDSAY
PAPA WESTRAY
WESTRAY
ROUSAY
SANDAY
STRONSAY
SHAPINSAY
EDAY
BURRAY
SOUTH RONALDSAY
HOY
MAINLAND
Kirkwall
Pentland Firth
Duncansby Head
Sinclair's Bay
Wick

Dunnet Head
Thurso
Helmsdale
Morven 705 m
Strathy Point
Ben Hope 927 m
Cape Wrath
Loch Shin
Lairg
Dornoch Firth
Moray Firth
Nairn
Elgin
Spey
Dee
Kinnaird Head
Peterhead
Fraserburgh
Aberdeen
Stonehaven

Ben More Assynt 998 m
Eddrachillis Bay
Peninsula Enard Bay
Loch Maree
Ullapool
Loch Ness
Loch Mree
Bairn Dearg 1 081 m
Inverness
Caledonian Canal
Fort Augustus
Loch Lochy
Loch Arkaig
Loch Linnhe
Fort William
Ben Nevis 1 343 m
Loch Eil
Ben Macdui 1 309 m
Loch Ericht
Ben Lawers 1 214 m
Loch Rannoch
Loch Tay
Tay
Forfar
Montrose
Arbroath
Dundee
St Andrews
Perth
Loch Leven
Buckhaven
Kirkcaldy
Firth of Forth
North Berwick
St Abb's Head
Berwick-upon-Tweed
Tweed
HOLY ISLAND

Butt of Lewis
GREAT BERNERA
Stornoway
LEWIS
Clisham 799 m
SCARP
TARANSAY
Sound of Harris
PABBAY
BERNERAY
NORTH UIST
BALESHARE
BENBECULA
SOUTH UIST
BARRA
VATERSAY
SANDRAY
MINGULAY
BERNERAY
ST KILDA
ERISKAY
CANNA
RUM
EIGG
MUCK
COLL
TIREE
SCALPAY
RAASAY
SCALPAY
SOAY
SKYE
Mallaig
Point of Ardnamurchan
MULL
Ben More 967 m
ULVA
IONA
COLONSAY
Oban
LISMORE
Loch Awe
SCARBA
JURA
Sound of Jura
ISLAY
GIGHA
Rhinns Point
Port Ellen
RATHLIN

Kintyre
ARRAN
Loch Lomond
Dumbarton
Helensburgh
Dunoon
Greenock
Paisley
Glasgow
Clyde
Irvine
Saltcoats
Prestwick
Kilmarnock
East Kilbride
Motherwell
Hamilton
Coatbridge
Bothgate
Falkirk
Stirling
Alloa
Dunfermline
Edinburgh
Biggar
Blood Low
Ayr

Loch Katrine

TORY ISLAND
Malin Head

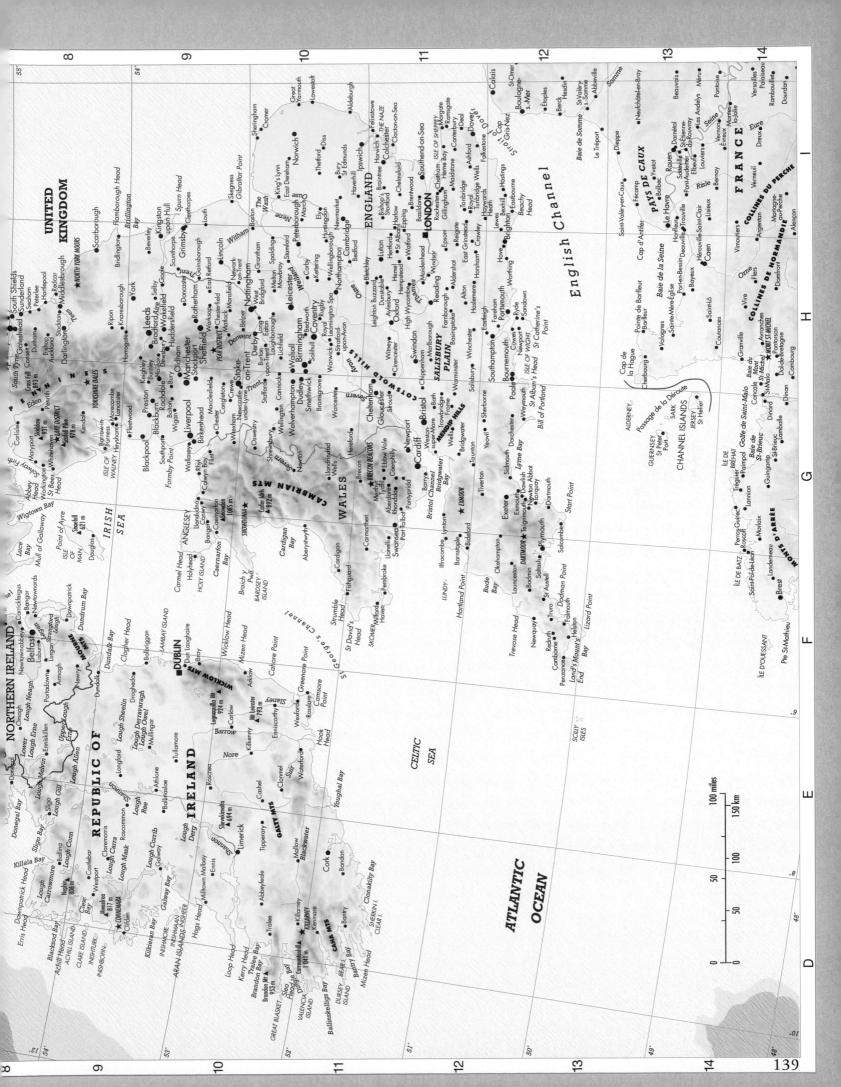

France (north) • Belgium • Netherlands • Germany (west)

E F G H I

9
Balbriggan
LAMBAY I.
DUBLIN
Dun Laoghaire
WICKLOW MTS.
Bray
Carmel Head
Holyhead
ANGLESEY
HOLY ISLAND
Llandudno
Conwy
Rhyl
Colwyn Bay
Flint
Caernarfon Bay
Bangor
Caernarfon
Chester
Blackpool
Preston
Keighley
Leeds
Selby
Beverley
Southport
Blackburn
Burnley
Halifax
Bradford
Dewsbury
Wakefield
Goole
Kingston upon Hull
Formby Point
Bolton
Bury
Oldham
Huddersfield
Wigan
Doncaster
Scunthorpe
Spurn Head
Wallasey
Liverpool
Birkenhead
Manchester
Stockport
Sheffield
Rotherham
Grimsby
Cleethorpes
Macclesfield
Worksop
Gainsborough
Louth
Congleton
Chesterfield
Retford
Crewe
Matlock
Mansfield
Lincoln
Skegness
Gibraltar Point
Newcastle-under-Lyme
Stoke-on-Trent
PEAK DISTRICT
Belper
Newark-on-Trent
Aire
Trent

10
Snowdon 1085 m
SNOWDONIA
Braich'y Pwll
BARDSEY ISLAND
Oswestry
Cader Idris 892 m
Shrewsbury
Stafford
Cannock
Lichfield
Derby
Burton-upon-Trent
Long Eaton
Loughborough
West Bridgford
Nottingham
Grantham
Boston
The Wash
Sheringham
Cromer
Mizen Head
Arklow
Cahore Point
Wicklow Head
CAMBRIAN MTS
Newtown
Wellington
Wolverhampton
Walsall
Dudley
Birmingham
Smethwick
Solihull
Bedworth
Leicester
Melton Mowbray
Spalding
Stamford
King's Lynn
East Dereham
Norwich
Great Yarmouth
Lowestoft
Aberystwyth
Cardigan Bay
Llandrindod Wells
Bromsgrove
Coventry
Rugby
Royal Leamington Spa
Corby
Kettering
Peterborough
March
Ely
Thetford
Diss
Strumble Head
St David's Head
Cardigan
WALES
Worcester
Warwick
Stratford-upon-Avon
Northampton
Wellingborough
Huntingdon
Newmarket
Bury St. Edmunds
Aldeburgh
Fishguard
SKOMER ISLAND
Milford Haven
Carmarthen
Hereford
Severn
Avon
Bedford
Cambridge
Haverhill
Ipswich
St George's Channel
Pembroke
Brecon
ENGLAND
Felixstowe
THE NAZE

11
Llanelli
Merthyr Tydfil
BRECON BEACONS
Aberdare
Rhondda
Ebbw Vale
Caerphilly
Cheltenham
Gloucester
Stroud
COTSWOLD HILLS
Witney
Cirencester
Oxford
Leighton Buzzard
Dunstable
Aylesbury
Luton
Hemel Hempstead
St Albans
Hertford
Harlow
Bishop's Stortford
Braintree
Colchester
Clacton-on-Sea
Swansea
Port Talbot
Pontypridd
Newport
Cardiff
Barry
Bristol Channel
Weston-super-Mare
Bath
Chippenham
Marlborough
Swindon
Reading
Maidenhead
Windsor
LONDON
Rochester
Chatham
ISLE OF SHEPPEY
Margate
Ramsgate
Chelmsford
High Wycombe
Watford
Epping
Brentwood
Basildon
Southend-on-Sea
Severn
Thames
Ouse

12
LUNDY
Ilfracombe
Lynton
Bridgwater Bay
SALISBURY PLAIN
Warminster
Farnborough
Basingstoke
Aldershot
Epsom
Reigate
Herne Bay
Maidstone
Canterbury
Deal
Hartland Point
Barnstaple
Bideford
EXMOOR
MENDIP HILLS
Wells
Bridgwater
Frome
Trowbridge
Salisbury
Winchester
Alton
Haslemere
Horsham
East Grinstead
Crawley
Tonbridge
Royal Tunbridge Wells
Ashford
Dover
Folkestone
Bude Bay
Taunton
Tiverton
Yeovil
Sherborne
Eastleigh
Southampton
Fareham
Portsmouth
Hove
Brighton
Worthing
Lewes
Bexhill
Hastings
Eastbourne
Beachy Head
Strait of Dover
Cap Gris-Nez
Calais
Trevose Head
Okehampton
Launceston
Exeter
Sidmouth
Exmouth
Dorchester
Poole
Bournemouth
Cowes
Newport
Ryde
Sandown
Boulogne-s.-Mer
Newquay
Bodmin
DARTMOOR
Teignmouth
Dawlish
Newton Abbot
Torquay
Weymouth
Lyme Bay
St Alban's Head
ISLE OF WIGHT
St Catherine's Point
Étaples
Redruth
Camborne
Truro
St Austell
Saltash
Plymouth
Dartmouth
Salcombe
Start Point
Bill of Portland
Berck
Penzance
Falmouth
Helston
Dodman Point
Land's End
Mount's Bay
Lizard Point
English Channel
Baie de Somme
St-Valéry-s.-Somme
Abbeville

13
ALDERNEY
Cap de la Hague
Pointe de Barfleur
Cap d'Antifer
Saint-Valéry-en-Caux
Dieppe
Neufchâtel-en-Bray
GUERNSEY
St Peter Port
SARK
Passage de la Déroute
Cherbourg
Barfleur
Baie de la Seine
Fécamp
PAYS DE CAUX
Bolbec
Yvetot
Le Havre
Valognes
Sainte-Mère-Église
CHANNEL ISLANDS
JERSEY
St Helier
Port-en-Bessin
Honfleur
Deauville
Trouville
Rouen
Darnétal
Sotteville
St-Étienne-du-Rouvray
Beauvais
Bayeux
Pont-Audemer
Elbeuf
Les Andelys
Méru

14
Saint-Lô
Hérouville-Saint-Clair
Caen
Lisieux
Bernay
Louviers
Vernon
Pontoise
Coutances
Risle
Seine
Évreux
Mantes-la-Jolie
Argent
ÎLE DE BATZ
Perros-Guirec
Tréguier
ÎLE DE BRÉHAT
Paimpol
Golfe de Saint-Malo
Granville
Vire
Orne
COLLINES DE NORMANDIE
Vimoutiers
FRANCE
P
Roscoff
Saint-Pol-de-Léon
Lannion
Baie de St-Brieuc
Baie du Mont St-Michel
Flers
Argentan
COLLINES DU PERCHE
Verneuil
Dreux
Versailles
Palaise
ÎLE D'OUESSANT
Morlaix
Guingamp
St-Brieuc
Cancale
St-Malo
MONT ST-MICHEL
Avranches
Domfront
Mortagne-au-Perche
Alençon
Bellême
Rambouillet
Chartres
Brest
Landerneau
MONTS D'ARRÉE
Dinard
Dol-de-Bretagne
Dinan
Pontorson
Combourg
Fougères
Mayenne
Mamers
Nogent-le-Rotrou
Dourdan
Étampes
Pte St-Mathieu

15
Crozon
Châteaulin
Aulne
Carhaix-Plouguer
MONTAGNES NOIRES
Loudéac
MER D'IROISE
Pte du Raz
ÎLE DE SEIN
Douarnenez
Audierne
Quimper
Pontivy
FORÊT DE PAIMPONT
Rennes
Vilaine
Vitré
Laval
La Ferté-Bernard
La Flèche
Le Mans
Saint-Calais
Châteaudun
Pte de Penmarc'h
Pont-l'Abbé
Concarneau
Quimperlé
Pont-Aven
Blavet
Oust
Josselin
Ploërmel
La Guerche-de-Bretagne
Château-Gontier
Sablé-s.-Sarthe
Segré
Orléans
Vendôme
La Ferté St-Au
Hennebont
Lorient
Î. DE GROIX
Vannes
Redon
Nozay
Châteaubriant
Loir
Loire
Château-du-Loir
Blois
Amboise
Golfe du Morbihan
Î. HOUAT
Quiberon
BELLE-ÎLE
Le Palais
Ancenis
Angers
Trélazé
Pithiviers

0 ___ 50 miles
0 ___ 50 ___ 100 km
48°

140

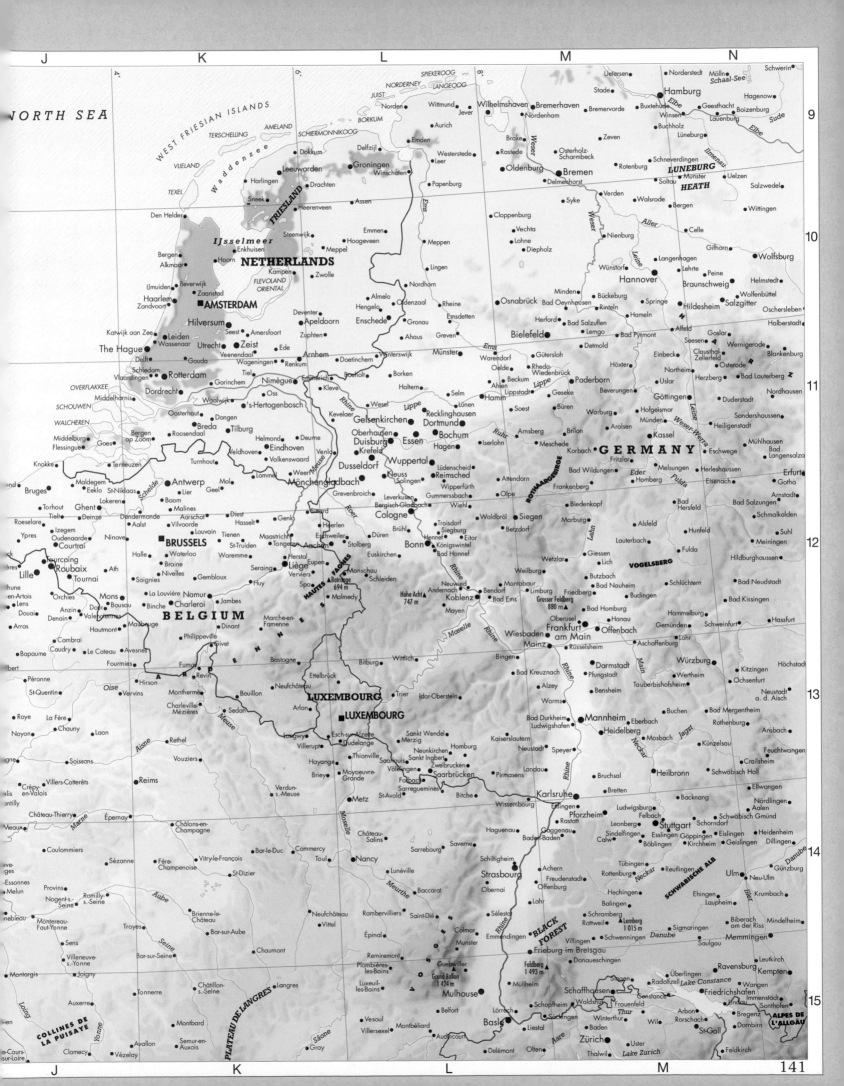

France (south) · Corsica · Switzerland

MER D'IROISE

Crozon · Châteaulin · Carhaix-Plouguer · MONTAGNES NOIRES · Fougères · Mayenne · Mamers · Bellême · Nogent-le-Rotrou · Brou

Pte du Raz · ÎLE DE SEIN · Douarnenez · Aulne · Loudéac · Rennes · Vilaine · Vitré · Mayenne · Laval · La Ferté-Bernard · Châteaudun · Pithi...

48° · Audierne · Quimper · Pontivy · Oust · FORÊT DE PAIMPONT · Le Mans · Saint-Calais · Orléans · La Fer... Saint...

Concarneau · Quimperlé · Josselin · Ploërmel · La Guerche-de-Bretagne · Sablé-s.-Sarthe · Vendôme · Loir · Château-du-Loir

Pont-l'Abbé · Pont-Aven · Redon · Châteaubriant · Segré · La Flèche · Loir · Château-du-Loir · Blois

Pte de Penmarc'h · Hennebont · Lorient · Nozay · Angers · Trélazé · Tours · Amboise · Montrichard · Romorantin-Lanthenay

15 · Î. DE GROIX · Vannes · Ancenis · Loire · Saumur · Azay-le-Rideau · Chinon · Che...

Quiberon · Golfe du Morbihan · Î. HOUAT · La Baule-Escoublac · St-Nazaire · Nantes · Rezé · Vertou · Chinon

BELLE-ÎLE · Le Palais · Le Croisic · Pornic · Lac de Grand Lieu · Cholet · Thouars · Châtellerault · Châteauroux

47° · ÎLE DE NOIRMOUTIER · Beauvoir-sur-Mer · Challans · Les Herbiers · Bressuire · Poitiers · Le Blanc · Châtillon-sur-Indre

16 · Saint-Jean-de-Monts · ÎLE D'YEU · Saint-Gilles-Croix-de-Vie · La Roche-s.-Yon · Parthenay · HAUTEURS DE GÂTINE · SÈVRE NANTAISE · Argenton-sur-Creuse · La C...

Les Sables-d'Olonne · Luçon · Fontenay-le-Comte · Niort · Poitiers · Montmorillon · Dun-le-Palestel · Chatelus-Malvaleix

46° · Ars-en-Ré · ÎLE DE RÉ · Courçon · La Rochelle · Melle · Bellac · Guéret

Rochefort · St-Jean-d'Angely · Boutonne · Charente · FRANCE

17 · ÎLE D'OLÉRON · Le Château-d'Oléron · Saintes · Cognac · Jarnac · La Rochefoucauld · Rochechouart · Saint-Junien · Limoges · Bourganeuf

Pointe de la Coubre · Royan · Angoulême · Nontron · St-Yrieux-la-Perche · Uzerche · PLATEAU DE MILLEVACH...

Soulac-sur-Mer · Girond · St-Genis-de-Saintonge · Brantôme · Périgueux · Vézère · Tulle · D...

45° · Lac d'Hourtin-Carcans · Isle · Brive-la-Gaillarde

ATLANTIC OCEAN · Lac de Lacanau · Libourne · Bergerac · Mussidan · Souillac

18 · Mérignac · Pessac · Bordeaux · Talence · Dordogne · Labastide-Murat

Bassin d'Arcachon · Cap Ferret · Arcachon · La Teste-de-Buch · Langon · Marmande · Figea... Decazev...

Lac de Cazaux et de Sanguinet · Grande Leyre · Garonne · Tonneins · Villeneuve-s.-Lot · Cahors

Lac de Biscarosse et de Parentis · Parentis-en-Born · Petite Leyre · Villefranche-de-Rouergue

Étang d'Aureilhan · Mimizan · Agen · Caussade

Bay of Biscay · Morcenx · Castelsarrasin · Montauban

19 · Étang de Soustons · Mont-de-Marsan · Condom · Fleurance · Graulh...

Adour · Adour · Midouze · Mauvezin · Garonne

St-Vincent-de-Tyrosse · Dax · Auch · Colomiers · Toulouse

19 · Anglet · Biarritz · Bayonne · Salies-en-Béarn · Orthez · Luy de France · Gers · Save · Muret · Villefranche-de-Lauragais

Bermeo · San Sebastian · Irun · St-Jean-de-Luz · Gave d'Oloron · Gave de Pau · Pau · Mirande · Ma...

20 · Eibar · Durango · Talosa · Mauléon-Licharre · Oloron-Ste-Marie · Tarbes · Lannemezan · St-Gaudens · Pamiers · Limou...

St-Jean-Pied-de-Port · Lourdes · Bagnères-de-Bigorre · Saint-Béat · Ariège · Foix

Vitoria · Pic d'Anie 2 504 m · Laruns · PYRÉNÉES · Pic du Midi de Bigorre 2 865 m · Bagnères-de-Luchon · Saint-Girons · Tarascon-s.-Arriège · Lavelanet · Quillan

Pamplona · Estella · Arga · PYRÉNÉES OCCIDENTALES · Les Posets 3 367 m · Pic d'Aneto 3 404 m · Viella · AIGÜESTORTES · Pic d'Estats 3 141 m · Ax-les-Thermes

20 · Logroño · Ebro · Aragón · Jaca · ORDESA · Río Cinca · ANDORRA · ANDORRA-LA-VELLA

21 · Calahorra · SPAIN · SIERRA DE GUARA · Río Gállego · Río Segre · Berga... · La Seu d'Urgell · Puigcerda

Tudela · Tarazona · Huesca · Barbastro · Ebro · Río Llobregat

Corsica inset

M · ISOLA DI CAPRAIA · Cap Corse · 43°

CORSICA · Saint-Florent · Bastia · Calvi · Vescovato · Golo

Monte Cinto 2 710 m · Corte · Évisa · Monte Rotondo 2 622 m · Cap Rosso · CORSE · PLAINE D'ALÉRIA

Cap di Feno · Ajaccio · Monte Incudine 2 136 m · 42°

Cap di Muro · I. DE CAVELLO

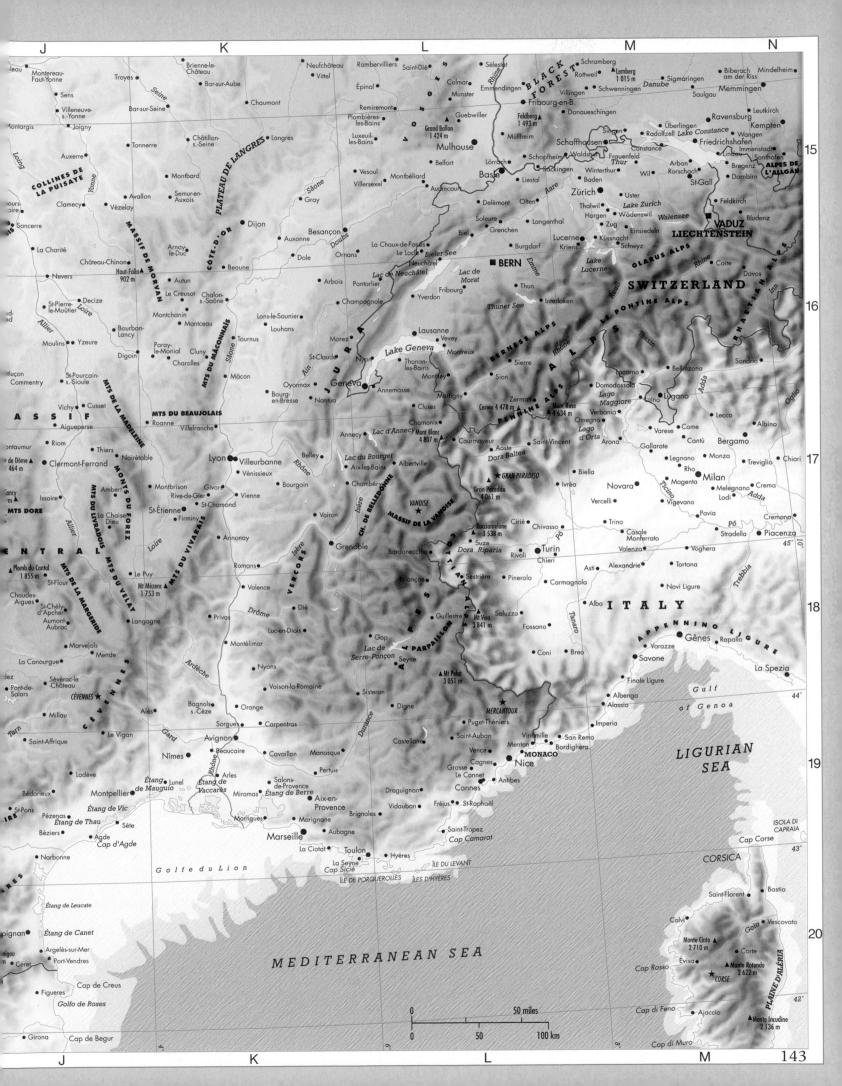

Western Europe: the statistics

The countries of Western Europe make up a complex mosaic of peoples and cultures.

IRELAND

Official name: Republic of Ireland (Eire)
Capital: Dublin
Area: 27 136 sq miles (70 282 km²)
Population: 3 810 000
Population density: 133 per sq mile (51 per km²)
Religions: Catholic 93%, Protestant 5%, others or none 2%
Currency: Euro
HDI*: 0.929
GDP per head: $25 616
Languages: English, Irish Gaelic
Government: Republic with a president as head of state, a multiparty government and a parliament of two houses – Senate and House of Representatives (Dail).
Flag: Tricolour – the emblem adopted in 1848 by Thomas Francis Meagher, a founder of the Irish Confederation. Green (the Gaelic colour), orange (for Protestant supporters), white (dividing the two sides).

UNITED KINGDOM

Official name: United Kingdom of Great Britain and Northern Ireland
Capital: London
Area: 94 217 sq miles (244 022 km²)
Population: 59 000 000
Population density: 624 per sq mile (241 per km²)
Ethnic minorities: 5.19% (Indian 1.44%, Afro-Caribbean 0.85%, Pakistani 0.6%, Chinese 0.2%, African 0.2%, Bangladeshi 0.2%, others 1.7%)
Religions: Christian 79.5% (Catholic 21.4%, Anglican 20.2%, Presbyterian 14.2%, Methodist 5.3%, Baptist 2.6%), Muslim 3.4%, Sikh 4.3%, Hindu 1.5%, Jewish 1.2%, others or none 2.6%
Currency: Pound sterling
HDI*: 0.931
GDP per head: $24 484
Language: English
Government: Constitutional monarchy and a parliament consisting of two chambers (the House of Lords (upper) and the House of Commons).
Flag: The Union Flag, also known as the Union Jack. The flag combines the cross of St George (red on white background) for England, the cross of St Andrew (white X-shaped saltire on blue background) for Scotland, and the cross of St Patrick (red saltire on white background), the last to be added in 1801, for Ireland.

FRANCE

Official name: French Republic
Capital: Paris
Area: 211 204 sq miles (547 020 km²)
Population: 59 700 000
Population density: 275 per sq mile (106 per km²)
Ethnic minorities: 5.78% (North African 2.4%, other African 0.3%, Portuguese 1.12%, Turkish 0.34%, Italian 0.44%, Spanish 0.38%, other European 0.49%, Asian 0.15%, others 0.16%)
Religions: Catholic 67%, Protestant 2%, Jewish 1%, others (including Muslims) or none 30%
Currency: Euro
HDI*: 0.946
GDP per head: $22 080
Language: French
Government: Republic with a president as head of state and a parliament with two houses (Senate and the National Assembly).
Flag: Tricolour dating from 1794 and the French Revolution. The blue and red are probably derived from colours of Paris, the white, formerly the royal colour, represents the nation.

SWITZERLAND

Official name: Swiss Confederation
Capital: Berne
Area: 15 943 sq miles (41 293 km²)
Population: 7 230 000
Population density: 456 per sq mile (176 per km²)
Ethnic minorities: 19% (Italian 5%, from former Yugoslavia 4%, Portuguese 2%, Spanish 1.5%, German 1.5%, Turkish 1%, others 4%)
Religions: Catholic 44%, Protestant 38%, Muslim 2%, Jewish 0.25%, others 2.2%, none 13.55%
Currency: Swiss franc
HDI*: 0.93
GDP per head: $34 384
Languages: German, French, Italian, Romansch
Government: Federal state with a president as head of state, and a Federal Assembly consisting of two legislative houses (Council of States (upper) and National Council).
Flag: Dates from the 14th century and has been the national flag since 1848.

LIECHTENSTEIN

Official name: Principality of Liechtenstein
Capital: Vaduz
Area: 62 sq miles (160 km²)
Population: 33 000
Population density: 500 per sq mile (193 per km²)
Religions: Catholic 80%, Protestant 7%, others or none 13%
Currency: Swiss franc
GDP per head: $35 910
Language: German
Government: Constitutional monarchy with a parliament (Landtag).
Flag: Blue and red bands, gold crown.

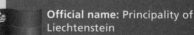

BELGIUM

Official name: Kingdom of Belgium
Capital: Brussels
Area: 11 785 sq miles (30 525 km²)
Population: 10 300 000
Population density: 857 per sq mile (330.9 per km²)
Ethnic minorities: 9% (Italian 2%, Moroccan 1.4%, French 1%, Turkish 0.8%, Dutch 0.8%, Spanish 0.5%, German 0.3%, others 2.2%)
Religions: Catholic 79%, Protestant 1.3%, Jewish 0.4%, others or none 19.3%
Currency: Euro
HDI*: 0.932
GNP per head: $22 048
Languages: French, Dutch, German
Government: Federal constitutional monarchy with two assemblies (Senate and Chamber of Deputies).
Flag: Tricolour of black, yellow and red vertical bands, dating from the 1830 revolution, with colours relating to the arms of the Duchy (now province) of Brabant, where the revolt began.

THE NETHERLANDS

Official name: Kingdom of the Netherlands
Capital: Amsterdam (seat of government: The Hague)
Area: 13 104 sq miles (33 940 km²)
Population: 16 000 000
Population density: 1190.5 per sq mile (459.5 per km²)
Ethnic minorities: 5% (Turkish 1.3%, Moroccan 1%, German 0.3%, British 0.2%, Surinamese 0.2%, Belgian 0.15%, others 1.85%)
Religions: Catholic 31%, Dutch Reformed and other Protestant churches 22%, others 6%, none 41%
Currency: Euro
HDI*: 0.94
GDP per head: $24 250
Language: Dutch
Government: Constitutional monarchy with a parliament (States General) of two houses (the First Chamber (upper) and the Second Chamber).
Flag: The flag dates from 1630, with the colours of the States General of the United Provinces. Previously the upper band was orange, relating to the ruling House of Orange.

GERMANY

Official name: Federal Republic of Germany
Capital: Berlin
Area: 137 853 sq miles (357 041 km²)
Population: 82 100 000
Population density: 592.8 per sq mile (228.8 per km²)
Ethnic minorities: 5% (Turkish 2.24%, from former Yugoslavia 1%, Italian 0.7%, Greek 0.42%, Polish 0.34%, Austrian 0.23%, others 0.07%)
Religions: Protestant 41%, Catholic 35.6%, Muslim 3%, others or none 20.4%
Currency: Euro
HDI*: 0.924
GDP per head: $23 071
Language: German
Government: Federal republic with a president as head of state, and a parliament with two houses (the Federal Council (Bundesrat) (upper) and the Federal Diet (Bundestag)).
Flag: The three colours of the Lützow volunteer regiment were first adopted as the national flag in 1848, again in 1918, and once more in 1949.

LUXEMBOURG

Official name: Grand Duchy of Luxembourg
Capital: Luxembourg
Area: 998 sq miles (2586 km²)
Population: 450 000
Population density: 410.8 per sq mile (158.6 per km²)
Ethnic minorities: 28% (Portuguese 12.6%, Italian 4.9%, French 3.7%, Belgian 2.9%, German 2.4%, others 1.5%)
Religions: Catholic 97%, Protestant 1%, others or none 2%
Currency: Luxembourg franc/Euro
HDI*: 0.899
GDP per head: $42 444
Languages: French, Letzeburghish
Government: Constitutional monarchy and parliament with two houses: the main legislative body is the elected Chamber of Deputies, while the supreme administrative tribunal is the Council of State, which is nominated by the Grand Duke.
Flag: Horizontal stripes in the colours of the Counts of Luxembourg, dating from the 13th century: similar to the Dutch flag, but with a lighter blue.

AUSTRIA

Official name: Republic of Austria
Capital: Vienna
Area: 32 376 sq miles (83 855 km²)
Population: 8 170 000
Population density: 247 per sq mile (95.4 per km²)
Ethnic minorities: 6.4% (from former Yugoslavia 2.5%, Turkish 1.5%, Germans 0.5%, others 1.9%)
Religions: Catholic 84.3%, Lutheran 5.6%, other Churches 3%, Jewish 0.9%, others or none 6.2%
Currency: Euro
HDI*: 0.932
GDP per head: $23 463
Language: German
Government: A federal republic with a president as head of state and two legislative assemblies (the Federal Council (Bundesrat) (upper) and the National Council (Nationalrat)).
Flag: Horizontal red and white stripes. The stripes date back to the 13th century, when they were the colours of the ruling dukes.

MONACO

Official name: Principality of Monaco
Capital: Monaco
Area: 0.77 sq miles (2 km²)
Population: 33 000
Population density: 41 558 per sq mile (16 045 per km²)
Ethnic minorities: 77.5% (French 37.7%, Italian 15.7%, British 4%, German 2%, American 1.3%, others 16.8%)
Religions: Catholic 90%, Protestant 5%, others or none 5%
Currency: Euro
GDP per head: $24 739
Language: French
Government: Constitutional monarchy with a Minister of State and an elected National Council.
Flag: The prince's colours, red and white.

*HDI: Human Development Index – an index prepared by the UN Development Programme, on a scale of 0-3, based on longevity, knowledge and income.

Climate and landscape

Western Europe has a temperate, well-watered climate that generally keeps the thermometer at comfortable levels, and is seldom afflicted by extremes. The landscape is green, gently contoured – and productive.

The maritime influence

The Atlantic Ocean and its attendant seas – the North Sea, English Channel, Mediterranean and Baltic – sweep some 6000 miles (9650 km) of coastline in Western Europe. Seven countries lie on the front line of a maritime climate, with comparatively small temperature differences between summer and winter, and high levels of precipitation (rain and snow).

Moderate and temperate

Situated between 41° and 61° north, Western Europe sits in the middle of the Northern Hemisphere's temperate band. Rainfall is abundant in all seasons. The constant clash between cold air from the Arctic and warm air from the tropics, generally pushed in by Atlantic Westerlies, means that the weather is highly changeable. Only in the areas farthest from the coast – south-eastern Germany, Austria, Switzerland and Liechtenstein – is the climate more continental, with harsher winters anddrier summers. Summer aridity is most marked in the far south of the region, along the Mediterranean coast of France, which is also where the highest temperatures are recorded.

CLIMATES ▼

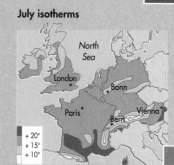

Climate
- ☐ Maritime (temperate)
- ☐ Continental
- ☐ Mediterranean
- ▨ Mountains

SEASONAL VARIATIONS ▼

January isotherms

+ 5°
+ 0°
- 5°

July isotherms

+ 20°
+ 15°
+ 10°

MEAN TEMPERATURES

	January	July
Dublin	+5.1°C (41.2°F)	+15°C (59°F)
London	+3.5°C (38.3°F)	+16.5°C (61.7°F)
Utrecht	+2.2°C (36°F)	+16.8°C (62.2°F)
Berlin	-0.4°C (31.3°F)	+17.9°C (64.2°F)
Paris	+3.4°C (38.1°F)	+18.4°C (65.1°F)
Geneva	+0.7°C (33.3°F)	+19.1°C (66°F)
Vienna	-0.7°C (30.7°F)	+19.7°C (67.5°F)
Marseille	+6.4°C (43.5°F)	+23.7°C (74.7°F)

Tropical Scotland *Plockton, on the west coast of Scotland, is on the same latitude as Hudson Bay, and farther north than Moscow, yet palm trees grow there due to the warming effect of the Gulf Stream.*

PRECIPITATION

	Total	Wettest month	Driest month
Dublin	28.8 in (731 mm)	Dec: 2.6 in (76 mm)	July: 2 in (50 mm)
London	29.7 in (754 mm)	Dec: 3.1 in (79 mm)	July: 1.8 in (45 mm)
Berlin	23.3 in (591 mm)	June: 2.8 in (71 mm)	Feb: 1.5 in (37 mm)
Paris	25.6 in (650 mm)	May: 2.5 in (63 mm)	Feb: 1.8 in (46 mm)
Geneva	35.6 in (904 mm)	Nov: 3.5 in (88 mm)	April: 2.4 in (61 mm)
Vienna	23.9 in (607 mm)	June: 2.9 in (74 mm)	Jan: 1.5 in (38 mm)
Marseilles	21.5 in (545 mm)	Oct: 3.1 in (78 mm)	July: 0.5 in (14 mm)

HOURS OF SUNSHINE
(Per year)

	Total
Dublin	1432
London	1574
Utrecht	1477
Berlin	1625
Paris	1750
Geneva	1694
Vienna	1771
Munich	1660
Marseilles	2835

The blessings of the Gulf Stream

The Gulf Stream is so named because it begins in the Gulf of Mexico, before heading into the Atlantic, where it splits into the North Atlantic Drift and the Canary Current. Shifting 1950 million cu ft (55 million m³) of water per second at 25°C (77°F), the Gulf Stream has a major warming effect on the climate of Western Europe. Its effects can be seen in western Ireland, Cornwall, Brittany and the Isles of Scilly, where microclimates support vegetation such as palm trees, which usually grow at least 600 miles (1000 km) farther south.

Some unusual records

Source : Météorologie-France.

RAINFALL
Fussen, Bavaria, Germany: 5 in (126 mm) in 8 min on May 25, 1920.

TEMPERATURE
Cannes, southern France: 25.8°C (78.4°F), on February 14, 1990 – twice the usual temperature for the time of year.

WAVE
Off the coast of Ireland: 67 ft (20.4 m) high, September 12, 1961.

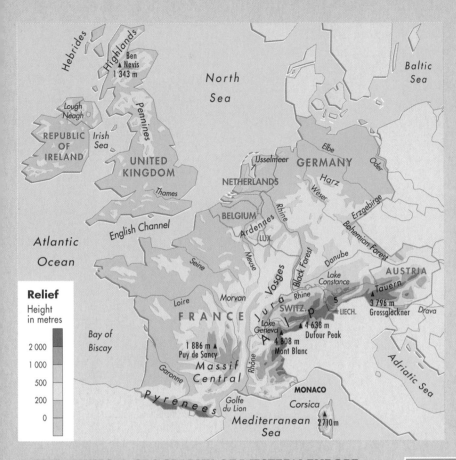

Relief
Height in metres

2 000	
1 000	
500	
200	
0	

HIGHEST PEAKS

Mont Blanc (France)	15 774 ft	(4808 m)
Dufour Peak (Monte Rosa) (Switzerland)	15 217 ft	(4638 m)
Weisshorn (Switzerland)	14 803 ft	(4512 m)
Matterhorn (Monte Cervino) (Switzerland)	14 705 ft	(4482 m)
Dent Blanche (Switzerland)	14 295 ft	(4357 m)

Famous peak *Ice has eroded the Matterhorn into its distinctive shape.*

▲ THE PHYSICAL GEOGRAPHY OF WESTERN EUROPE
Diverse terrain

The highest mountains of Western Europe, the Alps and the Pyrenees, rise only in the eastern and southern edges of the region. Apart from them, the landscape offers few obstacles to the westerly winds from the Atlantic, which carry with them rain-laden ocean air.

The huge North European Plain, with its undulating hills, extends into sedimentary basins in the heartlands of Western Europe, such as the Thames Basin, the Paris Basin and the North German Basin, formed in the early Tertiary era about 60 million years ago. They are overlooked by more ancient hills and mountains, their summits rounded by erosion, dating from the Hercynian period (late Palaeozoic) some 300 million years ago. These include the Scottish Highlands, culminating in Ben Nevis 4406 ft (1343 m), the Vosges, the Black Forest and the Harz Mountains. The rise of

FOREST COVER
(Percentage of total area)

Luxembourg	33%
Germany	30%
France	28%
Belgium	20%
United Kingdom	10%
The Netherlands	10%
Ireland	6%

the Alps some 70 million years ago set off a period of volcanic activity. The effects of this are seen, for instance, at the Puy de Sancy, which rises to 6187 ft (1886 m), the highest peak of the Massif Central of France.

Climatic variation and the diversity of relief have combined to produce a broad array of landscapes and natural environments. Areas with the moderate temperatures and high rainfall associated with a maritime climate favour deciduous forest, with oak, beech, sycamore (plane tree), ash, lime (linden) and hornbeam. These have often had to give way to the more profitable evergreens: since the 19th century conifers have been planted in managed forests, as in the Ardennes in Belgium; they have also been used to fix the dunes and marshlands of the *landes* of south-west

Forged by fire *The weathered puys of the Auvergne region of the Massif Central in France were formed by volcanic activity, still evident in the area's thermal spas.*

France. The mountains present a series of ecological layers. Up to about 4000 ft (1200 m), deciduous hardwood forests predominate; then the dark-leaved fir trees, spruce, and larch take over, before giving way to alpine meadows above 6000 ft (1800 m). The south of France has a mainly Mediterranean ecology, with forests of pines, holm oaks and cork oaks. The dry scrubland or *garrigues* of Provence are thinly spread with low shrubs. The Corsican *maquis* is similar but more impenetrable, with broom and thorny shrubs rising to 6 ft (1.8 m) or more.

LONGEST RIVERS

Danube	1771 miles (2850 km)
Rhine	807 miles (1298 km)
Elbe	700 miles (1127 km)
Loire	629 miles (1012 km)
Rhône	505 miles (812 km)

Crossing boundaries *The Rhine rises in the Swiss Alps and runs north through Germany and the Netherlands to the North Sea. In Germany, it cuts a winding path through the Rhine gorge.*

LARGEST LAKES

Lake Geneva (Lac Léman) (Switz/France)	224 sq miles (581 km²)
Lake Constance (Bodensee) (Ger/Aust/Switz)	208 sq miles (540 km²)
Lough Neagh (N. Ireland)	147 sq miles (381 km²)
Lake Neuchâtel (Switzerland)	84 sq miles (218 km²)
Étang de Berre (France)	60 sq miles (156 km²)

Population and economy

Some 244.6 million people live in Western Europe. Most of its countries are fairly densely populated, heavily urban and – by world standards – rich. In this competitive environment, unemployment and the ageing population are major concerns.

SIZE OF WESTERN EUROPE COMPARED TO THE USA ▶

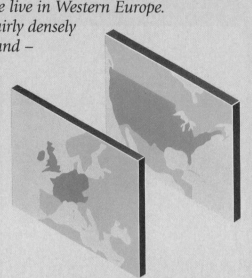

POPULATION DENSITY ▼

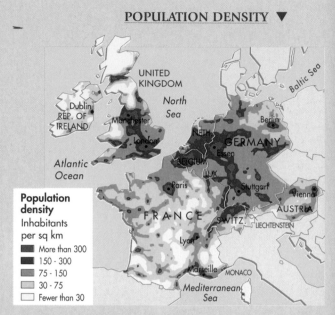

Population density
Inhabitants per sq km

- More than 300
- 150 - 300
- 75 - 150
- 30 - 75
- Fewer than 30

AGE PYRAMID ▼

IRELAND

GERMANY

30% 25% 20% 15% 10% 5%

under 15   15-29   30-44   45-59   60 and over   years

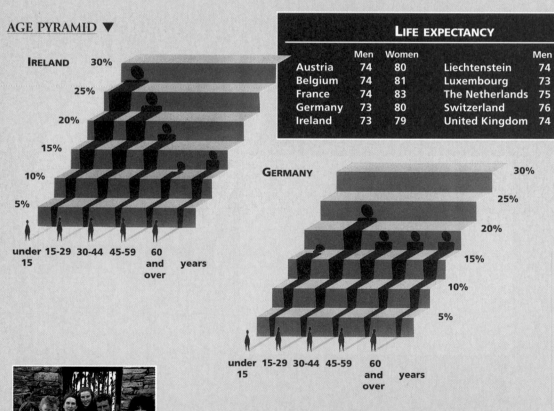

LIFE EXPECTANCY

	Men	Women		Men	Women
Austria	74	80	Liechtenstein	74	81
Belgium	74	81	Luxembourg	73	80
France	74	83	The Netherlands	75	80
Germany	73	80	Switzerland	76	82
Ireland	73	79	United Kingdom	74	79

NATIONAL POPULATIONS
(In millions of inhabitants)

Austria	8.1
Belgium	10.3
France	59.7
Germany	82
Ireland	3.8
Liechtenstein	0.03
Luxembourg	0.4
The Netherlands	16.0
Switzerland	7.2
United Kingdom	59

ECONOMIC HEART ▼

Ireland: the exception

Virtually all the Western European nations have populations in which the average age is moving upwards. The fear is that the working sectors of the population will increasingly be burdened with the cost of supporting an ageing population. Ireland is the only exception. It has the highest birth rate, with 1.9 children per woman. One in five of the Irish population is below the age of 15. In Germany, by contrast, where population growth would be stagnant were it not for immigration, the over-65s outnumbered adolescents in 2000, accounting for 16 per cent of the population.

A highly productive corridor links the largest population centres between London and the Po plain of industrialised northern Italy. It includes the Thames Valley, the Ranstad cities of the Netherlands, the light industries of Flanders, the industrialised Nord-Pas-de-Calais region, the Ruhr valley and the industrial cities of Bavaria. French economists and EU officials have given it the name the *banane bleue* (the 'blue banana').

Immigration

Germany, France and the UK have larger ethnic minority populations than other Western European countries. Germany's 4.1 million non-native inhabitants represent 5 per cent of the population. France has 3.4 million non-native inhabitants, or 5.78 per cent of the population; the UK has 3 million, or 5.19 per cent. Most Western European countries have ethnic minorities of around 5 per cent of the population, but Switzerland has 19 per cent, Luxembourg 28 per cent and Monaco 77.5 per cent.

The origins of the larger immigrant communities relate to historic circumstances. France, for instance, has a population of 1.4 million North Africans (or Maghrébins), a vestige of France's colonial connections with Tunisia, Morocco and, above all, Algeria. Algerians represent 19 per cent of the total immigrant population in France, but there are almost as many Portuguese (18 per cent). Britain's main ethnic minorities are from the Indian subcontinent and the Caribbean islands. Workers from Turkey and former Yugoslavia were drawn to Germany, Switzerland and the Netherlands by the call for labour from the 1950s onwards.

▼ DISTRIBUTION OF THE WORKING POPULATION

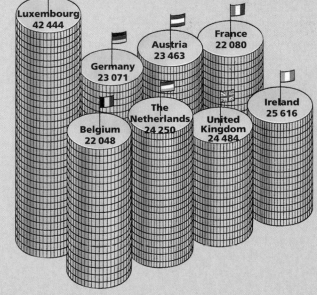

WORKING POPULATION AS A PERCENTAGE OF THE WHOLE
Germany: 49.1
United Kingdom: 49.9
France: 39.4

SERVICE INDUSTRIES
Germany: 65
United Kingdom: 74
France: 71.5

INDUSTRY AND MANUFACTURING
Germany: 33
United Kingdom: 24
France: 24.4

AGRICULTURE AND MINING
Germany: 2
United Kingdom: 2
France: 4.1

CAR PRODUCTION

PRODUCTION	(thousands of units)
Germany	5248.0
United Kingdom	4200.0
France	1626.0

PROPORTION OF WORLD PRODUCTION	
Germany	9.3%
United Kingdom	6.9%
France	3.7%

WORLD RANKING	
Germany	3rd
United Kingdom	6th
France	4th

UNEMPLOYMENT RATES

Austria	4.5%	Luxembourg	2.5%
Belgium	7.9%	The Netherlands	2.5%
France	9.2%	Switzerland	2.4%
Germany	10.4%	United Kingdom	4.8%
Ireland	4.3%		

▼ GROSS DOMESTIC PRODUCT PER INHABITANT (IN US $) (2001)

Luxembourg 42 444
Germany 23 071
Austria 23 463
France 22 080
Belgium 22 048
The Netherlands 24 250
United Kingdom 24 484
Ireland 25 616

FOREIGN TRADE OF THE ▼ UK, GERMANY AND FRANCE

The tail end of the arrows represents imports, and the point of the arrows represents exports, expressed in US$millions and as percentages of gross domestic product.

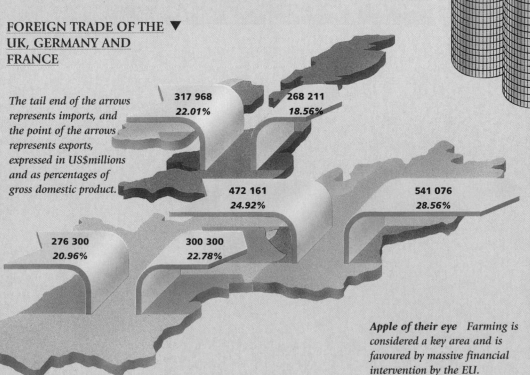

317 968
22.01%

268 211
18.56%

472 161
24.92%

541 076
28.56%

276 300
20.96%

300 300
22.78%

Apple of their eye *Farming is considered a key area and is favoured by massive financial intervention by the EU.*

151

Modest capital cities

In 1900, the capitals of Europe were among the biggest cities in the world. With the gathering pace of industrialisation, they had been expanding more rapidly than cities in other countries. From 1878 to 1898 Berlin, for example, grew at a quicker rate than New York. In 1900, London, with over 6.5 million inhabitants, was the largest city in the world. New York had reached 3 million, Paris 2.7 million, but this was still larger than Tokyo and Moscow. Over the next 40 years the population of Paris grew very little, while Tokyo expanded to 7 million and Moscow to over 4 million. London, with 6.7 million, still held the title. By the 1990s Tokyo had over 8 million inhabitants, but a world-beating 29 million if the Tokyo-Yokohama conurbation is included. Even the world's tenth-largest city, Calcutta, with 14 million, exceeded Europe's largest.

URBAN POPULATIONS ▶
(As a percentage of the total population)

Packed in tight London remains one of Europe's largest cities.

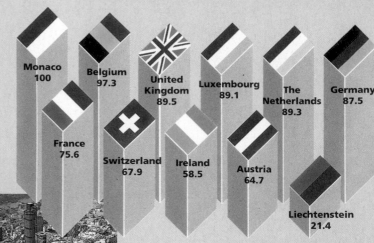

Monaco 100
Belgium 97.3
United Kingdom 89.5
Luxembourg 89.1
The Netherlands 89.3
Germany 87.5
France 75.6
Switzerland 67.9
Ireland 58.5
Austria 64.7
Liechtenstein 21.4

MAJOR URBAN AREAS
(Number of inhabitants)

Paris	9 644 507
London	8 897 000
Berlin	3 392 900
Birmingham	2 628 200
Hamburg	1 701 800
Vienna	1 562 676
Munich	1 193 600
Amsterdam	1 002 686
Rotterdam	989 956
Brussels	959 000

▼ TRANSPORT

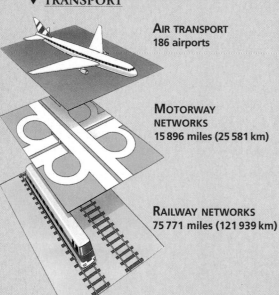

AIR TRANSPORT
186 airports

MOTORWAY NETWORKS
15 896 miles (25 581 km)

RAILWAY NETWORKS
75 771 miles (121 939 km)

BUSIEST AIRPORTS
(Annual traffic in millions of passengers)

London-Heathrow (UK)	64.2
Frankfurt-am-Main (Germany)	48.9
Paris-Charles-de-Gaulle (France)	48.2

international airport at Frankfurt-am-Main is second only to London's Heathrow as busiest airport in Europe, with Paris-Charles-de-Gaulle not far behind. All three airports rank among the ten busiest airports in the world: the other seven are in the USA.

HEALTH ▶ SERVICES

Road transport wins

Despite all the warnings about pollution, roads remain the preferred way of shifting freight across Western Europe. In France and Germany, over 50 per cent of commercial freight is carried by lorries: rail accounts for one-third. Canal and river networks link Germany, France, the Netherlands, Belgium and Austria, but water transport is in decline (averaging 20 per cent of freight transport in these countries). In passenger transport, rail outstrips the car and aeroplane in several countries: the French national railway, SNCF, carries over 700 million people every year. In Germany, 95 million people use air transport every year, and the

DOCTORS	HOSPITAL BEDS
(Per 1000 inhabitants)	
3.5	9.3
Germany	
3.02	8.9
Austria	
3.95	7.2
Belgium	
3.03	8.5
France	
2.19	3.7
Ireland	
1.31	3.85
Liechtenstein	
2.72	8.0
Luxembourg	
6.64	19.61
Monaco	
2.51	11.3
The Netherlands	
1.7	4.2
United Kingdom	
3.23	18.1
Switzerland	

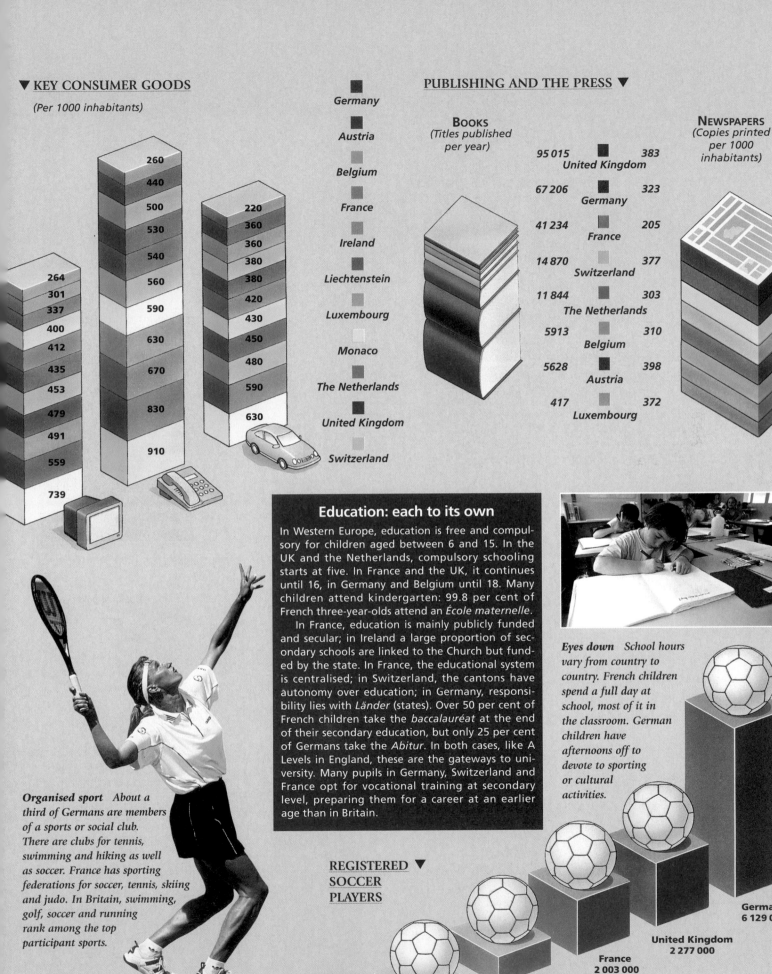

(Per 1000 inhabitants)

264
301
337
400
412
435
453
479
491
559
739

260
440
500
530
360
540
560
590
630
670
830
910

220
360
360
380
380
420
430
450
480
590
630

Germany
Austria
Belgium
France
Ireland
Liechtenstein
Luxembourg
Monaco
The Netherlands
United Kingdom
Switzerland

BOOKS
(Titles published per year)

95 015	United Kingdom	383
67 206	Germany	323
41 234	France	205
14 870	Switzerland	377
11 844	The Netherlands	303
5 913	Belgium	310
5 628	Austria	398
417	Luxembourg	372

NEWSPAPERS
(Copies printed per 1000 inhabitants)

Education: each to its own

In Western Europe, education is free and compulsory for children aged between 6 and 15. In the UK and the Netherlands, compulsory schooling starts at five. In France and the UK, it continues until 16, in Germany and Belgium until 18. Many children attend kindergarten: 99.8 per cent of French three-year-olds attend an *École maternelle*.

In France, education is mainly publicly funded and secular; in Ireland a large proportion of secondary schools are linked to the Church but funded by the state. In France, the educational system is centralised; in Switzerland, the cantons have autonomy over education; in Germany, responsibility lies with *Länder* (states). Over 50 per cent of French children take the *baccalauréat* at the end of their secondary education, but only 25 per cent of Germans take the *Abitur*. In both cases, like A Levels in England, these are the gateways to university. Many pupils in Germany, Switzerland and France opt for vocational training at secondary level, preparing them for a career at an earlier age than in Britain.

Eyes down School hours vary from country to country. French children spend a full day at school, most of it in the classroom. German children have afternoons off to devote to sporting or cultural activities.

Organised sport About a third of Germans are members of a sports or social club. There are clubs for tennis, swimming and hiking as well as soccer. France has sporting federations for soccer, tennis, skiing and judo. In Britain, swimming, golf, soccer and running rank among the top participant sports.

Steffi Graf

REGISTERED ▼ SOCCER PLAYERS

Belgium
455 000

The Netherlands
1 009 000

France
2 003 000

United Kingdom
2 277 000

Germany
6 129 000

Tourism in Europe

Tourism plays a major role in the economies of all Western European countries. France leads the field, being the most visited country not just in Europe, but in the world.

Treasure house of history The British Museum, the national museum of archaeology and ethnography, contains an extensive collection of ancient and medieval artifacts. It is the largest museum in the UK and one of London's most popular visitor attractions.

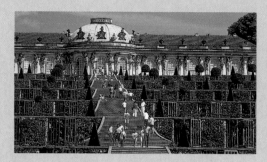

Rococo attraction The Sans-Souci palace at Potsdam, built in the mid 18th century, has been nicknamed the Prussian Versailles.

MOST POPULAR MUSEUMS AND ART GALLERIES
(Number of visitors per year)

British Museum, London	5 750 000
Louvre, Paris	5 200 000
National Gallery, London	4 470 000
Musée d'Orsay, Paris	2 400 000
Tate Gallery, London	2 230 000
Kunsthistorisches Museum, Vienna	1 460 000
Victoria and Albert Museum, London	1 440 000
Rijksmuseum, Amsterdam	1 000 000
Art Gallery and Museum, Glasgow	900 000
Gemäldegalerie, Berlin	860 000
Musée Van Gogh, Amsterdam	800 000
Centre Georges-Pompidou, Paris	800 000
Kröller-Müller Museum, Otterlo	780 000
Musée des Beaux-Arts, Brussels	600 000

Over 60 million tourists go each year to France. The majority are from Britain, Germany, The Netherlands and Belgium, but the figure also includes 2 million Americans and nearly a million Japanese, as well as a growing number of visitors from the old Soviet bloc. The next most-visited country in the world is the USA, with 45 million tourists. US income from tourism easily outstrips the rest of the world (about US$64 billion); Spain has the second highest income from tourism, but France comes close behind in third place, earning US$28 billion. Britain earns US$20 billion a year.

The French are more reluctant to go on holiday abroad than other Europeans – only 13 per cent of French people do so each year. By contrast, almost all the Luxembourgers, over 60 per cent of the Dutch and Germans, and 50 per cent of the Belgians, British and Irish spend their holidays in foreign countries, mainly in France and Spain. The Germans are the highest spenders, accounting for 14 per cent of annual world expenditure on tourism, or US$50 billion. The British spend about half this, or 7 per cent, the

The great chefs of France

Catering is an essential part of tourism, especially in France, which has a worldwide reputation for food. Every year, lovers of fine food and the restaurateurs await publication of the Michelin Guide. Since it first appeared in 1931, the guide has awarded stars to restaurants according to strict standards of inspection. Only about 20 restaurants have the right to claim Michelin's top ranking of three stars. Among the chefs who have survived longest at this pinnacle are Paul Bocuse at Collonges-au-Mont-d'Or and the Troisgros brothers at Roanne, who have held on to their crowns since 1965 and 1968 respectively.

Paul Bocuse

Giant visitors The superbly detailed miniature city of Madurodam is a popular attraction near the Hague in The Netherlands.

Resort of kings Palace Pier is a famous feature of Brighton. On England's south coast, the town became fashionable in the early 19th century when the Prince Regent built his Royal Pavilion here.

French 5 per cent, the Austrians 3 per cent, and the Dutch 3 per cent.

Britain receives about 26 million tourists a year, with London as the primary centre. About 2 million people every year visit the Tower of London, St Paul's Cathedral and Westminster Abbey. However, France wins for visitor figures: some 4 million people go up the Eiffel Tower, and nearly a million visit the Chateau de Chenonceau. But Disneyland-Paris puts all other attractions in the shade, with 11.7 million visitors.

TOP AMUSEMENT AND THEME PARKS
(Visitors per year)

Disneyland-Paris, France	11 700 000
Blackpool Pleasure Beach, UK	7 500 000
De Efteling, Netherlands	3 000 000
Futuroscope, France	2 800 000
Alton Towers, UK	2 700 000

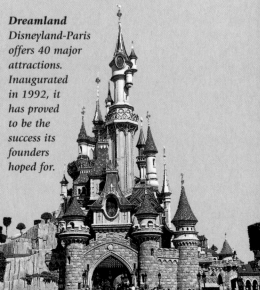

Dreamland Disneyland-Paris offers 40 major attractions. Inaugurated in 1992, it has proved to be the success its founders hoped for.

Index

The page numbers in *italics* denote illustrations. The letter and number references in brackets are the co-ordinates for places in the map section, p. 138-145.

Acknowledgments

Abbreviations: t = top, m = middle, b = bottom, l = left, r = right.

FRONT COVER: *Birkweiler, on the German wine route, in the autumn:* HOA QUI/ZEFA/Rossenbach.
BACK COVER: *Forest of Compiègne in Picardy, north-eastern France:* DIAF/TPC/M.Busselle.

Pages 4-5: DIAF/Y.Travert; 6-7: COSMOS/Geospace/SPL; 8b: DIAF/R.Mazin; 8-9t: DIAF/Pratt-Pries; 9: DIAF/IFA/Bilderteam; 10t: DIAF/J.Sierpinski; 10-11b: DIAF/TPC/M.Busselle; 11t: DIAF/Y.Travert; 12t: AKG Photo. Vienna, Naturhistorisches Museum; 12m: G.DAGLI ORTI/Reconstruction of the caves at Lascaux. Saint-Germain-en-Laye, M.A.N.; 12mr: AKG Photo. Graz, Steiermärkisches Landesmuseum Johanneum; 12br: MAGNUM/E.Lessing. Vaduz, Liechtensteinisches Landesmuseum; 13tl: AKG Photo. Graz, Steiermärkisches Landesmuseum Johanneum; 13tr: MAGNUM/E.Lessing. London, British Museum; 13b: DIAF/Eurasia Press; 14ml: G.DAGLI ORTI. Bonn, Rheinisches Landesmuseum; 14mr: DIAF/J.D.Sudres; 14-15t: RAPHO/Brake; 15t: AKG Photo. Hornhausen Stone, Halle, Landesmuseum für Vorgeschichte; 15bl: G.DAGLI ORTI. Jouarre, crypt of the ancient abbey; 15br: R.M.N. Fibula of Charnay. Saint-Germain-en-Laye, M.A.N. ; 16tl: B.n.F. The Life of Saint Aubin, 11th century manuscript Vikings ready to attack; 16tr: G.DAGLI ORTI. Charlemagne, bronze, 9th century, Paris, musée du Louvre; 16ml: AKG Photo. Chess piece, 12th century, island of Lewis, London, British Museum; 17t: AKG Photo. Chronicle of Aegidius Li Muisis (facsimile), Flagellants in Doornik, 1348; 17m: GIRAUDON/Bridgeman. Chronicle of saint Alban, battle of Agincourt. London, Lambeth Palace Library; 17b: G.DAGLI ORTI. Bayeux tapestry, centre William the Conqueror; 18ml: GIRAUDON/Bridgeman. att.G.Gower, Elizabeth I. Woburn, Abbey Art Gallery; 18mr: G.DAGLI ORTI. Jean Calvin aged 27. Geneva, bibl. universitaire et publique; 18tr: G.DAGLI ORTI. Lucas Cranach, Martin Luther. Florence, musée des Offices; 18-19b: G.DAGLI ORTI. F.Dubois. The St Bartholomew's Day Massacre. Lausanne, musée cantonal des Beaux- Arts; 19m: G.DAGLI ORTI. Titian, Charles V at the battle of Mühlberg. Madrid, Prado; 19t: G.DAGLI ORTI. V. der Meulen, View of the château de Vincennes with Louis XIV. Versailles, M.N.C. ; 19br: DIAF/R.Mazin. Woodwork in the King's Bechamber at Versailles; 20tl: GIRAUDON/Lauros. J.Huber, Meeting of Philosophers. Paris, musée Carnavalet; 20br: G.DAGLI ORTI. Dubois, Storming of the Bastille. Paris, musée Carnavalet; 20bl: Private Collection. Engraving for the *Encyclopédie* of Diderot and Alembert; 21tl: GIRAUDON/Lauros. A.E.F.Mayer, 'Le Redoutable' at Trafalgar. Paris, musée de la Marine; 21tr: AKG Photo. J.L.David, Napoleon in 1812. Washington, National Gallery of Art; 21br: AKG Photo. Congress of Vienna. Engraving by J.Zutz; 22ml: AKG Photo. A. von Menzel, Rolling Mill, 1875. Berlin, Alte Nationalgalerie; 22t:AKG Photo. J. M. W. Turner, Rain, Steam and Speed, 1844. London, National Gallery; 23ml: GIRAUDON. G. Doré, Scene of a London street. Paris, musée d'Orsay; 23mr: G.DAGLI ORTI London's Great Exhibition of 1851; 23bl: G.DAGLI ORTI. E. Hagnauer, The Watertower Fire in February 1848. Paris, musée Carnavalet; 23br: AKG Photo. A. von Werner, Proclamation of the German emperor. Friedrichsruh, Bismarck Museum; 24t: MAGNUM/E.Lessing. O. Dix, The War. Düsseldorf, Kunstsamm.N.W. © ADAGP 1998; 24bl: G.DAGLI ORTI. Engraving by A.Beltram for La Domenica del Corriere, Assassination at Sarajevo; 25tl: G.DAGLI ORTI. F. Flameng. A Bréguet-Michelin bomber. Paris, musée de l'Armée; 25tr: AKG Photo. W. Orpen, The Signing of the Treaty of Versailles. London, Imperial War Museum; 25bl: VIOLLET/Branger; 25br: G. DAGLI ORTI. Engraving from *Petit Journal*, British suffragettes, 1908; 26m: AKG; 26tl: AKG; 26bl: AKG/V. Yudin; 26-27: HULTON GETTY; 27m: SYGMA; 27tl: KEYSTONE; 27br: AKG/E. Bohr; 28-29: DIAF/Eurasia Press; 30-31: RAPHO/G. Sioen; 32tl: M. LANGROGNET. Monasterboice, Cross of the West, 10th century; 32bl: EXPLORER/Le Coz; 32ml: HOA QUI/J.M.Roignant; 32tr: COSMOS/A.Griffiths Belt/Aurora; 33tr: RAPHO/G.Sioen; 33br: DIAF/Pratt-Pries; 34bl: COSMOS/F.Perri; 34r: SCOPE/P.Borasci; 35b: DIAF/IFA/Bilderteam; 35t: RAPHO/G.Sioen; 36t: DIAF/G.Biollay; 36b: SYGMA/P.Vauthey; 37t: SYGMA/B.Annebicque; 37b: HOA QUI/K.Tomeï/Altitude; 38tr: HOA QUI/Ph.Renault; 38bl: GAMMA/Hodson-Greenpeace/Liaison; 38-39: SYGMA; 39m: EXPLORER/Ph.Roy; 39tr: HOA QUI/Morand-Grahame; 39br: DIAF/H.Ausloos; 40br: A.DREZE; 40ml: DIAF/Pratt-Pries; 40tr: Illustration from a photo by André Drèze; 41m: HOA QUI / Ch.Boisvieux; 41t: HOA QUI/Ch.Boisvieux; 42-43: MAGNUM/Fred Mayer; 44mb: DIAF/P.Sommelet; 44m: DIAF/J.D.Sudres; 44tr: DIAF/P.Sommelet; 44bl: DIAF/J.Miller/TPC; 44-45b: SCOPE/M.Guillard; 45m: SCOPE/J.Guillard; 45tl: STUDIO X/A.Reiser/Bilderberg; 45tr: MOET ET CHANDON. Courtesy of cuvée Dom Pérignon; 46ml: HOA QUI/J.F. Lanzarone; 46t: DIAF/R. Rozencwajg; 46b: STILL PICTURES/Thomas Raupach; 47ml: ENVIRONMENTAL IMAGES/Stan Gamester; 47tr: SYGMA/Th.Rousseau; 47b: SCOPE/J.L.Barde; 48m: NATIONAL COAL MINING MUSEUM/Phil Butcher Photography; 48t: SYGMA/Th. Orban; 48b: ENVIRONMENTAL IMAGES/Trevor Perry; 48bl: GAMMA/F. Demange; 49tl: COSMOS/G.Watson; 49tr: DIAF/D.Faure; 49ml: DIAF/M.Tiziou © TGV ®; 50ml: RAPHO/G. Uféras; 50t: SYGMA/F. Pitchal; 50b: SYGMA/F. Pitchal; 51br: HOA QUI/J. L.Manaud/Icône; 51t: HOA QUI/E.Streichen/Zefa; 51m: STUDIO X/Th.Ernsting/Bilderberg; 52m: DIAF/Pratt-Pries; 52bl: DIAF/G.Gsell; 52-53t: HOA QUI/P.Duval/Altitude; 53m: STILL PICTURES/Mike Jackson; 53br: COSMOS/G.Buthaud; 54t: EXPLORER/M.Seares; 54bl: DIAF/J.Sierpinski; 54mr: DIAF/J.Sierpinski; 55ml: ALLSPORT/Phil Cole; 55tr: KIT HOUGHTON; 55br: COSMOS/S. Bendow; 56-57: DIAF/C. Moirenc; 58m: SYGMA/T.Graham; 58tr: DIAF/D.Ball; 58b: CAMERA PRESS/Geoffrey Shakerley; 59m: SYGMA/L'ILLUSTRATION; 59tl: KEYSTONE/SYGMA; 59tr: SYGMA/R.Reuter; 59b: SYGMA/Th.Orban; 60t: RAPHO/J. Amos-P. Arnold; 60b: SYGMA; 61ml: HOA-QUI/M.Renaudeau; 61mr: SYGMA/C. Paris; 61tl: RAPHO/L. Kourcia; 61b: EXPLORER/Ch. Boisvieux; 62mr: VANDYSTADT/Allsport/B. Radford; 62tl: VANDYSTADT/Allsport; 62tr: ALLSPORT; 62b: VANDYSTADT/Ch. Guibbaud; 63t: VANDYSTADT/R. Martin; 63b: VANDYSTADT/Allsport/D. Rogers; 64mr: VANDYSTADT/Allsport/Ph. Cole; 64tr: VANDYSTADT/Allsport/B. Stickland; 64t: VANDYSTADT/R. Martin; 64bl: PRESSE SPORTS; 65tl: SYGMA; 65b: LA FRANCAISE DES JEUX/L. Barde; 66m: HOA-QUI/R. Manin; 66t: HOA-QUI/R. Manin; 66b: DIAF/J.D. Sudres; 67m: GAMMA/Y. Debay; 67t: GAMMA/V. Joanin; 67b: SYGMA/Ph. Eranian; 68m: SYGMA/A.Noguès; 68t: DIAF/Pratt-Pries; 69-70t: EXPLORER/Y.Layma; 69mr: DIAF/D.Ball; 69br: RAPHO/P.Koch; 70m: EXPLORER/Ch. Boisvieux; 70tr: SYGMA/A. Lewis; 70b: SYGMA; 71mr: GAMMA/M. Lounès; 71t: HOA-QUI/J. Hérault; 71b: DIAF/Ch. Bowman/TPC; 72mr: GAMMA/Bassignac; 72tl: HOA QUI/W. Buss. UN complex, Vienna, architect: Johann Staber; 72b: SYGMA/S.Ruet; 73bl: RAPHO/M.Baret; 73mr: SYGMA/A.Tannenbaum; 73tr: RAPHO/P.Lowe/Network; 74m: DIAF/A.Février/With the co-operation of Café de Flore; 74tl: HOA QUI/X.Richer; 74bl: DIAF/C.Moirenc; 74-75t: ARTEPHOT/A.Held. Van Gogh, Night Café. Yale, University Art Gallery; 75tr: HOA QUI/W.Buss; 75bm: DIAF/Pratt-Pries; 75bl: COSMOS/M.Horvath/Anzenberger; 76tl: DIAF/G.Guittot; 76br: DIAF/Pratt-Pries; 76-77: COLLECTIONS/Roger Scruton; 77ml: DIAF/J.D.Sudres; 77tr: RAPHO/H.Sykes; 77bl: RAPHO/B.Seed; 77tr: DIAF/A.Le Bot; 78mr: EXPLORER/Th.Borredon; 78tl: RAPHO/E.Luider; 78bl: STUDIO X/R.v.Forster/Bilderberg; 78br: EXPLORER/J.L.Bohin; 79t: RAPHO/Ch.Rausch; 79bm: DIAF/J.Miller/TCP; 79bl: RAPHO/H.Sykes/Network; 80tl: HOA QUI/E.Valentin; 80bl: EXPLORER/A.Philippon; 80-81: HOA QUI/Tréal-Ruiz; 81tr: HOA QUI/Ch.Vaisse; 81br: DIAF/D.Thierry; 82tr: RAPHO/J.M.Charles; 82bl: SYGMA/R.Bossu; 82-83m: RAPHO/Network/G. Mendel; 83mr: GAMMA/G.Mérillon; 83r: GAMMA/J.Sutton; 83tr: GAMMA/P.Siccoli; 84-85: VISA/H. Hughes; 86tl: RAPHO/F. Elkoury; 86m: DIAF/S. Viron; 86-87t: HOA-QUI/Altitude/Y. Arthus Bertrand; 87bl: RAPHO/E. Luider; 87tr: DIAF/R. Mazin; 87tr: DIAF/S. Viron; 88mr: DIAF/R. Mazin-© E.P.G.L.- The Louvre Pyramid. Architect: I.M.Pei; 88m: DIAF/D. Thierry; 88tm: DIAF/J. Kérebel; 88tl: DIAF/G. Simeone; 88bl: RAPHO/B. Wassman; 88br: DIAF/G.Simeone/© BIBLIOTHEQUE NATIONALE DE FRANCE, D. Perrault, Architecte/ADAGP, Paris 1999; 89mr: DIAF/C. Moirenc; 89t: DIAF/C. Moirenc. The Géode. Architect: Adrien Fainsilber; 89bm: EXPLORER/F. Chazot. The Bastille Opera. Architect: Carlos Ott; 89br: DIAF/R. Mazin; 90tl: DIAF/G. Simeone; 90tr: DIAF/G. Guittot; 90b: DIAF/G. Guittot; 91md: DIAF/Valdin; 91mg: HOA-QUI/W. Buss; 91br: M. LANGROGNET; 92bl: HOA-QUI/W. Buss; 92tl: HOA-QUI/W. Buss; 92br: EXPLORER/Schuster/Waldkirch; 93tr: STUDIO X/Bilderger/M. Engler; 93tl: HOA-QUI/W. Buss; 93m: EXPLORER/S. Grandadam; 94t: HOA-QUI/G. Rigoulet - Pont de Normandie - CCI Le Havre; 94b: EXPLORER/W. Geiersperger; 94mr: TONY STONE IMAGES/ Mark A. Leman; 95mr: RAPHO/H. Donnezan; 95t: G. CHENUET; 95b: GAMMA/Bassignac-Deville-Gaillard; 96t: DIAF/D. Ball; 96m: EXPLORER/P. Le Floc'h; 97tm: DIAF/Pratt-Pries/Architectehundertwasser; 97tl: DIAF/Eurasia Press; 97b: DIAF/Y. Travert; 98tl: M.LANGROGNET; 98tr: DIAF/Ph. Dannic; 98br: DIAF/Pratt-Pies; 98bl: DIAF/B.Morandi; 98-103: LONDON AERIAL PHOTO LIBRARY; 99mr: HOA QUI/S.Grandadam; 99m: DIAF/D.Ball; 99tr: DIAF/TPC/J.Miller; 99bl: DIAF/Eurasia Press; 99br: HOA QUI/W.Buss; 100t: M.LANGROGNET; 100bm: HOA QUI/W.Buss; 100bl: DIAF/G.Guittot; 100br: DIAF/TPS/Dave & Jacobs; 101tl: M.LANGROGNET; 101tr: DIAF/Eurasia Press; 101bl: EXPLORER/Geopress; 101br: HOA QUI/W.Buss; 102mm: HOA QUI/Gellie/Icône. The Lloyd's Building. Architect: Richard Rogers; 102mr: DIAF/M.Rosenfeld; 102mm: DIAF/TPS/Ch.Bowman; 102tl: SYGMA/B.Annebicque; 102tr: SYGMA/B.Annebicque; 102ml: DIAF/Bluntzer; 102br: DIAF/B.Simmons; 103br: DIAF/Eurasia Press; 103tl: HOA QUI/Morand-Grahame; 103tr: DIAF/TPC/Jacobs. Canada Tower. Architect: Cesare Pelli, sculpture 'Docklands Enterprise' by Wendy Taylor ; 103bm: FOTOGRAM STONE/J.Hawkes; 104tr: HOA QUI/Th.Perrin; 104l: HOA QUI/W.Buss; 104br: SYGMA/J.Jones; 105tl: DIAF/J.C. and D. Pratt; 105tr: DIAF/B. Régent; 105b: SYGMA/G. Barclay; 106-107: COSMOS/B. Sacha-© E.P.G.L.- The Louvre Pyramid. Architect: I.M.Pei; 108m: DIAF/G.Simeone; 108bl: EXPLORER/M.Smith; 108-109: DIAF/G.Simeone; 109mr: HOA QUI/W.Buss; 109tl: G.DAGLI ORTI. Turck, Portrait of Elisabeth of Austria, 1854. Château de Miramare (Italy) ; 109bl: DIAF/Pratt-Pries; 110bl: DIAF/R.Rozencwajg; 110t: DIAF/H.Gyssels; 111m: DIAF/G.Gsell; 111tr: DIAF/G.Gsell; 111b: DIAF/B.Régent; 112t: HOA QUI/Y.Arthus-Bertrand/Altitude; 112b: DIAF/Pratt-Pries; 113tl: R.M.N. Virgin Seated with Child. Forez, 12th century. Paris, musée du Louvre; 113tr: COSMOS/J.Zuckerman/Westlight. Rottenbuch (Bavaria), Church of the Virgin's Birth; 113br: EXPLORER/A.Tovy; 114tl: DIAF/Y.Travert; 114m: RAPHO/J.Pickerell; 114br: RAPHO/B.Wassman; 115tl: DIAF/E.Quéméré; 115tr: DIAF/Y.Travert; 116-117: DIAF/P.Cheuva; 118m: GAMMA/Ch.Hires; 118b: DIAF/J.Ch.Gérard; 119-120t: DIAF/B.Koch; 119tr: STUDIO X/W.Schmitz/Bilderberg; 119bl: SYGMA/B.Annebicque; 119br: DIAF/B.Régent; 120bm: RAPHO/F.Le Diascorn; 120tl: RAPHO/X.Testelin; 120br: RAPHO/E.Luider.Otterlo, Kröller Müller Museum. J.Dubuffet, Enamel Garden. © ADAGP, 1999; 121mr: RAPHO/E.Luider; 121t: DIAF/Pratt-Pries; 121bl: DIAF/Ouzounoff. Interior of the musée d'Orsay. Interior architect: Gae Aulenti; 122mr: KEYSTONE/SYGMA; 122tl: EXPLORER/A.Philippon; 122tr: STUDIO X/Sculpture by Renée Sinternes; 122b: KOBAL COLLECTION/October Films; 123m: SYGMA/R.Bossu; 123tr: SYGMA/S.Bassouls; 123br: RAPHO/J. Hilary; 124t: G.DAGLI ORTI. R. Van der Weyden, Polyptych of the Last Judgement. Beaune, Hôtel-Dieu; 124bl: GIRAUDON. J.Bosch, The Conjuror. Saint-Germain-en-Laye, musée municipal d'Art et d'Histoire; 124br: GIRAUDON. P.P.Rubens, Tryptych of the Descent from the Cross (detail). Anvers, cathedral Notre Dame; 125m: R.M.N./R.G.Ojéda. E.Degas, Dancer, Aged 14. Paris, musée d'Orsay; 125bl: GIRAUDON. C.Monet, Impression: Sunrise. Paris, musée Marmottan-C.Monet.©ADAGP,1999; 125br: G.DAGLI ORTI. P.Cézanne, Apples and Oranges. Paris, musée d'Orsay; 126t: RAPHO/J. Ch. Bourcart; 126bl: GAMMA/Allen/Liaison; 126br: GAMMA/P.Piel; 127m: GAMMA/A. Benainous; 127t: STUDIO X/Deborah Polaski & Wolfgang Schmidt in Siegfried; 127b: COSMOS/Anzenberger/M. Horvath. The Magic Flute, director of music Bernard Haitink, m.e.s. Johannes Schaaf; 128-129: COSMOS/G.Ludwig-Visum; 130tm: MARIE-CLAIRE IDEES/M. Faver; 130tr: SYGMA/R. Reuter; 130b: SWATCH; 131m: GAMMA; 131t: GAMMA; 131b: HOA-QUI/Valentin; 132m: SYGMA/J.M.Charles; 132r: SYGMA/S.Cardinale. Haute Couture Christian Dior created by John Galliano - Model Sheherazade, Spring-Summer 1998. ; 132bl: TONY STONE IMAGES/Joe Cornish; 133mr: SYGMA/E.Robert. Broderie chez Lesage; 133t: VIEW/Chris Gascoigne. 134mr: AIRBUS INDUSTRIE; 134m: GAMMA/Liaison; 134tr: COLLECTION VIOLLET; 135m: ESA/CNES; 135tr: GAMMA/P. Aventurier; 136-137: RAPHO/G.Sioen; 152b: DIAF/J.M. Leligny; 148: DIAF/TPC/J.Miller; 149t: DIAF/J.P.Langeland; 149bl: TONY STONE IMAGES/Stephen Studd; 149br: DIAF/R.Mazin; 150: COSMOS/Griffiths Belt/Aurora; 151: DIAF/A.Le Bot; 152h: DIAF/D.Ball; 153mr: HOA QUI/A.Félix. Primary school at Lavaur; 153bl: VANDYSTADT/C.Brunskill/Allsport; 154mr: SYGMA/A.Brucelle; 154m: DIAF/J.Miller; 154tl: DIAF/IFA; 154tr: VIEW/Dennis Gilbert; 154bl: HOA QUI/Morand-Grahame; 154br: DIAF/D.Ball.

Printing and binding: Printer Industria Gráfica S.A., Barcelona

Colour separations: Station Graphique, Ivry-sur-Seine

Paper: Perigord-Condat, France

160

617-002-4